Practical CARPENTRY
Percy Blandford

MACDONALD & CO
London & Sydney

A MACDONALD BOOK

© Macdonald & Co (Publishers) Ltd 1984

First published in 1984 in hardback
and in 1986 in paperback
by Macdonald & Co (Publishers) Ltd
London & Sydney

A member of BPCC plc
Reprinted 1985

ISBN 0 356 09748 X (hardback)
ISBN 0 356 10406 0 (paperback)

Illustrations by Clive Spong

Filmset by Text Filmsetters Ltd, Orpington

Printed and bound in Great Britain by
Hazell Watson & Viney Limited,
Member of the BPCC Group,
Aylesbury, Bucks

Macdonald & Co (Publishers) Ltd
Maxwell House
74 Worship Street
London EC2A 2EN

Contents

Introduction

The working of wood was practised in prehistoric times. Through more recent centuries it has been an important occupation in its many branches, and the man skilled in using his hands to make things from wood has been an honoured member of the community. For nearly all this time the work has been done almost exclusively with hand tools. The skills involved probably reached their peak only about two centuries ago with the work of the great cabinet-makers. Not long afterwards came the Industrial Revolution, in which machinery began to take over some of the functions not only of woodworkers but of all sorts of hand craftsmen. The benefits of power were seen in the way some of the heavier and more routine tasks were performed by machines, leaving the hand craftsman to do the more skilled and less laborious tasks.

Unfortunately, further developments included the wider use of power tools and the adaptations of designs so that more and more tasks could be done mechanically. The result has been the mass-production of furniture. This may have given acceptable and often attractive pieces to people who could not have afforded hand-made furniture, but in the demand for uniformity many of the benefits of real craftsmanship have been lost.

In more recent years shortages and greater costs of the better hardwood have led to the production of manufactured boards to take their place. Such boards certainly have many uses, but the design of much of the furniture that is quantity-produced and widely available incorporates plain rectangular panels to such an extent that we are in danger of accepting these functional boxy items as the norm.

Gone are the days of the traditional craftsman, with his chest containing a large number of hand woodworking tools and nothing else. In must come the craftsman of today, who has many hand tools but also makes use of the multiplicity of power tools, small and large. These can lessen his labour and help him do, with accuracy, things that might have been beyond his ability with hand tools only. This is the modern breed of woodworking craftsman, the carpenter of today. His encouragement is what this book is all about.

There will always be a place for wood. There will always be a place for the modern woodworker, whether amateur or professional, who can take the best from the past and use the benefits of modern equipment to do craftsmanlike work, not to copy what is being produced in factories, but to make individual pieces of woodwork in which, instead of design making concessions to machines, machines support the hand processes. The result is something to be proud of as a piece of twentieth-century craftsmanship.

Fortunately, I have had the benefits of following generations of family craftsmen and have spent a lifetime mainly devoted to various aspects of woodworking, and I have kept pace with the changes in equipment and materials. In this book I have pointed the way for the individual woodworker who wants to master the skills of his craft using the tools and equipment available today.

Percy W. Blandford

Chapter 1
WOOD

Wood is one of the most widely-used and versatile constructional materials. Fortunately for us, it regenerates and what we use is replaced by new growth. Today trees do not replace themselves as quickly as wood is used, but supplies are plentiful still, even if some of the particular species we would like are not always available when we want them. Sometimes wood has been taken in excessive quantities, as when English forests were denuded of oak trees in the days of the building of wooden warships. The slow-growing oaks have not yet recovered. Sometimes nature takes a hand: in many countries the terrible plague of Dutch elm disease, for example, has removed that wood from common use.

With modern methods of transport timber may be brought to almost any port from almost any part of the world. This means that we can now use woods that were unknown to carpenters even only a few years ago. Many of the traditional and well-known woods are still available, but others have been added to them and it is sometimes difficult to know the characteristics and suitability of the woods we are being offered. It was sometimes difficult to identify even the comparatively few woods in general use up to a few years ago. Now it is increasingly difficult, particularly if you want to use a common name. For instance, there are some widely-different species that are all called 'mahogany'. Even a prefix in front of it may not be sufficiently specific. A name like 'Brazilian mahogany' can be used to embrace a group rather than refer to one type. There are scientific names, which are essential if you need to state exactly which wood you mean. But, if you use them when buying wood, it is unlikely that the average timberyard man will know what you are talking about. Fortunately, the woods on offer are usually sufficiently limited in range for each type to be identified by a common name, and the seller will probably know enough about the characteristics to tell you how a new wood compares with another you know already. There are many thousands of different species of tree yielding timber suitable for various branches of woodworking, but those available at any particular time or place will be comparatively few.

Anyone with a little experience can identify some woods by their appearance, if only in very general terms. But even amongst the common woods there are varieties that show subtle differences when you work them. The only true way to identify wood is by microscopic examination, and as most of us do not have facility to do this, we have to take the word of the suppliers.

Trees can be broadly divided into hardwoods and softwoods. In most cases that is a fair description of relative hardness, but there are a few softwoods harder than some hardwoods. Most softwoods come from coniferous, needle-leaved trees that keep their leaves during the winter. Hardwoods have broad leaves, and in more severe climates these tend to be shed during the winter. Softwood trees are commonest in the colder parts of the world, while many hardwoods grow in the tropics, but there is a considerable range of both varieties in all sorts of climate.

Softwoods grow quickly, maturing in 20 to 50 years. Some of them are grown to be pulped and made into newsprint. Hardwood may take hundreds of years to grow large enough for conversion to timber. The relative density of hardwoods is much greater than that of softwoods; some hardwoods are so dense that they will not float in water, which obviously makes them unsuitable for use in boat-building or similar work.

CONVERSION

When a tree grows it develops from the centre outwards, producing a ring of grain each year. The earlier rings become compressed and hardened as they form the strong heartwood around an almost invisible pith. The newer sapwood outside is not as strong or as durable as the heartwood. In some woods there is a very obvious division between heartwood and sapwood, but in others it is more gradual and therefore less obvious. As far as possible, sapwood should be avoided, but in some woods the difference in quality is slight. Wider boards will usually be cut across the heartwood, although there may be some sapwood at the edges. Narrow battens and strips may come from offcuts near the outside of the log and be entirely sapwood. If you want to ensure having heartwood, it may be better to cut down your own narrow pieces from wider boards.

The outside of a log is no use for general woodwork. Usually, the bark and the cambium layer under it should

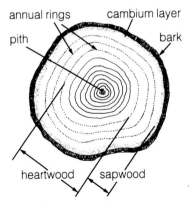

1.1 As a tree grows it forms annual rings outwards and these are the visible grain markings in cut wood. Bark is usually removed from the outside.

have been removed (fig. 1.1), but for decorative outside woodwork these outer layers may be retained, giving a board with a waney edge.

The part of the log from which a board comes can be found by examining its end grain. This is better grasped if the methods of cutting are understood. The simplest way to convert a log to planks is to make a series of cuts straight across (fig. 1.2a). Another way is to turn the log through 90° between cuts, so that its section as it is reduced is square (fig. 1.2b). With both of these methods you can examine the end grain and see, to fairly close limits, where the board came from and how far it was from the centre of the tree. This could be important in relation to warping possibilities.

Another method of cutting is radial or quarter-sawing (fig. 1.2c). Making every cut truly radial is wasteful and cutting is usually done in steps with a quarter section (fig 1.2d). With this method only a few pieces are near radial. In addition to the annual rings around a section of log there are medullary rays, which radiate from the centre. They occur in all woods, but in most they are too fine to be seen with the naked eye. Oak is the best-known exception. The medullary rays can be seen at the end grain and when cut radially they produce a pattern known as *figuring*. Wainscot, or figured, oak is cut in this way.

SEASONING

The lifeblood of a tree is sap, which becomes excess moisture in the wood when the tree is felled and converted to boards. Most of this moisture must be removed before you use the wood, and this process is called seasoning. The traditional way is called 'air' or 'natural' seasoning, when the boards are stacked with spacers between them (fig. 1.3) and left to dry out to an acceptable level of sap content. The rule of thumb is one year of drying for every 2-3cm (1in) of thickness, so natural seasoning is a slow process. There are several ways of speeding the drying, usually with some form of kiln, which can reduce the period to weeks. Too hasty drying, however, causes warping, cracking and some other problems.

A small amount of moisture is normal and acceptable in wood, and, as wood is a natural material, it will always absorb and lose moisture, according to the temperature and relative humidity of the atmosphere. As wood dries, it shrinks, so if wood is stored in a workshop that is normally unheated, and then an object made from it is kept in a well

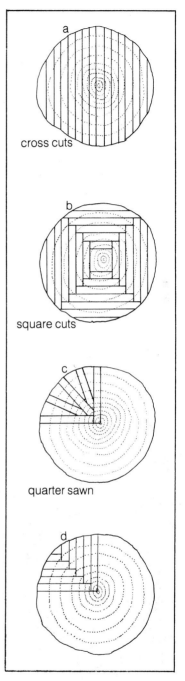

cross cuts

square cuts

quarter sawn

1.2 A log may be cut 'through and through' (a), it may be cut in alternate directions for different grain markings (b), it could be cut radially (c) or near radially (d) for the sake of figuring, particularly in oak.

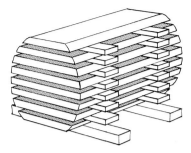

1.3 *For natural seasoning boards are stacked so air can circulate.*

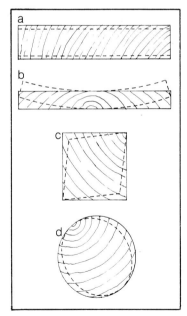

1.4 *Wood may shrink the direction of the grain lines as seen at the end, so a board with lines across gets thinner (a), one cut away from the centre of the tree will warp (b), a square will become a diamond section (c) and a round will become elliptical (d).*

heated room, parts may shrink or warp enough to spoil appearance or construction. Before making an object, it is advisable to store the wood for some time in the same sort of atmosphere, and temperature, as that in which the finished object is likely to be kept. In any case, it is always good practice to buy a stock of wood well before you need it, and to keep it for further natural seasoning before making something from it.

Shrinkage tends to reduce the length of the annual rings. If the board has been cut radially, with the annual rings appearing across the end from top to bottom, it will get thinner as it dries (fig. 1.4a); but any cross-wise shrinkage will be negligible. If the grain lines on the end show that the board was cut across the trunk of the tree further out from the centre, it will cast or warp as it dries. You can anticipate what may happen by imagining the grain lines trying to straighten out (fig. 1.4b). If you start with a square section, shrinking in the direction of the annual rings will pull the shape towards a diamond section (fig. 1.4c). Similarly, a circular cross-section will reduce to an elliptical section (fig. 1.4d).

Those examples suggest what may happen. If the wood has been properly seasoned, it may never shrink or warp enough to be noticeable. If you are aware of what might happen, you can allow for it during construction. For instance, a wide solid wood top can be held to rails with wood buttons engaging in slots, so that the top may get slightly wider or narrower without causing splits or joint failures.

SIZES

The maximum width and thickness of boards that can be cut from a tree must depend on the size of the tree. When allowance has been made for cutting off the bark and the outer sapwood, the available width may not be as great as expected, and further allowance must be made for the taper of the trunk and for cutting out any flaws. An extra charge is often made for particularly wide boards, so do not order wood wider than you need. In fact, you may get a better result by gluing together two narrower boards to make up a required width, as you can arrange the end grains so that any tendency to warp in one is reversed in the other.

Some wood is available in very long pieces, but for convenience in transport and storage it is usually supplied in lengths of about 6 m (20 ft) or less. If you need a single piece longer than the maximum normally available, you will probably have to place a special order. Do not order timber that is longer than you need. For example, if you want four pieces 4 m (13 ft) long, do not order one piece four times that length. A piece that long might not be in stock, while the yard man could probably find wood to cut the four pieces and you might gain some extra ends that he did not think worth cutting off.

If you buy your wood already planed (PAR), the sizes quoted will refer to dimensions as measured before planing. With power planers of the sizes used, your wood will probably be about 3 mm (⅛ in) undersize in each direction.

Knots in a board come where there was a branch leading off the trunk. A tree grown in a forest will have few knots because there were no branches in the lower part of the trunk. A tree grown in isolation may have many knots due to branches in its lower part. Knots must be accepted and may even be regarded as decorative in the grain pattern of polished work. However, knots weaken the wood. If the part is load-carrying, a knot that is large in relation to the wood section should not be accepted. In softwoods, in particular, a black ring round a knot indicates a 'dead knot', one that is no longer bonded to the surrounding wood. A dead knot may fall out, and whether it does or not it contributes nothing to strength, so discard the wood or use it where this weakness does not matter.

Trees develop shakes, which are cracks due to the tree swinging and twisting in the wind. They may radiate from the centre or follow the lines of the annual rings. They are not apparent until the tree is felled and cut into boards. Usually wood can be cut to size around them. End cracks may occur during seasoning, but these should be cut off before the wood is sold.

Before ordering wood, prepare a cutting list showing all the pieces you need, correct to section, but allowing a little extra on the lengths. If you show this to your supplier, it will save him time and trouble in finding suitable pieces from his stock – and the saving should be reflected in the price. If you expect to be making considerable use of your workshop and have a good idea of the types of project you will undertake, it is worth buying more wood than you need for the immediate job, so that some can go into stock. This gives you something to draw from, and stops you having to go out again for just a small amount. Storing the wood in your workshop will also stabilize it by further seasoning. Aim to reach a stage where you have enough wood on your racks to tackle some projects without having to buy wood specially.

SOFTWOODS

Besides being soft, most softwoods are light, both in weight and in colour. Because they come from tall straight trees, boards tend to be available in good lengths, but the sections are not very wide. Some softwoods have many knots, which are acceptable if they are small – although knotty pine panelling, in which large knots are a feature, has enjoyed a vogue. In many softwoods the grain lines on the surface are not very obvious. In some woods there is a considerable amount of resin, which imparts durability and causes dark and light grain lines. Resin may not show up much in the paler softwoods except where it comes to the surface at knots. The knot can be sealed, usually with shellac (see p.185), then painted or varnished over so that the resin does not spoil the finish.

Softwoods are confusingly named and the common names are not always the same in every place. Spruce, fir and pine may be found applied to the same woods. These are the names of trees as well as the cut wood. Sitka spruce is the lightest and straightest-grained wood with the minimum of knots. Because of this it has been used in aircraft construction and in making wooden yacht masts, although its durability in wet conditions is poor. Firs are mostly natural poles, stripped of bark and used for rustic and other outdoor purposes. The word pine is not always correctly used, but it has found a place in furniture as 'stripped pine'. Yellow pine is a stable, easily-worked softwood that has been popular in patternmaking for metal casting.

At one time the common softwoods in Britain were red deal and white deal, with the red version being the better quality. The names have changed, and they are now known as Baltic redwoods. In America there are giant redwoods, which are not to be confused with the Baltic woods.

Most softwoods are not durable in damp conditions, although the modern method of impregnation with preservative makes them suitable for outdoor use. Larch is a softwood that is more durable outdoors than many others, and it can be used for boat planking. Several varieties of cypress have similar properties and are used instead of larch, particularly in America.

The wood with the most resin is pitch pine, which is obtainable in large sizes. It is strong and heavy, but the amount of resin makes it unsuitable for painting. Columbian and Oregon pines are straight-grained and have less resin, and can be used for spars and other parts requiring strength in the length with small cross-sections.

Cedar is a name given to both hard and soft woods, most of which are soft and light with a fragrance that makes them attractive for lining linen chests. Parana pine is variegated, with brown and occasional red streaks, and may be used as a general-purpose softwood.

In general, softwoods are not furniture woods, although they can be used internally and for parts that do not show. They are the woods for general carpentry and tend to be much cheaper than hardwoods. Such things as floors and roof trusses in ordinary buildings are made from softwoods, as is much domestic woodwork – usually painted, rather than given a clear finish. However, although softwoods suffer more from wear and tear than hardwoods do, it is possible to protect them with tough modern clear finishes. If the object being made has to be as light as possible, softwood should be used. Softwoods are more amenable to nailing, and can be used in situations where hardwoods would need joints cut or the parts screwed together.

HARDWOODS

Hardwoods of furniture quality mostly come from specialist suppliers, who are often knowledgeable on their stock and its properties for cabinetwork. This is important because there are many woods on the market, sometimes for short periods only, that are welcome alternatives to some of the more established furniture woods, and we need to know their characteristics before using them. With the enormous numbers of different hardwood trees growing in the world, and the different names applied to some of them, it is not always easy to find details in reference books, so accurate information from the man on the spot is invaluable.

The seasoning of hardwood is important, but it is a comparatively slow process. It is advisable to buy hardwoods well ahead of your needs, if possible, so that the wood can dry or stabilize in your store for a few months. The yard expert may be able to give you an idea of how the wood was seasoned, how long it has been in stock and what its present state should be.

Such things as shakes and knots will show, whether the wood is bought planed or unplaned, but it is not always easy to visualize the final appearance of the woodgrain if it is bought 'from the saw'. If you are unfamiliar with the type of wood, it is advisable to buy it planed or have one surface planed so that you can see the grain pattern. You are not necessarily looking for straightness of grain or freedom from knots and other flaws. If the purpose of the wood is structural, straight grain may be important, but in furniture much of the beauty of the wood is in wavy grain and other markings, provided that you are able to plane and work them smooth.

There is a great variety of hardwoods available. The ones listed below may be regarded as the standards for comparison if you are offered woods with which you are unfamiliar. You need to know the qualities of a new wood before you use it, and, if you are planning to make several matching pieces, whether supplies of it will be maintained.

English oak is a darkish brown, fairly hard and with many pockets in the grain. It is rather coarse and tended to be used for fairly massive furniture, although it can be carved in quite fine detail. The medullary rays are quite prominent and quarter-sawn boards show them cut through to make the well-known figuring. English oak is a strong structural timber and very durable, and there are examples of its use in architecture and furniture surviving after many centuries. Japanese oak has a very similar appearance, with prominent medullary rays, but it is softer and much easier to work. Chestnut is a wood sometimes used with or in place of oak. It comes from the sweet chestnut tree, not the horse chestnut. Its appearance can be matched closely to oak, but as its medullary rays are invisible it cannot be used where figuring is required. It is less durable, but for indoor furniture it will last as long as required.

Elm has almost disappeared from the market because of Dutch elm disease. In fact, the disease only affected the outside of the tree, so a good deal of useful wood could still be cut from the logs of a diseased tree. Elm has a similar brown colour to oak and has similar hardness. Much of its grain is very twisted, and finishing a surface can be difficult. It is a good wood for outdoor furniture, particularly as it is available in very wide boards, and with a waney edge, if required.

Because of its complicated grain an elm board has fairly equal strength in all directions; other woods, with straighter grain, are weaker across it. This makes elm suitable for seats and other broad expanses that may have to take loads in all directions. It is used for seats of Windsor chairs as well as milking stools.

Beech, another widely-used timber, is reddish-brown, and the reddish tinge may be intensified during seasoning. Once seasoned, it is very stable, which has made it the choice for wooden planes, mallet heads and many other tools. Beech does not have the sort of grain that makes it a feature on the surface of furniture. It is close and not prominently marked, and although medullary rays may be seen on the end grain, they are only visible as small flecks on a surface. However, it is good structurally and as a backing for veneer. It is one of the most easily turned woods, cutting fine detail with little risk of the grain breaking out. It is not very durable, so is unsuitable for outdoor use, unless treated.

Ash is a greyer brown than oak, but with a similar open grain. It is not durable, but in the past its flexibility and springiness, made it the best wood for shafts of a cart, hammer hafts, and similar applications where the springiness was needed to cushion the load. It is still used for furniture – although usually very wide boards cannot be obtained – and tools and farm implements. Ash can be steamed and bent to tighter curves and in thicker sections than most other woods. Hickory, smoother than ash, but with similar springy properties, is often used for hammer and axe handles instead of ash.

Mahogany is a name that covers a large range of woods, some of which are not truly of the mahogany family. This is the wood of the great cabinetmakers. All mahoganies come from the hotter countries, and species are usually known by their country of origin. Honduras mahogany is sometimes considered *the* high-class furniture wood, but very similar types come from other Central American countries. All have a reddish tinge that tends to intensify with exposure to light, but it is common in furniture-making to stain mahogany redder before finishing. These mahoganies come from large trees, so wide boards are often available. The woods are mostly used in the rather short lengths needed for furniture. Some furniture is made with choice mahogany veneers on a plainer and cheaper wood backing.

African mahogany is a browner red and straighter-grained lighter wood than these. Some of it, such as Gaboon, does not belong to the same family as the mahoganies from the other side of the Atlantic. With longer straighter lengths available, it is used in boat building.

Walnut has been used extensively in furniture and there are plenty of antique walnut pieces around, but its use now is not as common as it once was. It is brown or brownish-red with a close, fairly hard-textured grain and little prominent marking. The darker variety may be called 'black walnut'. Both varieties are strong and fairly easy to work, so surfaces can be brought to a good finish.

Teak is fairly costly as a solid wood, but it has become better known as a veneer on commercially-produced chipboard panels. It is a light brown wood with fairly straight grain. Its characteristic is an oiliness, which has a good preservative quality and makes teak one of the best woods for use in boat building. Because of the oiliness teak is better not treated with any of the usual furniture finishes. Sometimes it is left untreated, or given an oiled finish.

Afromosia comes from Africa. It looks similar and is very similar in character to teak, and can be used in place of it, usually at a lower cost.

Maple is a light-coloured furniture hardwood, chiefly seen only as veneer. It can be cut to show an attractive 'birds-eye' figuring, and such boards may be sold as 'birds-eye maple'.

Sycamore and plane are names for similar trees, although the wood from either may be called sycamore, or buttonwood. This near-white close-grained hardwood has a clear, smooth appearance. It stains easily and is sometimes matched to other woods. It is stable, but not very durable. It can be turned easily and is used in making some musical instruments. Large sizes are available and a board makes a good bench-top.

Lime is not used much today, although it is one of the easiest woods to work and was used to create some of the famous carvings of the past. It is lightweight and near white, without any strong markings.

Obeche is one of the woods that are technically hardwoods, although it is actually lighter and softer than some softwoods. It has a uniform cream colour with little prominence to the grain, which may interlock and be difficult to chisel across. It can be stained to match other hardwoods, and can be used for shelving and similar purposes instead of softwoods.

PLYWOOD

While solid wood has its attractions, it also has some limitations, particularly when wide, thin pieces are required, as can be seen in some of the cracked distorted panels and backs in old furniture. Plywood gives wide stable panels of wood in sizes bigger than most woodworkers will require. For door panels, cabinet backs and similar purposes, plywood is the material to use. Much early plywood was made of three plies held with glue that was unreliable, and that gave plywood a bad name, but modern plywood is nearly all bonded with a synthetic resin glue that holds well and is either water-resistant or fully waterproof.

Plywood is made with at least three veneers glued together with grains crossing (fig. 1.5a). There may be any number of veneers and they can be of different thicknesses within one overall thickness. A larger number of thin veneers is stronger than a smaller number of thick ones in the same total thickness. For example, five thicknesses (fig. 1.5b) within an overall depth of 9mm (⅜in) is stiffer than three thicknesses in the same total depth (fig. 1.5c). The total is always an odd number, so the grain of the outside veneers goes the same way – normally along the length of a sheet.

Many woods are made into plywood, provided that they can be cut from a rotating log with a knife to make veneers. A softwood used in large quantities is Douglas fir which has a coarse open surface, but most other plywoods are fairly smooth. Plywood can be given an extra face of choice veneer, either by the craftsmen or during manufacture, and in this way a plywood panel can be made to match a surrounding frame of solid wood.

Building-quality plywood may be bought with knots and other defects in one or both surfaces. In better plywood knots have been cut out and patched, or the veneers are of a type that is free of knots. Exterior-grade plywood is used for outdoor work. It should be a durable wood bonded with fully-waterproof glue. In some inferior plywood, joints in inner plies show gaps, which are weak spots. Of better quality than exterior-grade is marine-grade plywood, in which the core plies as well as the outside ones are of good quality and close-fitting. Marine-grade and much exterior-grade plywood are made of mahogany-like woods.

Metric measurements are usually used to specify the thickness of plywood, but imperial measurements are often used for standard surface sizes. Common thicknesses are from 6mm (¼in) to 25mm (1in) or more, but other boards now are usually used in place of the thicker grades. Although 3mm (⅛in) is usually the thinnest plywood available, some aircraft plywood goes down to three plies within an overall thickness of 1mm (1/24in). Sheets can be made up to suit needs, but the usual maximum size is 2400 × 1200 mm (96 × 48 in), that being the largest that one man can reach across and carry (a woodworker's reach was considered standard before metric measurements were introduced). Plywood is good stock and it is much cheaper to buy standard size sheets to cut yourself than to ask the supplier to cut pieces to suit your immediate needs.

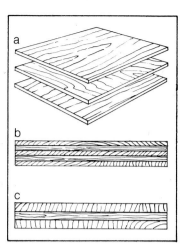

1.5 *Plywood is made with veneers having their grains crossing (a) – either a large number of thin veneers (b) or a greater number of thick ones (c).*

HARDBOARD

Hardboard must not be confused with hardwood. Hardboard is made from wood that is pulped and compressed to make sheets usually 3mm (⅛in) thick. The face surface is smooth and hard, and the other side is rougher, with a pattern of crossed lines. Some hardboard is little better than cardboard, but other boards are compressed to a very hard state. The toughest hardboard is treated with oil and described as oil-tempered. This kind has a resistance to damp, but the other grades soften and deteriorate if they get wet.

The chief advantage of hardboard is that it is cheaper than plywood or any other form of board. It takes strain and can be used with solid wood, but it cannot be disguised because of its lack of grain. It can be used for such things as the backs of cupboards and the bottoms of drawers, and for side or door panels in less-important painted assemblies. Sizes are similar to those of plywood.

Hardboard can be bought with a regular pattern of holes, either for a ventilating panel or for use with hooks on which to hang tools. It may also be found in a form that has a pattern on the surface, such as a series of ridges, which can be cut across and used as moulding. This may suit something like a bar front, but is not a traditional furniture treatment.

Softboard is similar to hardboard, but deliberately made softer. It is sometimes used for insulation. Pins can be stuck into one grade, and this may be framed for use as a noticeboard.

BLOCKBOARD

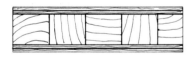

1.6 Blockboard is thicker than most plywood and has a core of solid wood strips.

Instead of plywood being made up to a great thickness, the inside may be made of solid wood strips – giving blockboard, battenboard or solid-core plywood. Usually blockboard has two veneers on each side, their grain going the same way, with strips of a solid wood laid together on the inside (fig. 1.6). Thicknesses are from about 19mm (¾in) upwards. Thinner boards are more likely to be like normal plywood – all veneers. Blockboard provides a stiff panel suitable for table-tops and similar large areas. Compared with solid wood, blockwood and plywood are stable, so there is no fear of a broad top expanding and contracting in relation to the supports below. This means that, although in solid wood the joints used have to take account of this factor, a plywood or blockboard top can be fixed down rigidly.

CHIPBOARD

Boards made with particles of wood embedded in synthetic resin are sold as chipboard or particleboard. Usually the proportion of wood to resin is enough for edges to be sawn and planed in a similar way to wood. The untreated surfaces are smooth and level, but an unattractive drab grey in colour. In that form the material is used in place of floor boards and in other situations where appearance is unimportant. For household and furniture use chipboard is sold already surfaced in many ways. A common finish is a white plastic veneer on surfaces and edges, so a board may be bought already suitable for use as, say, a shelf. There are plastic surfaces that have simulated wood grain effects, which are often seen in mass-produced furniture. While that treatment may be acceptable for some purposes, wood-grain plastic cannot be used alongside, real wood. For use in furniture making, there are chipboard panels available already veneered with wood, but the range of veneers is limited, so it may be necessary to start by selecting other woods to match what can be obtained on chipboard.

For furniture making veneered panels are available – usually veneered on the surfaces and edges, but not the ends. There is not much choice of thickness. That most commonly available is about 18mm (¾in). Many stock widths and lengths can be had, and it is best to design the other parts around these.

For covering cut edges, strips of self-adhesive veneer can be bought. These are made slightly too wide, to allow for trimming after fitting (fig. 1.7), and can be pressed on with a hot domestic iron.

Chipboard is heavier than comparable solid wood or plywood, but it provides broad stable panels of reasonable strength. Any furniture shop shows how the material has revolutionized the mass-production furniture industry. The individual craftsman may not want to make one-off copies of the product of a factory, but within the limits of good design veneered chipboard has a place in furniture construction.

1.7 Chipboard made from wood particles and resin may have veneer on the surfaces and edges.

LAMINATED PLASTIC

What was originally designed as an insulating material made of paper embedded in resin has been developed into an attractive hard-surface material, a well-known trade name being *Formica*. This gives a hard kitchen top or similar working surface. It needs a stable base, such as plywood or blockboard, to which it is attached with a special contact adhesive. The regular plastic surface supplied on chipboard is not hard enough to stand up to kitchen and similar work, but laminated plastic is the treatment to use in making anything of that sort.

Laminated plastic is no more than 2mm (just over ¹⁄₁₆in) thick. Until it is fixed down the material is brittle and can be cracked, so careful handling is necessary.

Chapter 2
HAND TOOLS

Not very long ago all woodworking had to be done by hand methods. Some of it was very laborious and time-consuming and was mostly concerned with the preparation of wood for the skilled processes involved in finally fitting together and applying a finish to a piece of work. Fortunately, we now have power tools that can not only take out much of the hard work in the preparation of wood but also do certain later processes – often with greater precision than might be achieved by hand methods.

However, there is still an important place for hand tools. It may be possible to make some furniture and other wooden assemblies almost entirely by machine, but those designs are planned to suit the method, and lack the features that indicate craftsmanship. The pieces will be identical mass-production products, which have a place in modern life, but they cannot compare with the one-off products of a skilled craftsman. Even if similar pieces are made to the same plan, there will be slight subtle differences.

Anyone who wants to call himself a craftsman in wood needs hand tools. They are more important to him than power tools, as it is possible to buy wood already machined, so that a project can be completed by hand work. But it is advisable to have *some* power tools, if much work is to be tackled without outside help. Mostly, hand tools are accumulated and we discover from the work being tackled what we need. But a bewildering array can be had, so it is possible to be attracted by a tool and buy it – to discover later that, although it might be appropriate for more limited uses, it is not the best for the general run of work being tackled. Of course, no good quality tool is valueless, but in some cases another might have been a better buy.

Hand tools are only good investments if they are good quality. Tool catalogues show what is available. British woodworking tools have a reputation for quality, and they are often used in preference to locally-made tools in many countries of the world. If a few catalogues are examined, some manufacturers' names (not always of the large firms) will be found to occur often in connection with certain types of tools: some specialists, for example, make only carving tools. This shows they are the recognized makers of those tools for craftsmen. Their tools are not usually cheapest, but in general price is a good guide to quality.

Many woodworking tools have to cut. It is the quality of the steel in them that controls their ability to take and keep a sharp edge. A good tool by a recognized maker can be given a sharper edge and it will hold it longer than a cheap tool from an unknown source. So if it is necessary to be economical when buying tools, it is advisable to spend what you must to get good cutting tools, while settling for something cheaper when buying tools for other purposes. It may even be better to spread the purchase of tools, getting good ones at intervals as funds allow. Most tools will give a lifetime of service, so get the best you can and make sure they are appropriate to your needs.

SAWS

Heavier cutting of wood to size may be done with power tools, either before you buy the wood or with your own workshop equipment, so some of the larger traditional handsaws are no longer essential. For cutting along the grain a rip saw – with large teeth sharpened for such cutting – used to be used. If one is available it is worth keeping in your kit, but lengthwise cuts are now normally made with a circular saw. For cutting across the grain you will still need to use a hand or panel saw, 500 mm (20 in) to 650 mm (26 in) long and with teeth about 8 per 25 mm (1 in) (fig. 2.1). If most of your work is in hardwoods, it is better to use saws that have slightly finer teeth than the ones used on softwoods. You may still use a circular saw for many cuts across the grain, but there are times, if – for instance – you are away from a workshop, when the handsaw is essential. It is interesting to note that although most Western craftsmen use saws that cut on the push stroke, in the Far East it is more usual for saws to be sharpened so that their teeth cut on the pull stroke. With normal saw handles you get the best control if you hold with your forefinger pointing along the blade, and allow the teeth to cut without putting excessive hand pressure on the saw.

Your most important handsaw is a backsaw, for precision cuts when working at the bench (fig. 2.2). The larger version may be called a tenon saw and a smaller one is a dovetail saw, but both saws are used for many things besides cutting those joints. The most expensive saws have brass backs,

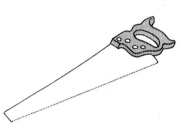

2.1 *A hand saw is the general-purpose tool for cutting to size.*

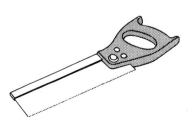

2.2 *A backsaw is the benchwork tool for precision cuts.*

2.3 A coping saw is for cutting curves in thinner wood.

2.4 A compass saw may have several blades to fit the handle for cutting curves.

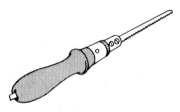

2.5 A keyhole saw is used for fine internal cuts.

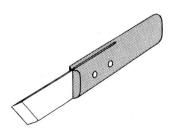

2.6 A marking knife is used instead of a pencil for greater accuracy in marking out.

which are heavier than the cheaper steel backs. Apart from the attractive appearance, the extra weight is an advantage. The teeth are sharpened for cutting across the grain and should be fairly fine. About 15 teeth per 25 mm (1 in) will suit a tenon saw, and a dovetail saw should have slightly finer teeth. There is no need to buy both saws in the first instance. A 300 mm (12 in) tenon saw will do its own and a dovetail saw's work, although the latter has advantages for small and delicate cuts.

Curves are most accurately and conveniently cut on a bandsaw, but if at first they have to be cut by hand the most suitable hand tool is a coping saw with some spare blades (fig. 2.3). These tools are all the same size, and the normal blades have rather coarse teeth. There are limitations, particularly in the distance a cut can be from the edge, but the blade can be turned in relation to the frame and with a little ingenuity it is possible to use the tool in many applications.

If you have a power bandsaw or a jigsaw, the coping saw need be the only handsaw for curves in your kit. But, if you want to cut curves far from an edge or in thicker wood than a coping saw will manage, there are narrow-bladed handsaws, often sold with three blades of different widths to fit into one handle, which may be described as compass saws (fig. 2.4). If of good quality steel, they are worth having, but more than the usual proportion of inferior standard goods may be on offer when you are looking for this tool.

A useful narrow one-ended saw is a keyhole saw (fig. 2.5). Its name describes its purpose. It is possible to get a pad handle with a slot through it that will hold a keyhole saw or a metal-cutting hacksaw blade. Saws very similar to keyhole saws are obtainable to fit into some holders for disposable knife blades. Any of these are cheap and give you the means of tackling awkward internal cuts. All are soft, bending instead of breaking if the cut does not go as you wish, so do not expect the same stiffness as in other saws.

EDGE TOOLS

Much hand woodwork is done with chisels and other tools with sharp edges. It is in this sphere that the most bewildering variety of tools is offered. When getting a tool kit together, it is best to start with a few basic cutting tools and add to them as the work shows a need. As with other tools, it is unwise to accept any collection sold as a kit – you may be buying tools you never use.

All woodworkers have uses for knives. The cutting edge at the point is most important in a knife used for marking out across the grain: the rest of the knife can be almost any shape. There are special marking knives (fig. 2.6), but many craftsmen use ordinary pocket knives or one of the types sold with replaceable blades (fig. 2.7). A broken-off table knife can be sharpened to have a sloping cutting end for use as a marking knife. Some marking knives are sold with pointed awls at the other end. That can be dangerous, unless it has a cover. A marking awl has some uses, particularly for getting into places where a marking knife cannot go, such as around dovetail pins, but any pointed steel rod can be used for this (fig. 2.8). A sharpened steel knitting needle in a handle is suitable.

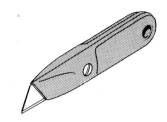

2.7 An alternative to the marking knife has replaceable blades.

2.8 A fine awl has uses in marking out.

Chisels and gouges

The general-purpose chisels are usually described as firmer chisels. They can have square or bevel edges (fig. 2.9). The bevel edges allow the chisel to get closer into corners. They may be slightly less stiff, but in modern woodworking they do not get such tough treatment. New chisels bought should have bevel edges. For a first purchase, four chisels should be enough: 25 mm (1 in), 19 mm (¾ in), 12 mm (½ in), 6 mm (¼ in).

Longer and thinner chisels are called paring chisels (fig. 2.10). Thicker chisels are called mortise chisels (fig. 2.11), from their original use in chopping out mortises. Both types still have uses, but purchase should be left until the work justifies it.

2.9 Firmer chisels are for general use and may have square or bevel edges.

Many chisels are offered with plastic handles moulded on. These are tough and strong enough to stand up to hammering, but most craftsmen prefer wooden handles with brass ferrules. Traditional woods for chisel handles are beech and box, but others are used. If you have a lathe, you can buy chisels without handles and make your own – individual and cheaper. With individually-turned handles you soon get to recognize them easier among shavings on the bench. The tapered tang goes into a hole tapered in steps, so that it drives in tightly without splitting the wood. There may be a leather washer between the chisel shoulder or bolster and the handle if it is likely to have its end hit.

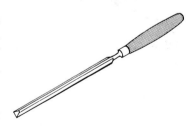

2.10 A paring chisel is longer and thinner than a firmer chisel.

Further chisels bought will be of intermediate sizes, with some larger ones. A broad long paring chisel is often useful, but you have to remember that it is not stiff enough to be hit. If you cut many mortise and tenon joints, it is worth getting chisels the same width as the mortises most commonly cut – 9 mm (⅜ in) is a popular width. Here you may prefer a square-edged chisel to a bevel-edged one.

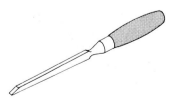

2.11 A mortise chisel is thickened to withstand levering.

2.12 *A paring gouge is sharpened inside.*

2.13 *A gouge sharpened outside is used for hollowing.*

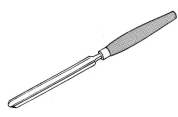

2.14 *A turning gouge is long and mainly used for roughing work to shape in a lathe.*

2.15 *A turning chisel is long and is mainly used for finishing turned surfaces.*

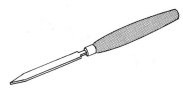

2.16 *A parting tool separates turned parts.*

Gouges are chisels with curved cross-sections. You can do a considerable amount of woodwork without owning a gouge or finding a need for one, so purchase might be left until you feel the need. If a gouge is described as in-cannelled its sharpening bevel is on the inside of the curve (fig. 2.12). If it is out-cannelled the bevel is on the outside (fig. 2.13). The first type is used for paring to curved outlines, while the other is needed for scooping out hollows. If you decide to start with one in your kit, you are likely to find most use for a 12 mm (½ in) in-cannelled gouge.

Carving tools are specialized and of no use for general woodworking, so do not buy them unless your work will include carving. Carving tools include gouges in many widths, with different curves in each width, and with many shapes in each length. The variety of carving gouges alone may total more than one hundred, and this does not include chisels, 'V'-tools and others. A carver certainly need not start with them all, but he needs quite a large assortment.

Tools for use in lathe work

Wood turning may come within the general woodworker's scope and it can add considerably to what he can make. The basic tools for turning are few. There are now many special tools offered, but they should be avoided, at least until you have mastered the basic tools, which will do almost all the turning you require.

The general-purpose roughing tool is a gouge that is sharpened on the outside with a curved finger-nail end (fig. 2.14), although some turners favour a square-ended one for some work. For most turning of furniture parts a gouge 20 mm (¹³⁄₁₆ in) or 12 mm (½ in) will do everything, but another 6 mm (¼ in) wide is also needed. Finishing work is done with a chisel, using slicing cuts. Its edge is angled and sharpened from both sides (fig. 2.15). Only a small part of its edge is cutting at any time, so width is not important – one 12 mm (½ in) would be a good first buy. A parting tool is like a narrow thick chisel (fig. 2.16). It cuts straight into the wood being turned, to cut off or mark a depth.

Turning tools do not have to withstand having their ends hit, so they are not given a shoulder where the tang enters the handle. However, leverage is important and the blades of turning chisels and gouges are much longer than the ordinary bench types; these are then fitted to long handles for even more leverage. Although handles may be bought with the tools, most turners buy them unhandled and make their own. Differing forms or woods make identification of tools easier among the chips of wood on the lathe bed.

The standard tools are made either in ordinary strength or 'long and strong'. The latter are for heavy work as the size and stiffness damp down vibration, which causes 'chatter marks' on the work. Most furniture turning can be done with the ordinary strength tools.

It is necessary to measure and compare diameters when turning. You cannot put a rule across the work, and the tool to use for this is a pair of callipers. They may have a screw adjustment, as used in engineering, but a cheaper simple pair with a friction joint – if you can get it – will serve just as well (fig. 2.17). There are also inside callipers, with their points turned outwards, but these are rarely needed and should not be included among first purchases.

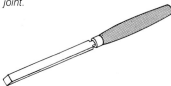

2.17 A simple form of calipers for checking diameters has a friction joint.

For bowls and similar items, the turning tools cut with a scraping action and are given obtuse angles. Ends may be square across for outside curves (fig. 2.18), or curved for use inside the object being turned (fig. 2.19). they may be bought, but can be adapted from chisels or straight pieces of tool steel, by grinding the ends. Some are made by grinding worn-out files. One straight and one curved scraping tool of somewhere near 25 mm (1 in) may make the start of a bowl turner's kit.

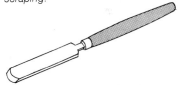

2.18 For bowl turning a straight-ended obtuse-angled tool is used for scraping.

2.19 A scraping tool is given a curved end for work inside a bowl.

PLANES

Traditional British planes have nearly always been made of beech. There are many still about and secondhand ones may be worth having, but any new planes bought should be metal. There is something to be said for the feel of a wooden plane and the way it slides over the wood being worked, but modern metal planes remain flat and have adjustments lacking in the wooden planes, which needed an acquired skill to deal with their crude means of setting.

Much wood is now machine-planed, so the heavy work of hand planing to prepare wood has gone. But the machine surface has to be followed by hand work to get the best results, and there are parts that cannot be machine-planed, so a craftsman still needs all the general-purpose bench planes.

The planes made by leading manufacturers are often similar, and vital parts suit various makes within a range of sizes. A minimum bench set consists of smoothing plane (fig. 2.20), a jack plane (fig. 2.21) and a trying plane or jointer (fig. 2.22). These planes differ only in the lengths of their soles, and if at first only one plane is bought, it should be a jack plane. The name comes from 'jack-of-all-trades': it is the

2.20 A smoothing plane is a finishing tool for bench use.

2.21 A jack plane is the general-purpose bench plane.

2.22 *A trying plane is longer and is particularly used for making straight edges.*

general-purpose plane. It can be used for removing machine plane marks from surfaces, and straightening edges or cuts across end grain. But the smoothing plane would be better for removing machine plane marks, and the long sole of a jointer is more suitable for bridging hollows and getting an uneven edge level.

In all these planes cutting is done by a blade, often called a plane iron. Although this is now made of steel, old wooden planes had blades of iron, with steel welded on to make the cutting edge. Over the blade goes a cap iron or chip breaker. This latter name, used in North America, is more appropriate, as the chip breaker breaks up the shavings as they come off the wood and prevents the surface tearing. For finishing work it is set quite close to the edge (fig. 2.23), but for coarse cuts it is brought back a little (not more than 1-2mm ($\frac{1}{16}$in)).

2.23 *The cap iron in a plane breaks off chips and is set close to the cutting edge.*

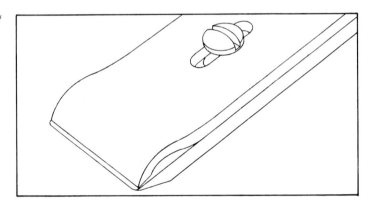

The planes also have adjustable mouths, and this is a control often ignored by users. A screw inside the sole behind the blade allows it to move the support of the cutting edge backwards and forwards a small amount, and so alter the width of the space ahead of the cutting edge. For fine finishing of hardwoods the mouth should be narrow, while for coarse cuts on soft woods, besides moving the cap iron back, it would be better to widen the mouth. If only one plane is available, these adjustments will have to be made to suit uses. But, if three planes are available, the jack can be kept set for coarser work, while the jointer has its cap iron closer to the edge and the mouth narrower, with the smoothing plane normally set finer than that.

The planes have a screw adjustment for depth of cut and a lever to regulate the tilt of the blade crosswise, so once the blade has been put in and the cap iron secured, adjustments may be made with the hand holding the tote or handle.

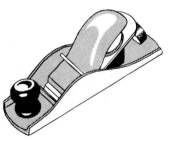

2.24 *A block plane is held in one hand for fine trimming and cuts across the grain.*

One other plane worth having is generally described as a block plane (fig. 2.24). This has a single iron, with its bevel upwards, fitted at a lower angle than in the other planes. This is a one-hand plane, particularly intended for use across the grain, but it can often be used to take off a sharp edge or make some other small cut. In the simplest block plane you have to adjust the cutter by moving it about by hand before locking it, but the better block planes have screw and lever adjustment as well as a means of altering the width of the mouth. They are worth the extra cost.

There are two operations that you may be able to do with power tools instead of using hand planes. These are cutting rabbets and making grooves. If you have suitable power facilities, purchase of the hand planes can be delayed; but in some woodwork you may reach a stage where you would be glad of the hand tools to follow, or take the place of, machine rabbeting (rebating) or grooving.

To cut a rabbet, the plane needs to cut the full width of the sole. There are planes made like the bench planes just described, but with the ends of the plane irons brought out through notches in the side of the sole, to give this effect (fig. 2.25). There are also narrower rebate planes to give the same effect, but in neither case is there any control of the depth or width of the cut. For this the plane is called a fillister (fig. 2.26). It is a rebate plane with a depth stop at one side and a fence on an extension at the other. The stop fence can be removed to make it a simple rebate plane. The type commonly available has a second position for the cutter close to the front of the plane, so that it can become a bull-nosed plane to get close into the end of a stopped rabbet, leaving only a small amount of wood to be removed with a chisel. The fillister may have a little side cutter ahead of the main edge, to sever the grain fibres and prevent the surface tearing up and leaving a ragged edge when a rabbet is being cut across the end of a board.

This desirable facility is not shared by the plough plane, the tool used for cutting grooves (fig. 2.27). It has a sole as narrow as the smallest of its cutters, but cutters from about 3 mm (⅛ in) to 12 mm (½ in) can be fitted. Like the fillister it has a depth stop, and a fence to regulate the distance of the groove from the edge.

There are combination planes that will make rabbets, plough, cut mouldings and form other sections. One is called a '55', since that is the number of planing functions it has. Although this obviously has some attractions, most craftsmen prefer a plane specifically suited to each job, and a combination plane should certainly not be an early purchase.

2.25 A rebate plane has its cutting edge the full width.

2.26 A fillister is a rebate plane with depth and width guides.

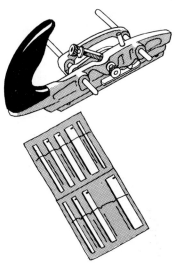

2.27 A plough cutter has several cutters for making grooves of many widths.

2.28 A hand router will level the bottom of a groove.

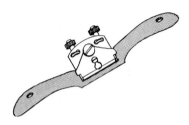

2.29 A spokeshave is a form of two-handled plane for use on curves.

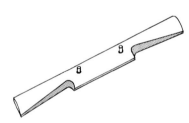

2.30 An older spokeshave is made of wood with a cutter that slices.

2.31 A brace holds bits for drilling and may have a ratchet for use when the swing is restricted.

The word 'router' is now accepted as referring to a power tool, but originally it was a type of plane with a projecting blade for levelling the bottom of a groove, such as a housing joint. Because of its appearance it was also known as an 'old woman's tooth'. The modern metal version (fig. 2.28) does not look so much like that, but it is a cheap and useful tool for this particular purpose.

Spokeshaves are like planes with handles at the sides. The modern metal version (fig. 2.29) has a wedged iron like a plane, but the older wooden type (fig. 2.30) has its cutter at a much flatter angle so that it makes more of a slice, and this may be found preferable when the tool is used to follow a curve. A spokeshave with a small flat sole is used on outside curves. One with a sole curved front to back is used on inside curves.

Much of the work of spokeshaves can be done with *Surform* tools. Spokeshaves belong to traditional craftsmanship, but *Surform* tools are quite effective, so the individual woodworker will have to decide which to buy and use.

DRILLING TOOLS

Old-time craftsmen talked of boring rather than drilling, but the latter term is more widely used. Almost up to the beginning of this century, when better drill bits for hand work began to appear, making holes was one of the less efficient processes in hand woodworking. By then, in any case, power drilling was becoming more common. Today it is probable that a craftsman who may have no other power equipment will have an electric drill. A hand-held electric drill or one of its more advanced variations takes much of the labour out of drilling and should produce cleaner and more accurate holes than boring with a brace and bit. However, there are steps in woodwork construction where a brace is necessary and a craftsman should include one in his tool kit.

It is worth getting a ratchet brace (fig. 2.31), as this allows you to turn the bit even when there is insufficient space for the handle to make a full circle. It also allows maximum leverage in a stubborn situation, as you can apply more turning power at some parts of the sweep than at others. Braces can be obtained with different lengths of sweep. A long sweep gives you more power, but you need more room to turn a full circle. The brace chuck is intended to take a standard square tapered end of a bit, but there are chucks to hold other shaped ends.

If an electric drill is available, most bits will be bought to fit that. These cannot be used in a brace. If bits are bought for the brace, they should be of the twist type, such as the *Jennings* type (fig. 2.32). These will drill shallow holes. An expansive bit to adjust to any large diameter hole is valuable, but not necessary as an early purchase. The usual bits have a central point that goes deeper than the main hole and may penetrate right through when the main hole is intended to be blind. The point is necessary to guide the drill as it penetrates. *Forstner* bits (fig. 2.33) are different, as they are guided by their circumference and have no extending central point. Besides making full holes, they can be used at an edge, where the circle breaks through the side. They are expensive, but should be remembered if the need arises.

Countersinking – hollowing for a screw head – is better done at the slow speed of a hand-turned brace than the high speed of an electric drill, so a suitable countersink bit for screws is worth having (fig. 2.34). A screwdriver bit should also be bought (fig. 2.35). More leverage can be applied to a stubborn screw with a bit and brace than by any other means.

Small holes for screws or other purposes, under about 6 mm (¼ in) diameter, are usually made with metalworking bits driven by the electric drill, but for the smallest sizes, under about 3 mm (⅛ in), this is rather clumsy and it is too easy to go too far. A simple wheel brace (fig. 2.36) gives better control and you are less likely to break the bits. The smallest wheel brace, with a chuck capacity of up to 6 mm (¼ in), is better than a breast drill or other large tool.

Gimlets are sold, but they should be avoided as they pull into the wood with a splitting action. An alternative to a small drill, for screws up to about 4 gauge, is a bradawl (fig. 2.37). Its chisel-shaped end is pushed in across the grain and quarter turns are given each way as it is pressed in. This severs the wood fibres and clears the way for the screw, but leaves the fibres ready to spring back and grip the screw threads, giving a stronger grip than in a hole where a drill has removed some of the wood as dust.

TOOLS USED FOR MEASURING AND TESTING

Apart, of course, from metrication in some countries there have been other changes in the way wood is measured and tested. The many versions of the folding carpenter's rule are almost obsolete. They have some uses, but should not be bought new. Most measuring is best done with an expanding tape or rule (fig. 2.38). Incidentally no craftsman talks

2.32 *A twist bit draws itself into the wood and keeps straight in a deep hole.*

2.33 *A Forstner bit is guided by its circumference and can make part holes.*

2.34 *A countersink bit prepares holes to take screw heads.*

2.35 *A screwdriver bit gives increased leverage on stubborn screws.*

2.36 *A wheel brace can be used instead of an electric drill for small bits.*

2.37 *A bradawl will make holes for small screws.*

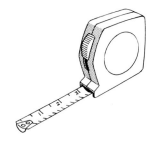

2.38 *An expanding tape/rule serves for most measuring.*

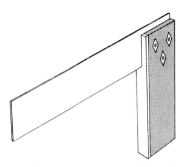

2.39 *Try squares are for marking and testing squareness.*

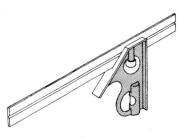

2.40 *A combination square measures and tests mitres and levels as well as squareness.*

2.41 *For special angles an adjustable bevel can be set and locked.*

about a ruler – there is no final *r*. The rule's length depends on your requirements, but for bench use 2 m or 6 ft should be sufficient, with another longer one for use elsewhere on large projects. Even with metrication some measurements will be required in Imperial measure, so both scales should be included.

Straight steel rules have two uses. They will measure, but they are also good straight-edges. A 300 mm (12 in) size is convenient to handle, but one twice that length is worth having. It can be sprung to draw curves as well as being a straight-edge. Markings on it should not be too fine – not less than 1 mm or 1/16 in for most of the length (although there could be finer markings for a short distance from one end) – and deep enough to be easily visible. Marks close together have to be shallower, which is one reason for close markings not extending too far along a rule. Stainless steel has attractions, but some stainless steel rules have very shallow markings.

Carpenters' pencils have rectangular section leads, so that they can be sharpened with a chisel end. Used on edge, it lasts longer between sharpenings than a round point. For accurate marking, where the cut line will not spoil a finished surface, it is better to cut distances across the grain with a knife, but pencils are frequently needed. Get them brightly coloured so as to be easily seen among shavings on the bench.

Angles and curves

Next to rules come try-squares, for marking and checking right-angles. This is another sphere where it is better to go for an all-metal square (fig. 2.39) than a wooden one with a metal blade. The all-metal square comes true and stays true. The truth of a square can be checked, even in the shop, by putting its stock against a straight edge and marking along its blade. Then turn it over and see if the mark matches.

A square with a 300 mm (12 in) blade will cope with most needs at the bench, but for marking out strips of wood of smaller section a smaller combination square (fig. 2.40) is more suitable. This is basically a rule with a sliding head on it that can be locked at any position. One side of the head is at 90° and the other is at 45° to the rule. Usually there is a spirit level in the head, so that it can be used to check whether something is vertical or horizontal. It may also have a small awl or scriber pushed into a hole in the head. Additional heads are available, less important for most woodworking. One is V-shaped, to allow the tool to be used to find the centre of a circle or draw a line square to a curve. The other is a head that can be adjusted to any angle to the rule with a built-in protractor. The basic combination square is more use than a small try-square; the other heads may be regarded as desirable, though not essential in a first tool kit.

The usual tool for marking angles other than square is an adjustable bevel (fig. 2.41). Some are made of wood, with a metal blade, but an all-metal one will stay accurate longer. There are various ways of locking the blade in position once it has been set. Some involve projections, such as levers or wing nuts. A flush screw that needs a screwdriver is better, as any fixture sticking out will stop it lying flat. Most angles to be marked or tested are fairly small, so a small adjustable bevel will do. If there is a need for a large one, it can be made from wood. Very large adjustable bevels are not usually available.

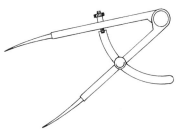

2.42 *Dividers must be stiff and lockable for marking wood.*

Large dividers are useful, not only for scratching circles, but for stepping off divisions along a line or around the circumference of a circle: a pair with 300 mm (12 in) arms will do (fig. 12.42). They should have stiff legs and a firm pivot, with a quadrant that locks firmly. Shaky dividers are no use. They are often called compasses, but a pair of compasses has one pencil point. For similar use, but a greater reach, trammel heads can be mounted on a strip of wood (fig. 2.43), but a strip of wood with two nails knocked through it serves the same purpose.

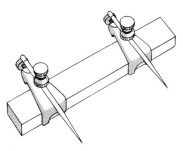

2.43 *Trammel heads will mount on a strip of wood for use as large compasses.*

Distances from an edge

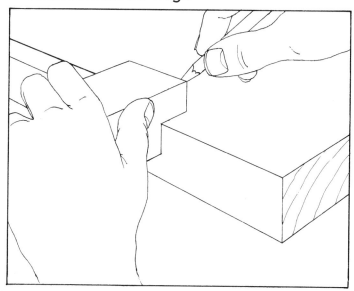

2.44 *Notched wood and a pencil will make a line parallel to an edge.*

2.45 *A combination square can be used in a similar way.*

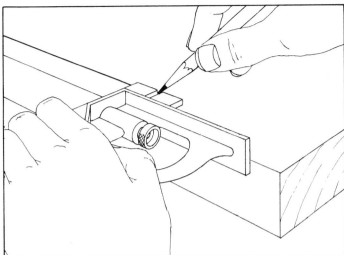

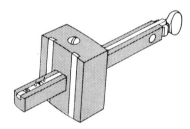

2.46 *A marking gauge is the general-purpose tool for scratching a line parallel with an edge.*

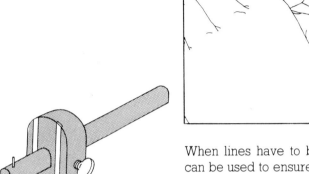

2.47 *A mortise gauge scratches two lines parallel with an edge, particularly for marking out mortise and tenon joints.*

2.48 *A cutting gauge cuts instead of scratches and is used for slicing veneers or marking cleanly across the grain.*

When lines have to be marked parallel to edges, gauges can be used to ensure accuracy and speed. It is possible to use a notched piece of wood with a pencil against it as it is drawn along (fig. 2.44). The end of a combination square can be similarly used with a pencil (fig. 2.45), but a marking gauge is more commonly used. Marking gauges are usually of wood with brass reinforcing on the face to take wear (fig. 2.46), but there are all-metal gauges. The thumbscrew in the wooden head is usually plastic, although older gauges have wood screws. The steel point is round, to scratch the wood.

A mortise gauge has two points (fig. 2.47), so that it can mark both sides of a tenon or mortise at the same time. Usually, one point is fixed to the stem, but the other is on a slide let into the stem, with a hand or screw adjustment to alter the distance between the points. Some of these gauges have a single point on the opposite side of the stem to the pair for mortises, so that they can be used as an ordinary marking gauge. It is not difficult to put a point in a mortise gauge bought without one, so avoiding the need to buy two gauges at first, although eventually you will probably be glad of more than one marking gauge.

A similar gauge, which may be needed as your work gets more ambitious, is a cutting gauge (fig. 2.48). Instead of the scratching point there is a blade sharpened on its end like a knife and held in place with a wedge. It will slice strips of veneer to width, cutting thicker strips by repeated passes from opposite sides. It can also be used as a marking gauge across the grain, making a cut instead of tearing the fibres as a round point does. A less-common marking or cutting gauge has a rotating wheel with a knife edge on the end of the stem. Besides its value for marking across the grain, it can be used close inside a rabbet or other obstruction – where the projecting end of the usual marking gauge could not reach.

CRAMPS

There are frequent occasions when you have to hold, pull or squeeze things together. Some improvisations are described later, and some devices are part of the bench or other fixed equipment, but there are a number of holding and gripping devices that are separate hand tools. Most prominent in your needs are 'G' cramps (fig. 2.49). They can be had in many sizes, described in terms of their capacity. Large ones are clumsy for holding small things, and some large cramps do not close fully, so a range of sizes is desirable. It helps to have two of each size, as cramping is often done in pairs. Much depends on the type of work being undertaken, but two at 75 mm (3 in) and two at 150 mm (6 in) could be your first purchases.

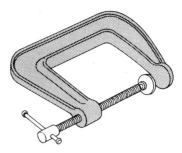

2.49 *G cramps, in many sizes, are general-purpose tools for squeezing parts together.*

There are several makes of adjustable cramp, and these allow one head to be slid to a convenient position (fig. 2.50). These can take the place of some fixed 'G' cramps. The cramps must hold their shape and the better ones are cast steel, but for light holding of small items bent strip metal cramps – sometimes described as fretwork cramps – can be used. A use in the workshop can be found for discarded domestic equipment with cramp action.

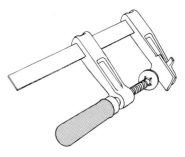

2.50 *An adjustable cramp, with one head movable, can take the place of several G cramps.*

For a greater reach than is possible with a 'G' cramp there are several versions of bar or sash cramps. Usually there is a sliding head on a bar, with a means of stopping it at many places, and a fixed head on the end of the bar to squeeze parts held between the heads (fig. 2.51). Much furniture is framed, and bar cramps are the best tools for pulling the joints together. Two with 900 mm (36 in) bars are needed for most work on furniture. Improvisations are possible (see Chapter 4), but if much furniture or other framed woodwork is to be made, bar cramps are quicker and more reliable. Extension bars are obtainable, but unless you need these it is better to start with plain bar cramps. A few bar cramps can have their heads turned round to provide an outward thrust if necessary.

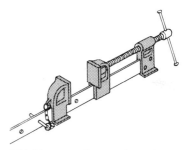

2.51 *A bar or sash cramp is used where a greater reach is needed than is possible with a G cramp.*

As a cheaper alternative to bar cramps, or a means of supplementing them with this extra facility, there are loose cramp heads for mounting on the edge of a board (fig. 2.52). They are effective, and allow a cramp to be made up to any length.

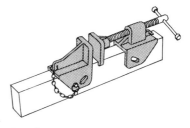

2.52 *Sliding cramp heads can be fixed on the edge of a board for setting to any distance.*

2.53 A dog cramps when driven into the end grain of two boards.

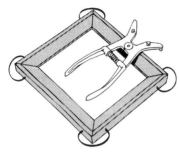

2.54 Circular spring clips are for cramping picture frame mitres.

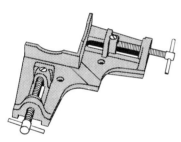

2.55 A corner cramp holds a mitre while it is being joined.

2.56 A general-purpose woodworking hammer has a Warrington-pattern head.

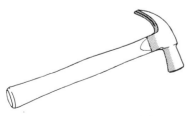

2.57 A claw hammer can withdraw nails.

Not all cramping needs are massive. Boards can be pulled together with joiners' dogs (fig. 2.53). These are made with wedge-shaped legs, parallel outside and tapered inside. When driven into the end grain of two boards that have to be pulled together they apply considerable compression on the joint. For a picture frame corner, or other light mitre, there are sprung circular clips (fig. 2.54), that have to be opened and positioned with a special tool with a pliers action. There are corner cramps (fig. 2.55) that hold mitres together, using screws in the same way as 'G' cramps do. 'G' cramps can be bought with a screw working through the body at right-angles to the main thrust, to put on a three-way pressure. These and other special cramps may be considered when your pattern of work has been settled, but plenty of 'G' cramps and at least two bar cramps should be given priority.

For smaller cramping needs there are tools with a pliers-like action. Simple pliers have limited uses, but the type that can be locked into position with a screw and lever action serve as small cramps to hold parts being worked on or while glue sets.

DRIVERS

At least one hammer is needed. Many modern hammers have the head and handle in one piece, with – in most cases – a rubber grip. These have no resilience, and shocks are transferred to your hand with every blow. That may not matter for occasional hammering, but a woodworking craftsman prefers a steel head on an ash shaft, where the wood cushions any shock. If the head is properly wedged and sealed, there should be little risk of the joint loosening or parting. For most woodwork on a bench a cross-pein hammer is usual, with a Warrington pattern head (fig. 2.56). There is a satisfactory balance, and the thin pein will get into restricted places. It is advisable to test the weight and balance of a new hammer, to suit yourself.

A claw hammer (fig. 2.57) is more the tool of a general outdoor carpenter, who assembles parts with nails and sometimes has to pull one out. If that is what you plan to do, get a claw hammer, but otherwise the Warrington pattern is more likely to suit you. As well as a hammer for general use, a very light similar one is useful for driving pins and tiny nails, if that is the sort of work you will be doing.

Pincers often have to be used with hammers. Some are made with narrow heads. Probably that was the easy shape for a blacksmith to make, but you get more leverage from a wide head (fig. 2.58). See that the ends meet and are bevelled inside only, so as to get close to the wood, but not so sharp that they cut off the nail-head.

Also used with hammers are nail punches or setts (fig. 2.59). They may be round and knurled for a grip, or of tapered rectangular section. The end should be slightly smaller than the nail head it is to drive, and some ends are hollow to prevent slipping. A few nail setts might be bought, but they can be filed from steel rod or even thick nails. It is worth getting a centre punch (fig. 2.60), which is really a metalworking tool but can be used on wood to locate with a positive dent the point where a drill bit should enter.

A tool with a steel head is a hammer, but if the head is of wood or any soft material it is called a mallet. The traditional English mallet has a squared beech head, with the handle as a taper through it. Centrifugal force then keeps the head tight on the handle (fig. 2.61). This is a fine tool to buy or make. It can be used on chisels or on wooden parts being assembled. The alternative is a cylindrical head on a wedged handle (fig. 2.62). The boxwood head on an ash shaft can swing a considerable weight in comparatively small bulk. Other mallets now have plastic heads, some with removable faces and others with lead shot inside. A carver uses a mallet with a round head in line with the handle (fig. 2.63) and this can be used with ordinary chisels if you wish. If you have a lathe, you could make such a mallet as a turning project.

Screwdrivers

Screwdrivers play a large part in some branches of woodwork. Ideally, you have a screwdriver that is an exact match for each size of screw being used, but in practice it is possible to make each blade work with a few sizes. Even then you need several screwdrivers. There are combination tools, in which you change the ends, but if many screws have to be driven it is more convenient to have a screwdriver that does not have loose parts, so in general it is best to start with plain screwdrivers. There are ratchet screwdrivers and some very good pump-action drivers. Both are useful if you have to drive hundreds of screws quickly, as may happen when building a boat, but – for occasional screws in normal assembly work – simple screwdrivers are cheaper and more effective.

Most screws for general use have slotted heads. There are screws for mass-production work that have star-shaped sockets and other patterns in the heads. Some of these may

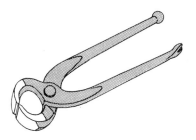

2.58 *Pincers grip and pull nails.*

2.59 *A nail punch has a small flat or hollow end for driving nail heads below the surface.*

2.60 *A centre punch will make a dent in wood or metal for starting a drill.*

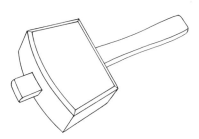

2.61 *The traditional woodworking mallet has a squared head on a tapered handle.*

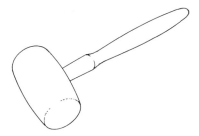

2.62 *A mallet with a cylindrical wooden head can also be used for general woodworking.*

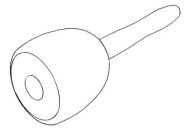

2.63 *A woodcarver favours a mallet with a round head.*

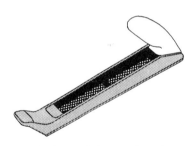

2.64 *A screwdriver with an oval handle is best for driving woodscrews.*

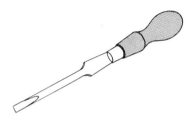

2.65 *Surform tools in many forms have disposable perforated blades.*

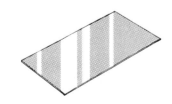

2.66 *A cabinet scraper is a flat steel plate sharpened with burred edges.*

be used by hand driving, and drivers with matching ends are needed. For the screw sizes likely to be used there are three sizes of sockets to be matched. Other screws have square sockets. For these special screws, which may be used only occasionally, you could use a driver with interchangeable ends, but it is better to avoid these screws and use only slotted ones.

To drive a screw you need leverage. Not much may be needed to drive a small screw, but a long driver exerts more leverage than a short one – because of the slight movement out of line as you turn – so get long screwdrivers. Choose oval heads for the same reason (fig. 2.64) (wood gives a better grip than plastic, but you may have to accept plastic). Another way of applying extra leverage is with pliers at the flat section at the top of the shaft just below the handle on some screwdrivers. There will be places where you cannot use the increased leverage of a long screwdriver, so have a few short ones. One should be broad in the handle and the end, for turning large-headed screws like the one in a plane cap iron. There are offset screwdrivers for awkard places, but they are rarely needed.

FILES AND SCRAPERS

At one time a carpenter used files very similar to those used on metal and rasps for coarser work. A file has teeth cut with lines across. A rasp has teeth individually cut. These tools are still of use, but their place has mostly been taken by *Surform* tools (fig. 2.65). The cutting parts have holes making teeth through sheet steel, and the strip blade is replaced when blunted. The common tools take flat or curved blades, but there are others. Their effect is very similar to that of planing, and the tools are particularly useful on shaped parts, such as rounded ends or hollowed edges for gripping.

When grain is wild and tends to tear up whatever way it is planed, the tool for smoothing it is a scraper. The traditional tool is a flat rectangular piece of tool steel (fig. 2.66) of a size to hold in both hands. Its edge is sharpened, so that a slight burr is turned over (see Chapter 8). If the scraper is held so that it is slightly bowed and tilted to get the burr cutting, a very thin shaving is removed. Scraping in this way may follow planing when the finest surface is required on hardwood. The scraper edge is maintained by rubbing with a hard steel burnisher, which is a piece of round, flat or elliptical section steel in a handle (fig. 2.67). It may be possible to use the back of a chisel or gouge, but a proper burnisher should be made or bought.

There are tools with bodies like planes and spokeshaves that will hold a cabinet scraper correctly, but hand holding is usual. Other scrapers are made in a hook form to mount in a handle, for pulling. The best-known make is *Skarsten*. The handles take several forms, but the actual cutter hooks into a holder and can be driven out and replaced when blunt (fig. 2.68). Some blades are intended for paint removal and other purposes, but with the appropriate blade the effect on wood is similar to using a cabinet scraper.

Sanding follows scraping, or may follow on directly after planing. There are ways of power sanding, but for hand sanding a flat surface the paper is wrapped around a block, usually of a size to take one quarter of a standard sheet, which is coated with glass or garnet – not sand. The block needs some resilience and cork has been found to be very suitable. These blocks may be bought, but one could be made by facing a wood block with hard rubber or something similar.

SHARPENING EQUIPMENT

Methods of sharpening are described in Chapter 8. Tool catalogues show a large range of sharpening devices, some of them very expensive, but sharpening any tool consists of rubbing the cutting edge thin with successively finer grits. That is all – the back-up equipment is not important.

If much metal has to be removed, some sort of rotating abrasive stone is useful (see Chapter 3), but a coarse flat stone will do the same thing almost as quickly. Abrasive stones may be lubricated with water or oil, and as oil and water will not mix, you must settle for one or the other. In most countries oil is preferred – this must be very thin lubricating oil or even paraffin. Old-time craftsmen had their own special mixtures of oil, but any oil that does not clog the pores of the stone or keep the tool edge away from it is suitable.

For general sharpening, a stone should be about 200mm (8in) by 50mm (2in) in surface area – and preferably mounted in a box or a hollowed block, which you can make yourself (fig. 2.69). In this case the tool is rubbed on the stone, but other smaller stones, called slips, are rubbed on the tool – inside a gouge for example (fig. 2.70).

Sharpening stones may be natural or manufactured. The manufactured stones give a control of grit size. Several grades are available and it is possible to get a combination stone, fine on one side and coarse on the other. This may be a good buy for a first stone. Manufactured stones produce an

2.67 *A hard steel burnisher is used to turn over the burred edge of a scraper.*

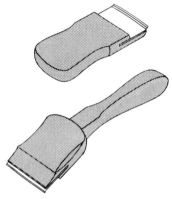

2.68 *Skarsten scrapers have disposable hooked blades.*

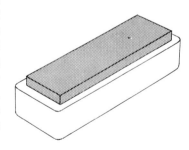

2.69 *An oilstone for sharpening tools is best mounted in a case.*

2.70 *A slip is an oilstone shaped for sharpening inside curved edges.*

edge good enough for most purposes, but for the finest edges they should be followed by a natural stone.

For the very finest edge the tool may be drawn along a strop, which is just a piece of leather on a wood backing, dressed with a special honing paste. For most woodworking there is no need to strop a tool, but you may need to use one when carving.

Chapter 3
POWER TOOLS

These are tools in which some power is provided to supplement the user's skill: they do not do all the work. It is wrong to think of them as production machines, though something of the sort may be used in industry for quantity-production. When used by a craftsman a power tool simply speeds his work, as well as lessening the labour and increasing accuracy in some processes. As with hand tools, there is a bewildering variety of power tools on the market and you should take care to select tools that suit your needs. It is no use paying extra for a particular facility, only to find that you rarely use it or that it does not do exactly what you want, so that you have to follow with hand work that could have accomplished the whole task with little more effort.

At one time power tools were not individually motorized and had to be driven by belts from shafting powered by one motor or engine. Those days have gone and it would be unwise to acquire a secondhand machine that needed outside power, unless that could be arranged compactly near it. Modern power tools have individual electric motors, built-in or closely connected by a belt or other drive mechanism. The power needed for many woodworking machines can be taken from a domestic supply via a simple plug, although it is better to have some machines wired in permanently.

Electric motors are graded in terms of their horsepower. For most machines this is expressed in fractions – ¼, ⅓, ½ etc. If a machine is offered with a choice of motor, it is usually better to choose the higher power. The initial cost may be more, but running costs are little different. The lower power may be sufficient for occasional and light use, but the more powerful motor is best for long and heavier use.

Many machines have a switch built in, and that will have been matched to the motor by the makers. If a switch has to be provided, do not choose a simple on-off one, but go for a push-button type with a cut-out that protects you and the motor in emergency. These have a prominent red button that you can feel, as well as see, to switch off quickly. If wiring has to be installed and connected, it should be done by an expert.

Power tools are broadly divided into portable and fixed ones. In general, besides being light enough to be lifted and moved about, a portable tool is taken to and moved over the work, while a fixed power tool has the work brought to and moved over it. Both types have their place, and the fixed ones can usually deal with heavier and larger work more successfully. For some work both types are suitable and a particular craftsman has to decide which will suit his purpose. There are a few machines adaptable to both functions. Much depends on the work being tackled. If what is being made is all done in the workshop, more fixed machines may be used than if outdoor carpentry or built-in furniture are the main products.

DRILLS

Portable electric drills are the most commonly-used power tools (fig. 3.1) and purchase is justified for most woodworking activities. Many that are offered are aimed at the amateur do-it-yourself market and have quite low prices. These have their uses, but if the drill is intended to be a craft investment, it is better to buy one intended for professional use: the motor will be better able to stand up to prolonged and heavy use.

An electric motor only develops maximum power if it can revolve at high speed. That means it must be geared down, and in many drills there is a selector at the chuck that gives a choice of two or more speeds. This is desirable, as if you want to drill large diameter holes in wood you need a lower speed than is suitable for drilling small holes in metal.

The chuck on an electric drill is self-centring, to take drills with round parallel shafts. The smallest usual capacity is 6 mm (¼), but many chucks open to take 9 mm (⅜) or more. The larger chucks go with increased power in the tool. If the main use for your drill will be in making holes for screws, the lighter small-capacity drill is more convenient to use, but for large holes, particularly in hardwood, the better reserve of power of a bigger drill is worth having. It can also be used for screw and similar small holes.

As the three jaws in the chuck have to grip a round shaft that will slip if not firmly held, their grip must be tight. Usually a key is provided, and it is important that it works in a way that puts adequate pressure on the chuck jaws. If a drill slips, it and the chuck jaws can be damaged. The key should be attached to the drill with a cord or in some other way, as the drill is no use without it and searching for a loose key is a waste of time.

3.1 *A portable electric drill is the most-used power tool.*

3.2 *An electric drill takes metalworking twist drills for use in wood and other materials.*

3.3 *For larger holes an electric drill is used with a spade bit.*

For ordinary drilling of small holes, where smoothness of the hole is unimportant, metalworking twist drills (fig. 3.2) are suitable. These can be obtained in sizes differing from screw sizes by much less than will matter in woodwork. There is no need for the more costly high-speed steel drills, but the cheap short 'jobber's' drills should be avoided. Carbon steel drills in standard lengths are suitable.

Drill bits for use in wood at the higher speed of an electric drill have a different form from those used in a hand brace. For fairly shallow holes there are spade bits (fig. 3.3) in diameters from 6 mm (¼ in) to upwards of 25 mm (1 in). Three flats on the shaft end reduce the risk of the chuck jaws slipping when subjected to the considerable torque of drilling with the larger diameters. For deeper holes there are drills with twists along their length and shafts whose diameter is usually 6 mm (¼ in) (fig. 3.4). They can be used to drill shallow holes too. Countersink bits are available for power drills, but this work is better done at the slow speed of a hand brace.

3.4 *For deeper holes there are special twist drills for power driving.*

DRILL STANDS

For accurate control of a drill bit, it should be mounted and driven in a stand. Ideally a separate drill press should be used, but the expense of this would be justified only in a large comprehensively-equipped workshop. For most purposes, satisfactory results can be achieved with a portable electric drill mounted in a stand (fig. 3.5). This can easily be removed for use freehand, although the state of work may justify keeping a second electric drill in the stand most of the time.

The main advantage of using a stand is that holes drilled with one are known to be square to the base in all directions, as is necessary in, for example, holes for dowels. The stand is usually equipped with a depth stop, so holes can be made to uniform depth. For freehand drilling there are depth stops to put on the bit. They work, but are inclined to rub the surface of the work, which the stop on the pillar of a stand does not.

Some bits are unsuitable for use freehand. A forstner bit is more easily controlled if a stand is used. The rather similar saw tooth centre bit is also designed for use with a pillar stand (fig. 3.6), although both bits can be used with suitable equipment in a lathe. They make clean holes from 9 mm (⅜ in) to 50 mm (2 in) in diameter. Another bit that can be used only with a drill in a stand or a drill press is a plug cutter – which is a sort of hollow drill (fig. 3.7) that cuts a ring

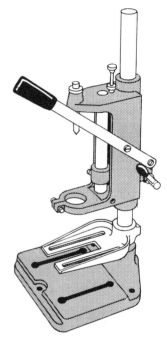

3.5 *A bench stand for an electric drill allows drilling with precision and permits other functions besides drilling.*

3.6 *A saw tooth bit can only be used with a drill in a stand.*

3.7 *A plug cutter, used with an electric drill in a stand, cuts small cylinders of wood.*

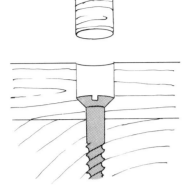

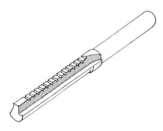

3.8 *The plugs cut by a plug cutter can be made to match surrounding wood when used to fill counterbored holes.*

3.9 *A hollow mortise tool, driven by an adapted electric drill, cuts square holes, so several adjoining holes can form a mortise.*

3.10 *A mortise miller bit cuts on its side and may be moved along to make a mortise.*

in the wood, so that the plug at the centre can be broken out and used with its cross grain matching surrounding wood, over the head of a counterbored screw (fig. 3.8).

A drill press or an electric drill in a stand can be used for making mortises. The tool used is a sort of hollow square chisel, down which a twist drill can work (fig. 3.9). With a suitable attachment the outer part is forced downwards to cut a square hole, while the twist drill removes the waste. The mortise is made with a series of adjoining square holes. Sizes available are from 6mm (¼in) to 18mm (¾in) across. You also need a sharpening tool, like a large countersink, to sharpen the square chisel.

There are alternatives to that mortise tool. If you are cutting only a few mortises, you may first drill and then use a hand-held chisel: your budget for new tools may not allow you to buy specialist tools at first. It is possible to use a router cutter to make a mortise with a rounded end, which can be squared off with a hand-held chisel. There are mortise miller bits (fig. 3.10), which quickly cut mortises when used with suitable equipment in a lathe or other machine. The method and equipment chosen will depend on your needs.

DRILL ACCESSORIES

A large number of accessories is offered for use with electric drills. Mostly they are aimed at the amateur, and most of them are unsuitable for the serious woodworker. Apart from the fact that many accessories are not sturdy enough for anything but light work, which may often be more easily done by hand, changing uses of power tool can be time consuming and it is better to aim at having one tool for each sort of job as soon as possible.

There are some attachments that allow you to groove and shape with an effect similar to that of a router, while the electric drill is still on its stand, but the router and its cutters are preferable. Pairs of cutters are available for making tongue and groove joints, but router or spindle cutters are better, as would be cutting by hand with fillister and plough planes.

If you expect to drive large numbers of screws, there is a screwdriver attachment that freewheels after the screw has been driven tight, but a hand-held pump action screwdriver may be preferred, as less likely to slip and mark the surrounding wood.

A rubber backing disc for a sanding disc is worth while (see the sanding section, pp.52-3). A circular wire brush mounted on an arbor to fit in the drill chuck is also useful for removing rust and for other cleaning jobs. A bench stand to hold the drill so that it is horizontal can be useful, with the above attachments and others. A stand that extends to form a lathe is of doubtful value, although if you do not have a lathe as well it allows you to turn small parts, up to the size of tool handles. Adaptors to make the drill into a portable circular saw, a jigsaw or even a planer, tend to be cumbersome and lacking in power.

One useful accessory is a dowelling jig. There are several types, of varying degrees of complexity, but their purpose is to guide the drill squarely, and at regular pre-set intervals, into both pieces to be joined (fig. 3.11). You can get the same results by careful marking out and drilling, but the jig ensures accuracy and is particularly useful when making dowelled joints in chipboard. Simple alternatives are a set of little pointed plugs (fig. 3.12). To use these you drill the holes in one part, put the plugs in the holes, and press the drilled part against the other to mark the centres to drill there. For many assemblies they are as effective as a jig.

A dovetail jig (fig. 3.13) allows you to use the electric drill to cut accurate dovetails, similar in appearance to those seen in mass-produced furniture, with the pins and tails the same width. If that is what you want, this is fine, but the mark of hand-cut dovetails is wider tails than the pins between them. If you want your drawers and similar parts to show the marks of hand craftsmanship, this jig is not for you.

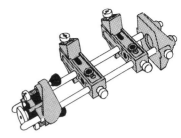

3.11 *A dowelling jig can be set to ensure holes matching in meeting parts.*

3.12 *Dowel points can be used in one set of holes to mark matching holes in another part.*

POWER SAWS

Next to an electric drill, among the power tools needed in most woodworking shops, is one or more power saws. Which to choose from the variety available depends on the work done. Of the hand-held power saws there are circular saws, which do much of the work of handsaws with little effort, cutting with the grain or across it, and jigsaws – which cut curves and will do a certain amount of straight cutting.

The best known fixed saw is a circular saw, available in capacities up to more than will be needed in most individual workshops. A bandsaw cuts curves in much thicker wood than a jigsaw can and it is also capable of straight cuts. It may be more use than a small fixed circular saw as the first power saw to be fitted in a workshop. A radial arm saw is a circular saw that can be moved across the wood on an arm. It may have a greater number of possible joint-cutting and similar functions, but the fixed saw – which may be called a table saw – is probably more use for cutting wood to size, and radial arm saws are not universally popular.

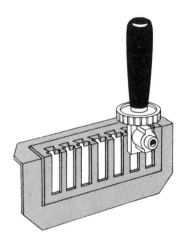

3.13 *A dovetail jig and its cutter driven by an electric drill will cut the parts of a dovetail joint.*

3.14 *A hand-held circular saw does general sawing that would otherwise be done with hand saws.*

Portable Circular Saw

A hand-held circular saw has the saw blade in a protective case, with below it a sprung guard that pushes out of the way against the wood being cut. There is a handle above the case and the motor projects to one side (fig. 3.14). A small one might be used in one hand, but most need two hands. The saw blade has much larger teeth than on a handsaw and they are usually of a form that is a compromise between cross-cutting and ripping along the grain. The sole through which the blade projects can be adjusted so that it is possible to limit the amount of blade projecting, for cutting grooves or rabbets or for tilting. There is an adjustable fence to guide its cut parallel to an edge, and a mark on the front of the sole serves as a guide for freehand cutting.

The power for some small circular saws is based on an adapted drill motor and this is unlikely to stand up to prolonged heavy use. Larger portable circular saws have more powerful motors, but are heavier; for some jobs you may find it simpler to use a handsaw or take the wood to a fixed circular saw.

A portable circular saw blade revolving rapidly can be dangerous: beware of the teeth below the wood as it cuts across. Its guard keeps it covered except when cutting, but care is needed to prevent the wood worked on from moving.

Jigsaw

The basic jigsaw has the motor horizontal and a handle above it, while a saw blade projects below a sole at one end, operating with a reciprocating motion (fig. 3.15). the cut is normally square to the sole, but in some jigsaws this can be tilted either way for angled cuts. A fence may be fitted to make cuts parallel to an edge, or the whole tool may pivot on a centre for cutting circles.

The blade cuts on the up stroke, so any roughness left is on the top surface of the wood. Some jigsaws have a blower to clear dust. The blade is held at the top by a clamping device, which is not the same in all makes. Blades are made with different teeth spacing, and in types suitable for plastics and metals as well as wood. There are wide blades for easier cutting of straight lines. The actual reciprocating motion is small, so on thinner woods only a few teeth get worn. In some saws it is possible to break off a blade and grind its top again to fit the clamping arrangements and give further use to the blade with other teeth.

A jigsaw is mainly a freehand tool and you can cut intri-

3.15 *A powered jigsaw is a hand-held tool for cutting curves.*

cate shapes down to about 12 mm (½ in) radius anywhere on a sheet, or follow a straight line reasonably well. The cut may wander from perpendicular to the surface, so some trimming of edges may be needed. The jigsaw lacks the precision of a bandsaw in this way, but gains by being able to be used at any distance from an edge.

Circular Saw

A fixed circular saw is often the first static power tool to be installed in a workshop. For one to be of maximum use there should be plenty of clear space all round, as at the start of a cut boards being ripped have to extend their full length at one end, and at the finish they must extend the same amount at the other end. There is a similar problem with cross cutting. Ideally, it should be possible to move a full standard 8 ft × 4 ft plywood sheet into position for a cut to be made anywhere on it. It may be impossible to achieve this, but this is the working area to be aimed at. If the table of the saw is higher than the things around it, it will be more versatile.

A circular saw is mounted on a spindle driven by a motor usually via a belt. It projects through a slot in a table and wood is pushed against it for cutting. The cut breaks through downwards, so any raggedness is on the underside. There is a fence alongside the saw to guide wood for parallel cuts. There is often a groove parallel with the blade, and an adjustable guide slides in this to hold wood being pushed through at an angle.

The table may be adjusted in height or the saw assembly may move up and down. The former is usual and preferable. This allows any amount of saw blade to project. The table may also tilt for making angled cuts.

The whole tool can be mounted on a bench (fig. 3.16) or be given legs or a stand to the floor. A considerable amount of sawdust is produced, and this must be led away via a chute or other means. There may be sealed bearings, or you may have to lubricate frequently.

Over the saw there is a guard that can be lifted and tilted, but it should be kept in position during cutting. At the far side of the saw is a riving knife, which is a steel plate that keeps the cut open as the wood passes across the blade. If you want to cut a groove, or otherwise use the saw only partly through the wood, the guard and riving knife must be removed. In some machines they swing out of the way, but in others nuts must be slackened.

A large table is an advantage, as it steadies large pieces of wood, but space available will limit this. Some machines

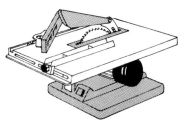

3.16 *Circular saw benches are made in many sizes and can be adjusted for cuts additional to straight cutting to length or width.*

have extending arms. With others you can make or buy stands with rollers at the same level as the table. These are particularly valuable when you are working single-handed.

Circular saw blades have central holes and are clamped between washers in these and portable power tools. They are made with many tooth spacings and shapes. A saw with a combination blade will do most general cutting of solid wood, but you may need a finer one for a cleaner cut in plywood, laminated plastic or chipboard. Blades are made in tool steel, but more costly ones have carbide or other tips, which keep their edge much longer. A tool steel blade can be sharpened by the user, but tipped blades have to be dealt with by an expert with special equipment.

The capacity of a circular saw depends on the projection of the blade through the table. With a 200 mm (8 in) blade you can expect about 50 mm (2 in) cut, but much depends on the wood and on the sharpness of the blade. Considerably more power is needed to push a blunt blade through hard wood, and overloading could cause the motor to stall even though it might have functioned easily with a sharp blade.

Bandsaw

A bandsaw has a continuous narrow blade passing over two or more wheels, with most of it enclosed, but the cutting part exposed through a table (fig. 3.17). The capacity in width depends on the throat between the blade and the solid support. Having three wheels allows this to be wider in a small machine. But, with two large wheels, less strain is put on the blade – so that it is less likely to break. For general woodworking the throat depth should not be less than 300 mm (12 in). The capacity in depth depends on an adjustable guide above the table, but in a small machine could be up to 75 mm (3 in) depending on the size of saw blade used.

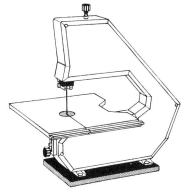

3.17 *A bandsaw has a continuous flexible blade and is used for cutting external curves.*

The body of the tool opens to allow blades to be changed. They run on rubber rims on the wheels and the tension of the blade can be adjusted. Several widths of blade can be used on a machine: wide blades are stronger and suitable for straight cuts as well as moderate curves; narrow blades – 6mm (¼ in) – will cut tighter curves. Several tooth sizes are available, but a useful type is 'gap tooth', in which there is a straight recess between teeth, which therefore make cleaner and freer cuts.

Cuts are clean and perpendicular, with any raggedness underneath. The table may have a tilting adjustment and it may be grooved to take a guide or fence for controlling the wood as it is cut. Besides its obvious use in cutting curves, the bandsaw is convenient for simple cutting off from strips, or for many other cuts that might otherwise be done with a tenon saw on the bench, provided that the edge of the board to be cut does not project more than the depth of throat of the machine.

Fretsaw

Intricate dust-catching patterns used to be cut from thin wood, often by hand with a fine blade in a long frame like a coping saw (see p.24), or with a treadle machine. There are power fretsaws that can be used with blades from hair-like thickness up to those like coping saws. If you are concerned with fine shaping this would be a useful tool, but otherwise a jigsaw or a bandsaw is more useful.

Radial Arm Saw

A radial arm saw may be likened to a portable circular saw mounted on an arm above the bench that supports the work being cut (fig. 3.18). In use the saw is moved along the arm. It has guards that open against the wood, and it can cut through partially into the surface of the work.

Adjustments give a precise control of depth, angle and direction of cut. It can crosscut or rip, squarely and at angles. With other attachments, the tool will cut grooves, mouldings and some joints.

It is necessary to weigh up the value of this against that of a table circular saw as a first buy: for straightforward cutting the table saw should be preferred. The radial arm saw has other features, but making use of some of its other capabilities involves changing equipment, so in the workshop it may be more convenient to use a router or some other tool.

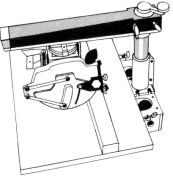

3.18 *In a radial arm saw a circular saw cuts when it is moved along a controlling arm.*

PLANER

A power planer is the obvious complement to a circular saw. Once you have sawn wood to the width you want, it is convenient to move to the planer and put a smooth surface on the edges and faces you have just sawn. The planer may be a separate machine, but it could be combined with a circular saw, to use the same motor and conserve space. It can be housed below the level of the saw table so that it does not interfere with overhanging boards.

A planer, sometimes called a jointer, uses blades mounted on a cylinder that rotates at high speed between two tables that can be adjusted in height to regulate the

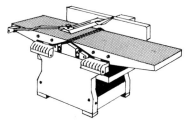

3.19 *In a planer the wood is moved over two tables each side of rotating cutters.*

thickness of cut (fig. 3.19). With a fixed planer, wood is fed over the tables and the cutters remove tiny pieces – leaving a series of ridges across the grain. In careful fine cuts these are not very obvious, but in quick coarse work they are very apparent. Such a surface is acceptable for some purposes, as it is basically flat and true, but in other cases some hand planing or sanding is necessary to produce a furniture-quality finish.

A planer is described in terms of the width of the cut it can make. The weight and size of castings, as well as the power needed (and therefore the price) increases considerably with cutting capacities, so a machine capable of dealing with wide boards may be desirable, but not justified within a given budget. A 125 mm (4 in) cut is useful, and the smallest planer worth buying has a capacity of at least 150 mm (6 in).

A planer has a fence to hold boards against when planing their edges. It is normally set square to the table, but can be adjusted for planing bevels. Guards go over the cutters and should be used. With this and the circular saws, push sticks of various sorts should be used, instead of bringing fingers near cutting edges.

One table can be dropped in relation to the other so that rabbets can be planed with the edge of the cutters. The machine may be equipped for 'thicknessing' – planing one surface, then putting the wood through to plane the other surface and bringing the wood to a set thickness – which is convenient if you want to prepare a large number of pieces of wood of identical section. some simpler machines do this with guides above the cutters. In others the wood can be fed back underneath.

There are portable planers with soles and handles something like normal hand planes, but blades on a cylinder similar to those of a fixed planer do the cutting. Portable planers are comparatively narrow, and their scope is little different from that of a hand plane, so they are not worthwhile alternatives to a fixed planer. They make similar small ridges, so for a quality finish they have to be followed by hand treatment.

Vibration can spoil the work of a fixed planer. It is important that castings should be robust in relation to their size, to ensure rigidity. Table length helps in maintaining the truth of a surface being planed. Practical considerations affect both requirements.

ROUTER

Modern powered routers are comparatively recent tools. They have a vertically-mounted electric motor, with a cutter bit gripped at the end of its shaft and a base through which the bit projects (fig. 3.20). The cutting edges, on its sides and sometimes on its end as well, must be sharp and must rotate at high speed. The name comes from the similarity to a hand router, and it is used chiefly for cutting housing or dado grooves across boards. But there are a large variety of cutters now available for doing other things.

In a standard router the base is adjustable for depth of cut and it can be used with its own fence or against guide pieces to get cuts in the right places. A plunge router is similar, but the cutter can be held above the surface and lowered or raised through it before and after cuts.

Bits have standard shafts to be gripped by a special chuck. The simplest makes grooves in any direction of grain. Others will make round or 'V' grooves and decorative moulded patterns. For edge decoration, from simple chamfers to various mouldings, the cutter has a projecting pilot to run along the plain part of the edge (fig. 3.21).

There are several pieces of equipment for use with a router and special cutters. A dovetail fixture allows for the cutting of dovetails similar to those possible with an electric drill (see p.45). A pantograph arrangement allows the router cutter to repeat a pattern from a guide: this can be used for cutting letters in signs and house name boards. A device something like a lathe uses the router to make round things and to cut patterns like spiral flutes on them. It will copy another piece, to make such things as identically turned legs.

Whether the variety of cutters and special equipment is justified or not depends on needs and the availability of other tools for doing the same work. A router is a versatile tool and much of its supplementary equipment may be justified if full use is to be made of it, but it cannot take the place of other power tools in all their applications.

A spindle moulder is a tool like a router, but with the cutter projecting upwards through a table and with an adjustable fence. A piece of wood pushed along the fence can have moulding or other pattern cut on its edge. This is a similar action to that of the router, with the wood being moved instead of the tool. A spindle moulder may have uses in a large production workshop, but a router is certainly the more generally useful and versatile power tool for the small domestic workshop.

3.20 *A router has a vertical motor that takes cutters for grooving and shaping.*

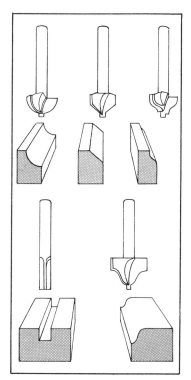

3.21 *Router bits will make mouldings as well as cut grooves.*

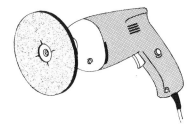

3.22 *A flexible sanding disc can be driven by an electric drill.*

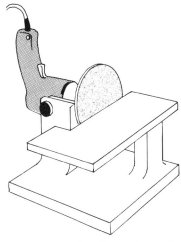

3.23 *A flat sanding disc can be used for smoothing and shaping.*

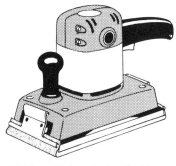

3.24 *An orbital sander is a finishing tool.*

SANDING

Sanding is primarily a finishing process, but there are some situations where abrasive can be used for stock removal on the surface or for shaping edges. However, for good craftsmanship coarse abrasive should not be used as a substitute for planing and other cutting processes.

Simplest is a sanding disc that is held with a central screw and washer to a flexible backing on a short arbor to fit into a drill chuck (fig. 3.22). The disc may tear away at the centre, so might not last long. It makes curved scratches on the wood, so is unsuitable for many applications. However, it is cheap and worth having, provided that you do not expect too much from it. Another disc is rigid or has a flat, padded surface. With a table in front of it to support the work, small pieces can be manipulated against it for sanding shaped edges (fig. 3.23). There are abrasive metal discs as alternatives to paper or cloth sanding discs.

For finishing sanding there are orbital sanders (fig. 3.24). The base takes a flat piece of abrasive paper and the motor and handle are set above it. The paper is moved rapidly with a small oscillating action and the effect on the wood is very similar to hand sanding. A dust-collection bag and an extractor for dust is attached in some cases.

A flap sander is a wheel with a large number of abrasive pieces that project radially as loose flaps (fig. 3.25). It may have its own portable motor, be used with an electric drill or be bench mounted – with wood being moved over it. This will sand into intricate shapes. It will also remove paint and do other coarse work, when fitted with flaps of suitable grit.

A belt sander may be portable or fixed. The portable type is handled something like a plane and the belt runs over a pair of rollers and a pressure plate between them in the opposite direction to which the tool is pushed (fig. 3.26). Depending on the grit used, this will level off rough surfaces or provide a finishing cut. With the lengthwise action the effect is more like hand sanding along the grain. However, on wide surfaces care is needed to keep the edge of the belt from cutting into the wood. The belt sander is particularly effective where end grain adjoins side grain.

Fixed belt sanders are more specialized. A rather longer endless abrasive belt works in a similar way to that of a portable sander, but its working surface is upwards or sometimes at an angle nearer vertical. It may have a flat pressure plate, so that wood held against the belt is sanded flat, or the whole or part of the exposed belt may be unsupported. With that sort of belt it is possible to hold wood against it to shape it. For instance a knife handle could be shaped completely from a square block by manipulating it on the belt. Much depends on what sort of work you intend to do. For most woodworking, the expense of acquiring and fixing a belt sander is not justified, but a portable belt sander may be useful.

3.25 *A flap sander uses a large number of abrasive pieces.*

LATHE

Whether you have a lathe or not also depends on what sort of work you intend doing. Some round things, such as bowls and lamp standards, can be made entirely on a lathe, but you can also make tool handles and such spindle work as table and stool legs. A lathe makes possible the production of parts of furniture or other assemblies that might have had to be bought, or for which a square part would have had to be substituted. The principle on which a lathe works is that the wood is mounted between centres and rotated, while tools are used on a rest to shape it by making circular cuts. For a bowl or similar shallow thing of large diameter the wood is mounted with a faceplate or chuck, without the aid of a second centre.

3.26 *A belt sander has the advantage of sanding in a straight line.*

A lathe has a headstock, which takes the power from a motor. This is mounted on a long bed, on which slides the tailstock, carrying the other centre, and the adjustable tool-rest (fig. 3.27). There are differences in construction between makes, but the principles are the same. For spindle turning, the capacity between centres should be 760 mm (30 in) or more, so that table legs can be turned. The height of the centres above the tool-rest attachment to the bed determines the largest radius that can be swung. This is usually more than enough for most spindle work, but if bowls have to be turned over the bed, the diameter is limited by the clearance. The specification of a lathe may give the

3.27 *A lathe is used to rotate wood, against which a tool is used for shaping. For discs and bowls too large to fit over the bed there may be a faceplate at the outer end of the spindle.*

centre height above the bed (radius), or the diameter that can be swung.

In many lathes there is provision at the outboard end of the headstock for a faceplate to be mounted there, so that a bowl or wheel of considerable diameter can be turned. There may be a mounting on the lathe end for the toolrest, and that will set the maximum size that can be swung. But in some cases the toolrest has a stand on the floor, so it should be possible to turn such a thing as a large round table top (which depends also on the power and speed adjustment available). A much slower speed is needed on a large diameter than on a small spindle. The load on a tool cutting at the edge of a large diameter is much more than it is with a smaller diameter. Lathe speed is usually controlled in the less ambitious machines by cone pulleys on motor and headstock spindle: moving the belt gives a choice of speeds – probably four. For very large diameters there may have to be some other arrangement for stepping down the spindle speed.

Turning is more a hand process than some other machine work, and the tools needed have been described in Chapter 2, but there are several pieces of equipment that go with the lathe. Drive for work between centres is provided by prongs pressed into the ends of the wood to be turned. At the tailstock the centre tapers to form an axle as it goes into a hollow in the wood. A plain centre there causes wear in the wood and has to be adjusted occasionally. It is better to have a revolving centre, with a bearing that lets the point rotate with the wood.

A screw centre at the driving end will hold small things, like egg-cups. For some lathes there are special small chucks for the same purpose. For larger diameters there are faceplates, to which the back of a disc of wood may be screwed while its face and edge are turned. If there is provision for turning discs on the outboard end of the headstock spindle, the thread there has to be left-handed to prevent the faceplate unscrewing in use; so faceplates cannot be changed round.

A drill chuck to mount at either end in place of a centre is almost essential. With a drill bit fixed at the tailstock end, wood can be drilled while it revolves, either to take a dowel or full length for the wire of a lamp standard. Having the drill chuck at the driving end, the lathe becomes very similar to a drill press for accurately making holes for dowels or other purposes, with the wood mounted on a pad at the tailstock or on a special table on the lathe bed.

Several lathe makers provide additional equipment to

mount on the lathe for other functions. As with other multiple tools, it is necessary to consider the time it takes to change from one purpose to another and the effectiveness of the machine when set up – in comparison with that of an independent power tool. Anyone concerned in the long run with doing serious woodwork should normally aim – as with other power tools – at separate machines for different jobs. But adaptations to a lathe have the advantage of compactness, so – if space saving is very important – they may be worth having.

GRINDER

Tool sharpening is dealt with in Chapter 8. Most of it can be dealt with by hand and with suitable coarse-grit stones you may do all of it. If grinding is needed, you may take tools occasionally to a specialist. However, it is helpful to have some means of grinding in your workshop.

The traditional means of grinding woodworking cutting tools was by use of a large sandstone. No modern way is better, but you are unlikely to find such a stone.

There are smaller sandstone grinders driven at a suitable speed with a motor (fig. 3.38). There are other grinders with the wheel on a vertical spindle, so that grinding is done on the side of this cylinder. Both are good for woodworking tools.

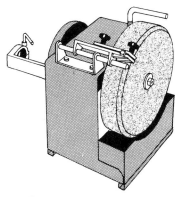

3.28 *Tools are best ground on a slow-turning sandstone wheel.*

The alternative is a smaller grinding wheel, used dry and protected with a casing, that revolves at high speed on a spindle projecting from a bench-mounted motor (fig. 3.29). Usually a second wheel or a polishing mop is mounted at the other end. This is really an engineering grinder, but many woodworkers use one. Care is needed to keep the bevel uniform and to prevent overheating. A container of water alongside can be used for cooling. Some grinders have a trough included, but that is for dipping tools, not for wetting the wheel, as is done with sandstone. The wheel should have a diameter of at least 150 mm (6 in).

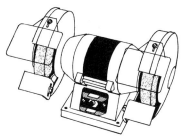

3.29 *A high-speed grinder requires care to avoid overheating and softening a tool being ground.*

There are geared hand- and foot-driven engineering wheels, but it is almost impossible to drive them fast enough to sharpen properly and avoid rapid wear of the stone, so they should be avoided.

A possible alternative for occasionally grinding tools is a disc sander, using a suitable grit on a rigid backing. This makes a true flat bevel easier to obtain than on the edge of a small grinding wheel, but the tool must still be dipped in water frequently to prevent overheating.

Chapter 4
EQUIPMENT

Tools are not much use without somewhere to use them. Some work may have to be done in position on site, but most woodworking processes are better performed in a workshop or, at least, on a properly-equipped bench. The surroundings and equipment can make a considerable difference to the quality of work, and to the ease and speed with which it can be done. If work has to be done in a room that is also used on other occasions for other purposes, that should be regarded as a temporary expedient if you mean to produce good work. But, even then, something better than a shaky table is required for working on.

4.1 *The Workmate is an alternative to a bench and vice for some purposes.*

There has to be a good flat solid surface that will withstand hammering and not bend or move under planing and other processes. In temporary accommodation you might use a stout plank on trestles. Besides the flat surface there is a frequent need for something to hold wood on edge, and the best thing for doing this is a vice. There are vices that cramp onto a plank, and they are suitable for light work, but a more substantial permanently-mounted vice is preferable. It could be fixed to the plank, to be put away with it when the area has to be cleared.

Ideally, work is done at about table level. But some things can be done at a lower level, so it is possible to manage with a board placed across stout trestles. An ingenious form of folding trestle, obtainable in several forms, is the *Workmate*. Its main attraction for anyone wanting a compact woodworking support is in the top, which opens like a long vice and can be used for holding and clamping wood (fig. 4.1). Other stops and attachments permit the gripping of wood in various ways, and there is provision for using your own weight to steady the trestle. For anyone who has to make do with temporary quarters for woodworking, or – even when your base workshop is well equipped – if you have to go out to do work on site, the *Workmate* is worth having.

BENCHES

A strong rigid bench is the most important piece of a woodworker's equipment. No matter how elaborate the assortment of power tools and the range of hand tools available, much work has to be done on a firm flat support. There has to be a surface known to be level, larger than the things that have to be assembled, and there must be provision for tackling the many hand operations that are involved.

Much of the work is done on the front part of a bench, so that is where the thickest and strongest part has to be. Even if other parts are of lighter section or less dense wood, the front should be very strong. Beech is most popular for bench-tops. It is dense and even-grained, with little tendency to warp or split. Ideally, the bench front board should be 75 mm (3 in) thick – certainly not less than 50 mm (2 in) – and about 300 mm (12 in) wide, with its top level and without twist, and its front edge square and straight.

For the average worker a height of 800 mm (32 in) is about right. You are unlikely to need it higher, so – if you make or buy a bench of that height, and then find it would be better shorter – you can cut off the bottoms of the legs. From back to front may be 600 mm (24 in) or more, if the bench is to go

4.2 A bench should be heavy and
rigid, with at least one vice.

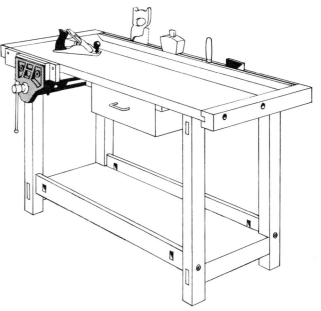

against a wall. For some work there is an advantage in being
able to work all round the bench, for dealing with large
assemblies, sheets of plywood and similar big things. In that
case it helps to have a wider one.

There are many benches for sale in many sizes and with
various arrangements of stops and vices. They are attractive
and obviously worth having, if you find one to fit your space
and needs. But prices are considerably more than the cost
of material to make your own, and that would have the
advantage of being tailored more exactly to your needs. A

4.3 An end vice is useful for an
additional grip on some work.

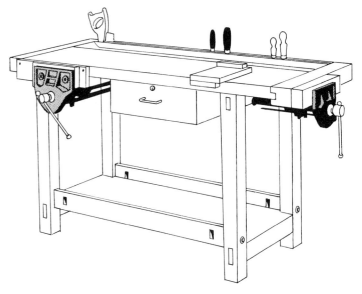

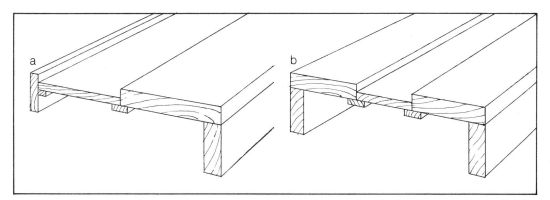

bought bench may have one vice, a drawer and tool rack (fig. 4.2). Sometimes there is a second vice at the end (fig. 4.3). The substantial legs are framed for stiffness, and the framing could be made into a tray. For some work it is convenient to have a bench that is level for its full width, but it is more usual to include a thinner plank to form the base of a tool well (fig. 4.2a), with the rear edge level with the front for supporting wide things. If the bench is to be used at both sides, the well is in the middle (fig. 4.2b). Sometimes the board forming the tool well can be lifted out. That allows cramps to be put through, to hold wood being worked on or to pull joints together.

4.4 A tool well goes at the back of a single bench (a) or between the sides of a double one (b).

Making your own bench

If you make your own bench, plan sizes in relation to where it is to be used. If you are able to attach it to a wall, that will help in maintaining rigidity – assuming that the wall is strong enough. But it may be advisable not to rely on the walls of – say – a wood-framed shed to take the place of legs or other framework, which must take the strain of working loads. Besides, you may want to re-organize your workshop one day, or take the bench with you when you move. Bear this sort of thing in mind.

Ideally, all of the bench (fig. 4.5) is made of beech or other hardwood, but it is possible to have a satisfactory bench with legs and underframing of softwood – provided that they are of large enough section, and that the vital working surfaces are hardwood.

It is better if you start with the front working surface and design other parts around it. It is also worth providing an apron, which is a vertical hardwood piece below its front (fig. 4.6a). Dowels may join these pieces squarely together. Besides providing a true surface for boards on edge to bear against, this gives rigidity to the bench, particularly under

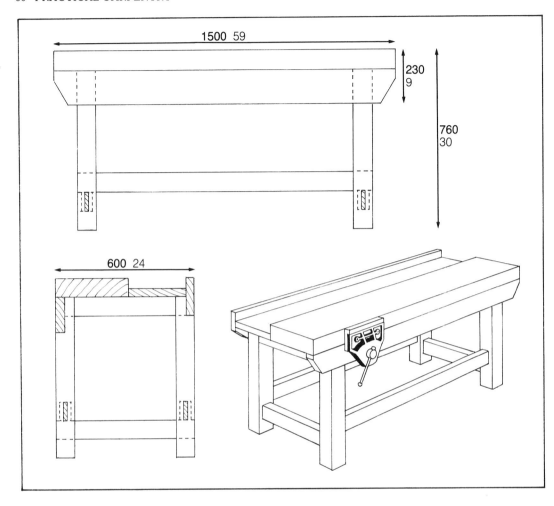

4.5 *A bench can be made in your own workshop.*

Note: Measurements in millimetres are given in **bold type**; measurements in inches are given in normal type.

the frequent lengthwise loads that are applied in planing and other processes. Many benches without aprons flex in the length after much use.

For a bench up to about 2m (6ft) long, two pairs of legs will be enough. For a longer bench there should be an intermediate pair. Legs may be 75mm (3in) square for a small bench, but 100mm (4in) would be better. Rails can be the same section or 100 × 75mm (4 × 3in). Deep rails provide stiffness from back to front.

The rails are best tenoned to the legs (fig. 4.6b). At the front, the leg is partially cut back to take the apron piece (fig. 4.6c). Treat the leg at the back similarly for the piece behind the tool well (fig. 4.6d). For a simpler construction, the parts may be halved and bolted (fig. 4.6e). In any case, be sure to get both leg and rail assemblies square and matching each other.

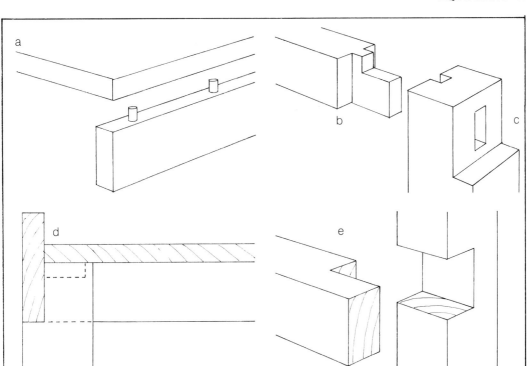

The top parts provide all the links that are needed between the leg assemblies, but lower down arrange lengthwise rails at a different level from those set across (fig. 4.7a), so that their tenons clear the others. If the lengthwise rails are notched instead of tenoned, do not halve them fully (fig. 4.7b), so as not to weaken the legs by cutting out too much. Allow for a small overhang each end, but not more than 150 mm (6 in) if the bench is free-standing.

The apron can be fixed with counterbored and plugged screws into the legs, and the back piece may screw into the legs. To hold the working top down screws may be driven upwards in deeply counterbored holes in the rails (fig. 4.7c). The holes should not be plugged, so that you can tighten the screws if ever necessary. It is best to avoid driving screws or other fasteners down through the top. But if you have to, counterbore and plug them, to make sure that there is no metal anywhere near the surface.

The tool well can be made with a thinner board, either fixed permanently or arranged to lift out. Supports on the front and back pieces are needed for such a board (fig. 4.7d). If it is to be lifted out, pieces may be fixed across it to prevent lengthwise movement (fig. 4.7e). The ends of the

4.6 In bench construction the apron is dowelled below the top (a), the top rails tenon into the legs (b), which are cut back for the apron (c) or for the back piece (d). Alternatively, halve the parts (e).

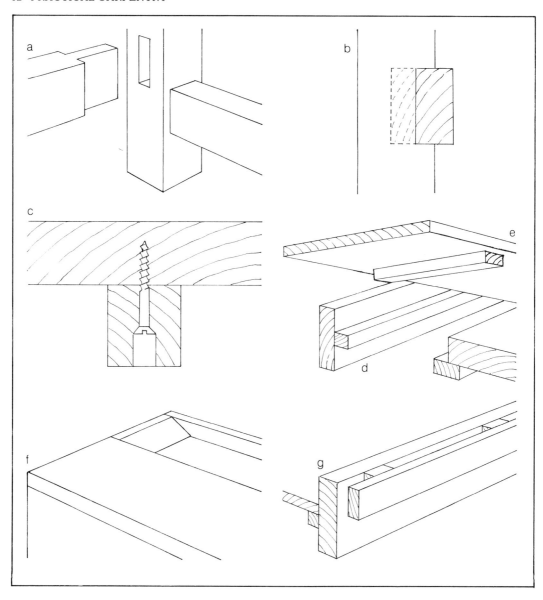

4.7 *Lower bench rails enter the legs at different levels (a) or they are notched (b). The top is screwed (c), but the tool well rests on supports (d) and will lift out (e). Its ends are improved with sloping pieces (f). A tool rack can go at the back (g).*

board should have pieces made up to the working height, preferably sloped (fig. 4.7f) for ease in cleaning and to act as rests for planes to keep their cutters clear of the wood surface.

If the back is to be made into a tool rack, you could fix a strip to it held off at intervals with spacers (fig. 4.7g). On a long bench you might have two parts with different width gaps; with this arrangement, saws, chisels and other thin tools can go in a narrow gap, while thicker things like hammer handles can have a wide one. However, it is a nuisance having to clear the racks to allow the wide boards to over-hang when you are working on them. So if there is a wall near, it is better to put there any tools that are not in the bench well.

There is a lot of spare space under a bench. Any boxing in to make drawers or cupboards is worth while, for the added stiffness as well as for added storage. The apron might be cut to admit a drawer, but one with a flush front. Closing in the back and ends under the bench with panels contributes to stiffness. If you are equipping a workshop from scratch it may be advisable to leave detailed bench storage until you are certain how it can most usefully be arranged.

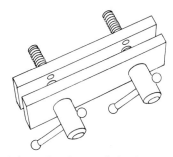

4.8 A wooden vice usually has two screws.

VICE

The one vice, traditionally located near the left-hand end of the bench front, is the most important piece of bench equip-ment. This is something on which you should not comprom-ise. There may be other vices and holding devices, but it is at this vice that you will do much of your detailed and preci-sion work.

Some benches are sold ready equipped with wooden vices. A wood screw lacks precision and in such a vice there may have to be two of them to adjust (fig. 4.8), but the main drawback is in the way the front jaw can wobble out of true if the wood being held does not pass right through the vice. It is better to have a metal vice with wooden jaws, and to get one large enough to cope with your needs. There are some light versions that may suit modelmaking, but for

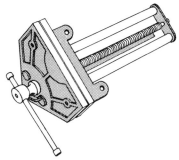

4.9 A metal vice has a single long screw and guides that go under the bench.

4.10 A metal vice should be fitted with wooden jaws (a). The vice has to be bolted through the bench top (b).

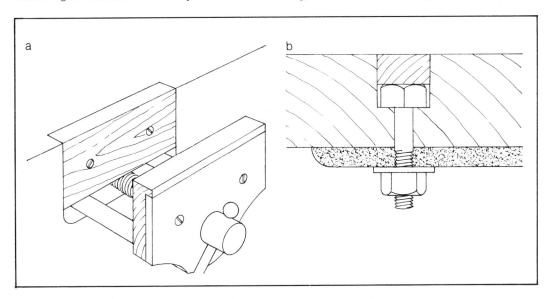

serious woodworking the vice should have jaws about 230 mm (9 in) wide, opening to 330 mm (13 in) (fig. 4.9).

The rear jaw is let into the front of the bench and most of the vice parts go under the bench-top. The front is attached to two slides and is worked in and out by a handle turning a substantial screw. A time-saver is a quick-release mechanism. By squeezing a lever near the handle you can free the vice to move in or out to any position, then releasing the lever re-engages the screw. If you expect to spend much time woodworking, this facility is worth the extra cost. Another feature available only on some makes of vice is a 'dog peg', which is a rectangular peg that can be raised on the moving jaw. With a stop on the bench-top, this can act as a cramping device.

The vice should be mounted so that there are wood faces on the jaws and on the upper surfaces, to prevent any metal from coming into contact with cutting tools (fig. 4.10a). The inner wood jaw has to be arranged flush with the front edge of the bench so that long boards are held level. A vice should be bolted to the top, but the heads of the bolts must be sunk below the surface and covered with wood plugs (fig. 4.10b). If coach bolts are used, their square necks pull into the wood to prevent turning. Use large washers under the nuts.

An apron must be cut away to admit the vice. That is best done before the apron is fitted, and the vice is most easily put in place before the top is attached to the underframing.

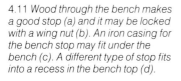

4.11 *Wood through the bench makes a good stop (a) and it may be locked with a wing nut (b). An iron casing for the bench stop may fit under the bench (c). A different type of stop fits into a recess in the bench top (d).*

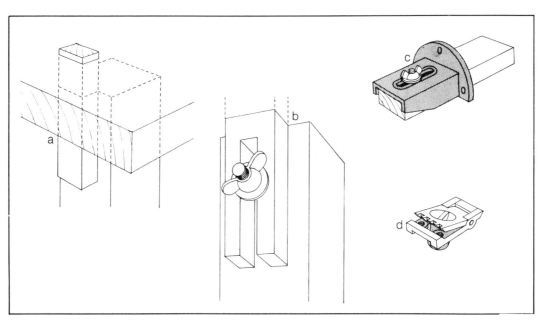

BENCH STOPS

The bench-top should be uncluttered with projections, and if possible it is advisable to avoid metal on the surface. However, there are several additions worth having. Of most use is a bench stop, which is just a piece of wood projecting through a hole near the end of the bench. In its simplest form that is all it is – just a length of hardwood positioned so that its lower part comes against the bench leg (fig. 4.11a). It can be adjusted by tapping up or down.

For greater precision the lower part can be split, with a wing nut providing locking (fig. 4.11b). You can buy a cast iron casing to screw under the bench-top to give similar adjustment (fig. 4.11c). On a wide top there can be a second stop level wth the first, to give steadier support when planing wide boards.

If the bench forms part of something longer or there is some other reason for not being able to arrange a stop through the top, a flush-mounted metal stop can be let into a recess in the top (fig. 4.11d). Height can be adjusted by means of a central screw, and the stop can be closed flush with the bench-top.

Old-time cabinetmakers made much use of a holdfast that could be pushed through a hole in the bench-top, where it was held by friction. The modern equivalent has a screw action and is valuable for holding wood down (fig. 4.12). A notched collar is let into the bench-top, then the rod fitted through it a suitable amount, so that tightening the screw forces the jaw on to the work. Collars can be put at several places on the bench-top, so that one or more holdfasts can be arranged to suit the work.

Holes may be drilled in the apron to take pegs for supporting long pieces when other parts of them are in the vice. The pegs can be simple roughly tapered pieces or parts turned like blackboard pegs. Cramps may also be used under or at the end of the apron.

If there is an end vice with a dog peg it is useful to have positions for other pegs, called 'bench dogs', further along the bench top. You can then use the vice as a cramp to bring parts tight for joining or working on. There are metal bench dogs (fig. 4.13) that need square holes, in which they are retained with springs. In a compact workshop you may want to mount a small machine on the bench, but it is advisable to arrange it with removable bolts, so that you can always revert to a flat top of maximum size. For the same reason, avoid any special attachments that could cause projections or unevenness.

4.12 A bench holdfast presses down on wood on the bench top and holds with its stem fitted through one of the collars let into the bench top.

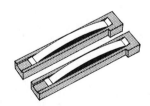

4.13 Wood may be held on the bench top by pressure from a vice against dogs fitted into holes in the bench. These dogs are metal with retaining springs.

4.14 *Bench hooks may be narrow and used in pairs (a) or wider (b) and cut back on alternate sides for sawing (c). Cuts can be made as mitre sawing guides (d). The hook will act as a stop when planing end grain (e).*

Note: Measurements in millimetres are given in **bold type**; measurements in inches are given in normal type.

BENCH HOOK

The bench-top should be kept in good condition for as long as possible. Such work as chopping or vertical paring with a chisel should be done over scrap wood and not directly onto the bench. This also applies to sawing: the bench-top can soon become scored with saw marks from careless sawing. Freehand sawing can be done over scrap wood, but it is help in holding the wood to have one, or preferably two, bench hooks.

Older bench hooks were narrow and cut from solid wood (fig. 4.14a). They were used in pairs spaced as needed along the length of wood being worked on, but they did not protect the bench-top. It is better to make wider bench hooks, with crosspieces dowelled on. They should not be so long as to go over the edge at the tool well (fig. 4.14b), but a long bench hook is of more use than a short one.

A suitable width is 125mm (5in), with crosspieces high enough to prevent wood being pushed over the end. Join with dowels rather than screws, so that there is no metal for a saw to touch. Keep the crosspieces cut back, so that a saw breaks through on to the hook and not the bench. Most craftsman become ambidextrous with a tenon saw, so cut back one piece for sawing with the right hand and the other for turning over to use your left hand (fig. 4.14c).

If your work involves mitring small pieces, you could cut saw guides in a bench hook (fig. 4.14d). With a bench hook it is possible to use a block plane across end grain, so that the bench hook is functioning as a small shooting board (see below). For that to be most satisfactory, the board should be just thick enough for an average piece of wood being worked on to come near the centre of the plane sole (fig. 4.14e).

Bench hooks should be regarded as disposable. They take cuts that would otherwise fall on the bench, so be prepared to replace them occasionally.

SHOOTING BOARD

With power tools to help, getting edges straight and square is easy. A circular saw cuts straight and a planer makes the edge flat and square to the surface. However, there are occasions when an edge has to be straightened by hand. It can be done with the wood held on edge in the vice, but then you have to rely on testing with a straight-edge and square to get your freehand planing right.

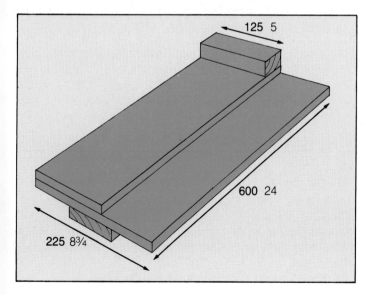

125 5

600 24

225 8¾

4.15 *A shooting board is for holding wood being planed on its edge with a plane resting on its side.*

Note: Measurements in millimetres are given in **bold type**; measurements in inches are given in normal type.

A shooting board is a guide for a long-soled plane to get an edge true. The plane is used on its side so that the cutting edge is vertical against the wood being planed. The board should be long enough for preparing such things as small table-tops to be joined, so 600 mm (24 in) is a minimum.

Some craftsmen use a board on which the wood rests, attached to one on which the plane slides, with a stop to press the wood against (fig. 4.15). A piece 18 mm (¾ in) thick will lift it sufficiently to make sure that the centre of the cutting edge comes against wood of average thickness. The shooting board may be used on the bench-top and held with dogs, or it can have a strip attached underneath for gripping in the vice. As in the bench hook, it is better to make sure that no metal is involved, by assembling with dowels rather than with screws.

Another shooting board can be made for planing mitres (fig. 4.16). Sizes should be compared to the ordinary shooting board, to give the plane a long guide in either direction and certainly not less than 450 mm (18 in) overall. The mitre stops need not meet at a point. Their grain will be less likely to break out if a small thickness is left.

4.16 A special shooting board can hold mitred pieces for planing.

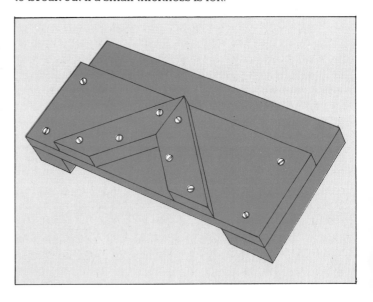

MITRE BOX

There are several devices available for cutting mitres, either with a separate backsaw or with one that is built in. If much mitring is to be done, one of these is worth having, particularly if it is a type that can also be used for cramping a corner joint.

Mitres on wider flat pieces are best marked with a mitre

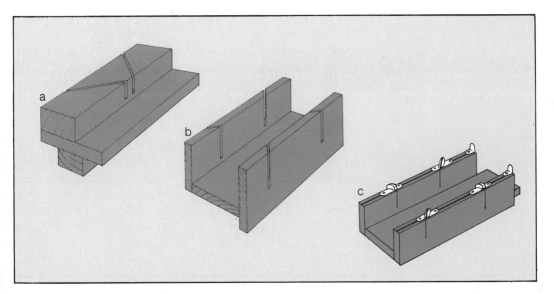

square or an adjustable bevel, then sawn to the line; but, for small picture-frame moulding and similar sections, it is a help to use a guide for a fine saw. The simplest guide is a mitre block, which works in a similar way to the bench hook cut as suggested on p.67. Making the guiding parts deep and wide gives the best control over the saw. A piece can be set underneath, for gripping in a vice (fig. 4.17a). The cuts need not continue right through to the base of the block; a piece of scrap wood may be put under the work to make up the depth and prevent the block becoming marked.

Using a saw guide at one side only is more liable to lead to error due to saw wobble than if you use guides at both sides. With guides at both sides the tool becomes a mitre box (fig. 4.17b). Although you may not cut very wide pieces in this way, it helps if you spread the parts bearing on the saw by making the inside of the box 75mm (3in) or more wide. Extending one side of the box downwards allows it to be gripped in a vice while the main part is on the bench-top. Some mitre boxes are supplied with metal saw guides (fig. 4.17c).

4.17 *A mitre block is a saw guide for cutting mitres on narrow pieces (a). A mitre box gives better saw control on wide pieces (b), and some mitre boxes have metal saw guides (c).*

WINDING STRIPS

It is possible to test a board with a straight-edge and find it flat in the length and across at various places, yet the surface is twisted, or 'in winding'. This can be checked by sighting along the board, when one end will be seen to be twisted in relation to the other. Winding strips are used to extend the width and make the twist seem more pronounced. Basically,

4.18 *Winding strips aid in checking twist (a). Pieces of contrasting colour make the ends clearer (b). Dowels can hold the strips together for storage (c).*

they are two wood straight-edges thick enough to stand on the board, so you can look along and see if one is tilted relative to the other (fig. 4.18a).

Length should be about three times the width of the board to be tested, and the wood should be a stable hardwood. For better sighting, at the ends of one piece you can let in pieces of wood of a contrasting colour (fig. 4.18b). For storage, two short dowels fixed in one piece press into holes in the other piece to hold them together (fig. 4.18c) and a hole at the end of one piece can be used to hang the pair on a nail. If the winding strips are made of an attractive hardwood and polished, their quality encourages you to do good work. This applies to many things you use – a good tool or piece of equipment encourages you to take care and get better end results.

TRESTLE

Not all work is most conveniently done at bench height. For some things, such as hand sawing downwards, it is better for the wood to be at about 450 mm (18 in) above the floor: sometimes old chairs can be pressed into use, or a *Workmate* can be set at a suitable height. For general workshop use it is worthwhile making two identical trestles of fairly substantial form, so that they are steady and will withstand hammering. Consider them as auxiliary benches. Much work can be done on one, but two will support long pieces of wood or provide a base for assembling a carcase or other framed work at a more convenient height than the floor or bench.

4.19 *A trestle is used instead of a bench for holding work at a lower level (a). The legs are splayed (b) and notched and gussetted to the top (c). Mark the leg lengths parallel with the top after fitting to it (d). An extension can be used to support higher work (e) and a trough will hold parts that might slip off (f).*

Note: Measurements in millimetres are given in **bold type**; measurements in inches are given in normal type.

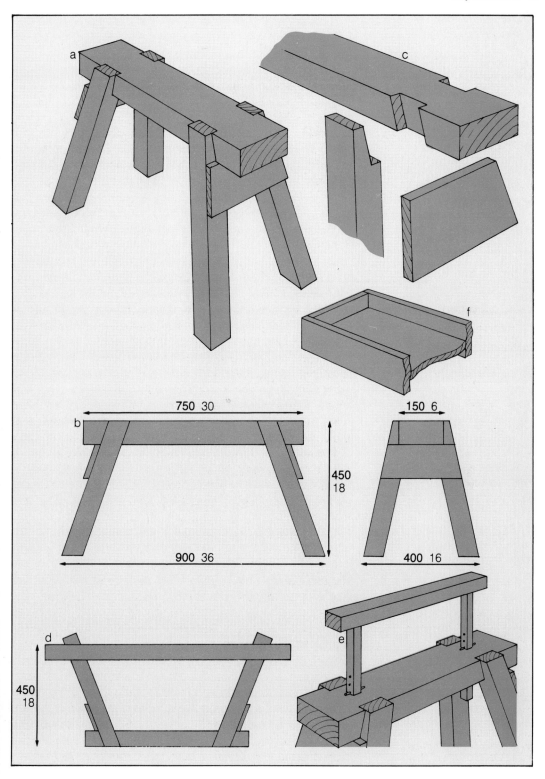

a

c

f

750 30

b

150 6

450
18

900 36

400 16

d

450
18

e

The standard trestle (fig. 4.19a) has four legs splayed outwards to points outside the plan of the top, so that the trestle will not tip over in normal use.

Metal parts are available for attaching the legs to the top. They give a rigid bolted assembly, and with some the trestle can be dismantled. Most trestles are made without such fittings.

The top of an all-wood trestle may be fairly wide (fig. 4.19b), to give a broad support to a board being worked on, or it can be narrower if you will normally use two trestles. The legs notch into it and there are gussets across the outsides of the legs (fig. 4.19c). Basic geometry will show that the legs should not be quite square on their corners, and the angles they make with the top should allow for the double slopes making the splay. In practice the differences in angles are slight and the parts can be positioned by trial and error: slight variations from the slopes originally drawn will not matter, provided that the result is symmetrical. And if two trestles are to be made, it is advisable to do all the stages in making them in step with each other, to get matching results. The legs should be left too long until after assembly. Then the ends are marked parallel with the top (fig. 4.19d) for cutting accurately.

Something similar to trestles could be made the same height as that of the circular saw table, to support long pieces of wood. Another way of dealing with this job is to make supports that can fit through holes in the ordinary trestle, either with permanent stops to set the height or – if you have more than one use for the extensions – with pegs to support work on several machines (fig. 4.19e). The top might be flat, or you could include a metal or rubber tube as a roller.

If you expect to work on chair seats or tackle upholstery, it is helpful to give the pair of trestles troughs to take two chair legs each. An upholsterer keeps trestles boxed round, but you can make troughs to slip into place and not affect the trestles for other uses (fig. 4.19f).

TOOL STORAGE

At one time any professional woodworker kept all his tools in a large chest that took at least two men to move, but in the usual workshop it is better to store tools around the place where they are accessible. If any have to be taken to outside jobs they can be carried in a smaller box: a rigid box can be fitted with drawers and racks, and – if made like an attache case with a partial door – it can open to show the contents in

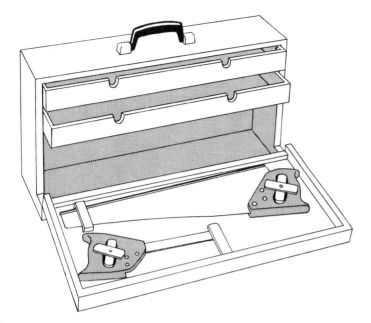

4.20 *A portable tool box can be made to open at the front.*

an orderly manner (fig. 4.20). If the outside work regularly requires the same tools, it may be worth equipping the box with duplicate basic tools. Besides having the tools always ready to take out, this allows the shop tools to be kept in the finest condition while the others take any rough treatment that may occur on a building site or in any similar situation.

Plenty of thought should be given to the layout of permanent tool storage and you may want to try temporary arrangements first. Consider where a tool is most often needed. You do not want to cross the workshop to get it and to put it back. Much depends on available wall space. Hanging tools should not interfere with work in progress or be knocked out of their racks when you move a job around. Sharp tools should not have their edges exposed, where they could get damaged or cause an accident.

Bags

The alternative to a rigid container, for temporary storage, is a bag. We have tradition to guide us there. The older outdoor craftsman took his tools to the job in a stout half-moon canvas bag with two handles (fig. 4.21a). A hammer, or other long tool, was pushed through the handles so that the load could hang from it over his shoulder. These bags are still available. Some may have inside pockets, but otherwise all the contents come tightly together. Such things as nails and screws could be kept in small bags or boxes with lids. Chisels can be kept in canvas rolls with pockets for up to nine chisels, giving good protection to their cutting edges

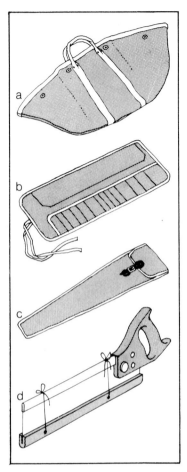

4.21 *Traditionally, a carpenter carried his tools in a bag (a). Chisels may be protected in a canvas roll (b). Saws may fit into a canvas bag (c) or be protected by a strip over the teeth (d).*

(fig. 4.21b). Similar rolls are available for drill bits. The usual handsaw is too long to be enclosed in the bag and may be carried projecting each side of this type of bag, but its teeth should be covered. Canvas cases with perhaps two compartments are available (fig. 4.21c), but a simple way of protecting a saw is with a strip of wood cut along one edge, and with cords to tie it on (fig. 4.21d). In any case, this is the best treatment for a tenon saw carried in the bag.

If a box or traditional bag is not wanted there are other bags – like canvas shopping or sports bags – that will take most tools, leaving long things to be carried separately. Strap fastenings allow adjustment to suit the contents, but zip fasteners with a lock are more secure. For better bags, at a greater cost, leather may be substituted for canvas. It is unwise to keep tools for long periods in cloth or canvas containers, as the material attracts moisture and could encourage rust.

Racks

Tools that are in fairly frequent use may be kept in racks. If the workshop is left out of use for long periods, and if heating is only used occasionally, it is better to have the tools in wall cabinets or cupboards, preferably those that give similar access to racks when the doors are opened (fig. 4.22). Tools that are only occasionally needed are better enclosed, in any case. Many small items are better kept in drawers, preferably arranged as a block under a bench or other work surface, so that it is easy to reach down and open one when you are working at the bench.

In general it may not seem advisable just to put a lot of tools loosely together in a drawer or box, but that will almost certainly happen with some of them. Giving each tool a rack or compartment is desirable but no matter how compactly you make the stowage, the tools and their fittings will take up much more room than they would if they were packed together. Many things, other than edge tools, do not suffer if kept in contact with each other. Unless you have almost unlimited space for tool storage, you will have to decide which of your tools to give individual racks and which will have to be stored together in drawers or elsewhere. There are many small things, such as bits for ratchet screwdrivers and cutters of many widths for a plough plane, that only get occasional use and may be lost. They are best kept in their own small boxes, with divisions if necessary, in a drawer – rather than in racks, where such items would get dusty and rusty. Small drills of the metalworking type are a similar

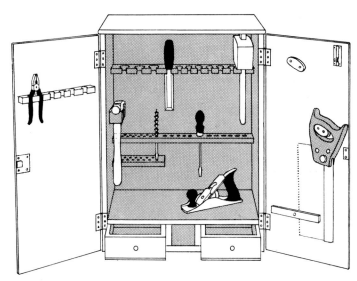

problem. They will blunt each other if stored loose, so ought to be in individual holes and protected by a cover.

For hanging things, perforated hardboard is available, with a regular pattern of holes, and wire hooks of various sorts provided for insertion where needed. The idea is attractive, but there can be wear after much use and hardboard storage is not best in a workshop that will get long and heavy use. However, the material is comparatively cheap and it allows you to experiment with rack arrangements that might be converted eventually into something more permanent. The hardboard has to be held off from the wall with battens, to give the hooks space when they are inserted, and a panel can be made attractive by framing.

If something can hang from a nail, there is nothing wrong with using a nail, but it will look more business-like if you cut off and file the end round, then tilt it upwards (fig. 4.23a). A large screw hook might suit your needs better – the straight cup hook (fig. 4.23b) being more use for most tools than the commoner round hook.

Spring clips are sold as tool clips, sprung in two ways. With the simplest (fig. 4.23c) the tool to be held needs to be quite close to the size of the clip. With the other (fig. 4.23d) there is more tolerance for different sizes. In both cases the clips can be bought with plastic coatings and this is less likely to mark wooden tool handles. A row of clips on a batten will accommodate a range of tools, with the advantage that you can take the tool you want by just pulling it forward.

Many tools will fit through round holes. A long screwdriver will hang upright under its own weight through thin wood

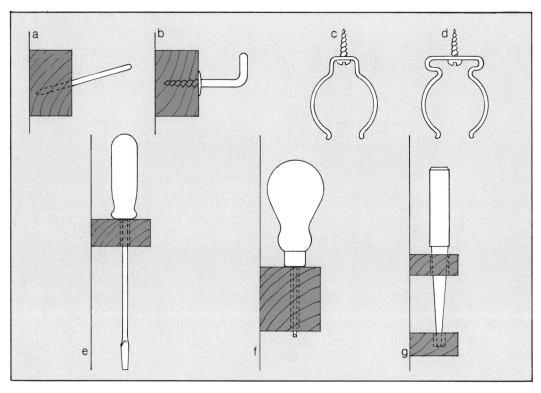

4.23 A tool may hang from a nail (a) or a hook (b). A simple spring tool clip (c) does not have as much tolerance as one with double bends (d). Some tools can hang through holes (e, f, g).

(fig. 4.23c), but it is better to hang a more top-heavy tool, like a bradawl, in a hole made through thicker wood (fig. 4.23f). Countersink holes slightly below as well as above, to prevent the grain breaking out, and some tools may need a second hole lower down (fig. 4.23g).

Chisels and gouges are best kept in separate slots, but side by side they take up a lot of space (fig. 4.24a). If slotted across the grain they weaken it (fig. 4.24b), so a compromise diagonal stowage may be better (fig. 4.24c). A piece of rigid transparent plastic will protect the edges and let you see which is which. Longer chisels, such as lathe tools, may be kept in individual spaces with their blades pointing upwards, with a retaining strip at the bottom and another higher up. With these or similar racks, leave a gap at the bottom, otherwise sawdust will fill the space (fig. 4.24d).

Some tools are best hung in a notched strip where they can be removed by pulling foward, rather than lifting from holes or slots. The strip should slope up, so that vibration will not make a tool fall out (fig. 4.25a). It may help if you work a hollow along the strip before cutting the notches (fig. 4.25b).

It could be that you do not want the same tools always available. A general rack that will take different tools would then be more suitable. This could be a strip with many

holes, but it is better if you provide it with one or more slots, similar to the arrangement described for the back of a bench. If the wall of the workshop is of stone or brick, put plywood behind the rack, then hold off battens with spacers at intervals (fig. 4.26a), making the rear one thick enough to hold tools and their handles clear of the wall. A wide slot behind a narrow one will cope with tools of different thicknesses, and the spacers between gaps stop tools falling over, particularly if many top-heavy ones are inserted together.

Having a number of racks for individual kinds of tool may use up more space than is available, and leave you with tools that have nowhere to go. But many ways can be found for storing different tools in the same rack. For instance, try-squares could go into slots on strips wide enough to have hooks or clips attached to the front (fig. 4.26b); or tools that fit into holes may be stored behind others that need clips or slots (fig. 4.26c).

4.24 Tool slots in line (a) take up more room than those across (b); the weak cross grain thus caused can be reduced by having diagonal slots (c). Long chisels are best stood on end (d).

4.25 Tools fitted into notches will hold in place better if the strip slopes up (a). A hollow along the top also helps in retaining tools (b).

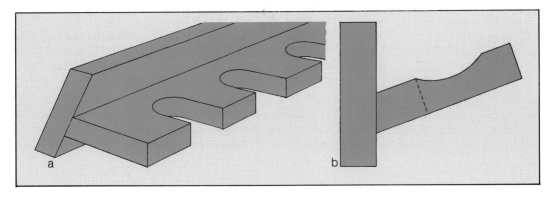

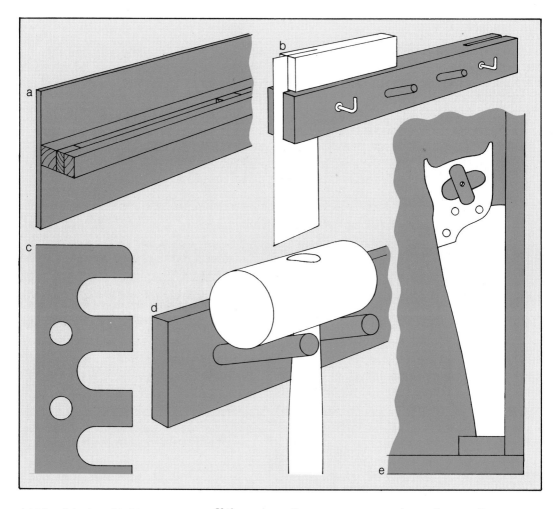

4.26 Parallel strips will hold some tools (a). One piece of wood can be arranged to support some tools in front of others (b). Holes for tools can go behind slots for others (c). Dowel rods into angled holes will support hammers and mallets (d). A saw fits conveniently inside a door (e).

If there is wall space, saws can hang from nails or dowel rods. Similar dowel rods in pairs will take mallets and hammers, always arranged on a slight tilt (fig. 4.26d). If there is space from back to front – perhaps 200 mm (8 in) – such things as saws and try-squares can go edgewise into a slotted shelf. A stack of shelves can be made into multiple racks, with the whole thing enclosed to make a cabinet with doors: besides protection from damp and dust, doors can have racks inside for tools such as saws, which do not need much depth (fig. 4.26e). However, there must be enough space for the doors to swing fully open without interfering with other things on the wall. Sliding doors only let you get at half the interior at a time and are a nuisance. Doors can be made to lift off, if there is no room for them to swing open, but you then need somewhere to put them.

Planes are a special case. They could go on a shelf below

the bench, so that they are end-on and you can recognize their backs. If the end of the bench is accessible, a rod across allows them to be placed so that they are held by the wedges (fig. 4.27c), but make sure there is sufficient space to lift a long plane clear. Other tools could go through holes in a board that is also serving as a plane rack. Such a rack at the vice end of the bench is convenient, as you can reach over and get the tools most often in use.

For a wall rack the planes most needed could go upwards into compartments, either with retaining strips at different heights (fig. 4.27b) or with the bottoms raised to use one

4.27 *Planes can fit behind a bar at the end of a bench (a), or they can go upwards into compartments on the wall (b, c). Another wall rack (d) may hold them in a similar way to the one at the end of the bench.*

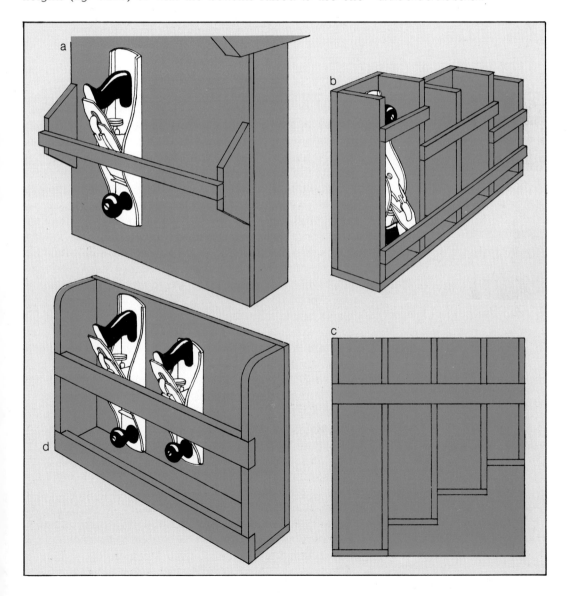

strip (fig. 4.27c). That gives space below the shorter planes for other tool racks. Another way is to provide a crossbar similar to that at the end of the bench, and put the planes downwards behind it (fig. 4.27d). The only snag with that is that, if it is placed high on a wall, the extra lift up to remove a heavy plane can be awkward.

Accessories and the tools to fit them to power tools should be kept near the machines, if possible, otherwise it is better to keep them in drawers with spare parts and accessories for hand tools. You will probably have some of these things that are rarely used, and can protect such tools from rust in storage by putting silica gel in the compartment. This, a chemical in crystal form that absorbs moisture, is supplied in two forms: sachets, or impregnated paper. In both cases you can dry out with warmth and use the sachet or paper again.

TIMBER STORAGE

As seen in the opening chapter, timber has to be looked after before use or it may suffer enough to make it useless for a particular project. Good wood is expensive and it is correct practice to store and use pieces down to quite small lengths and sections. Longer pieces should be kept straight. This means supporting at fairly close intervals and stacking boards neatly on each other, so that one does not get twisted in its length. This is particularly so with narrow battens, which may fall over and be left to take a distorted shape. Anything over about 1500 mm (6 ft) is better supported horizontally than stood on end, where it may bow between its top and bottom contacts.

Long pieces can often be put on crossbars high in the workshop, using space inside the roof or ceiling that would not otherwise be used. If the workshop has to double up with a garage, racks might go along one wall beside the car, with metal shelf brackets keeping obstruction to a minimum (fig. 4.28a). Part of the rack could be made into a shelf for shorter pieces of wood.

For pieces not long enough to store horizontally, a rack to take pieces on end is convenient (fig. 4.28b). Divisions can be made to prevent wood falling over when the rack is not full. Very small pieces still of useful size may be kept in a similar smaller rack, or on end in a box. If you have a circular saw, or a planer or a combination machine, small pieces of wood may be stored near or under it. With that equipment all sorts of oddments can be converted to sizes to suit the need of the moment.

Plywood, hardboard and similar sheet material is best

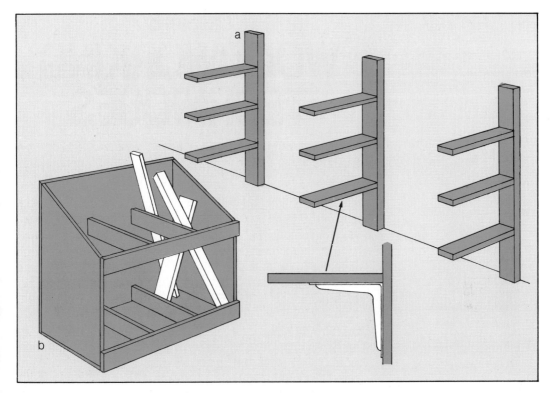

stored flat, but – with sheets of maximum size – that will probably involve more space than you can spare. If sheets are stored on edge for long, they should lean against battens to prevent them bowing. Thicker material, such as chipboard, will help to keep thinner materials flat.

4.28 *Long timber should be closely supported by racks (a). Shorter pieces may stand on end (b).*

Chapter 5
WOODWORKING TECHNIQUES

The difference between a craftsmanlike piece of work and one that is not as good as it should be can often be traced to the approach to the work. A good example of craftsmanship is probably the result of planning and an organized schedule as well as the ability to use tools. The work has been thought right through, and preparations for a later stage have been dealt with earlier before the assembly became more complicated. For instance, a beginner may put together a part of an assembly and discover that he should have cut mortises or ploughed grooves for a later part; they are now difficult, or impossible, to fashion cleanly and accurately. An experienced worker would have done all the work possible on each part in anticipation of later joints or other complications.

A drawing is always advisable, but it need not be a very full or detailed one, if you can visualize what you want to make. A scale drawing shows proportions, and may be the first indication that you have not got it quite right, so that you can correct sizes without wasting wood. The drawing gives you a chance to adapt sizes and design to suit available wood, or whatever sizes are more easily obtained.

There are a few design points to observe. This is not a book on design, but you can get more pleasing results if you understand a few principles. A rectangle, as part of a finished piece of furniture, is more pleasing to the eye than a square; so if you are planning some sort of a cabinet or table, try to avoid a square outline, no matter what angle it is viewed from. Part or the whole of an ellipse (fig. 5.1a shows a decorative cut under a rail) looks better than part of a circle (fig. 5.1b). An optical illusion makes lower heights look less than they are in relation to higher ones. So if you make a block of drawers all of the same depth, they will appear to get shallower towards the bottom (fig. 5.1c), and if you frame a door panel, it is usual to make the bottom rail noticeably wider (fig. 5.1d). Diagonal lines need care: they can be used, but sometimes they upset the overall appearance.

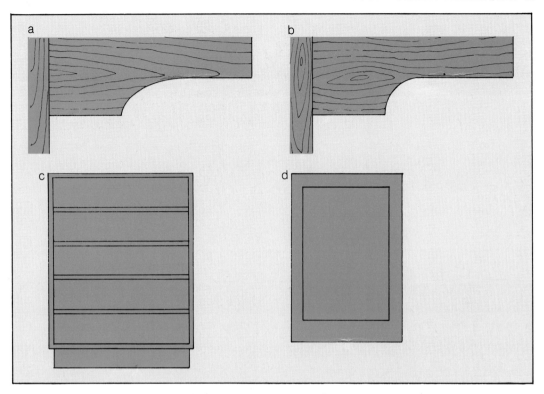

The drawing need not show the complete thing. If the finished article is to be symmetrical, half may be enough. For a table you can use drawings of half each of two elevations, and you may need a plan (fig. 5.2). From the drawing it always helps if you make a list of wood needed, showing widths and thicknesses, with a little extra added to each length. Remember to include enough for cutting joints. In the case of a table you can list the overall size of the top, but it may have to be made up from two or more narrower pieces ((fig. 5.3). The cutting list is a guide to what to cut from your own stock of wood, or it may be taken to your supplier so that he can select wood to suit.

5.1 An elliptical curve (a) looks better than a circular one (b). An even spacing appears to get narrower towards the bottom (c). Equal borders do not look as good as having the bottom one wider (d).

WOOD PREPARATION

There is a tendency with machined wood to assume that it is accurate, and to dispense with the traditional working from face side and edge, but for the best work this method should still be used. Look along the wood with one eye to sight for straightness. If necessary true one edge and face by hand planing. See that the edges are square to each other, then give them the traditional pencil marks (fig. 5.4a). If that is done on all pieces and you do your marking out from those

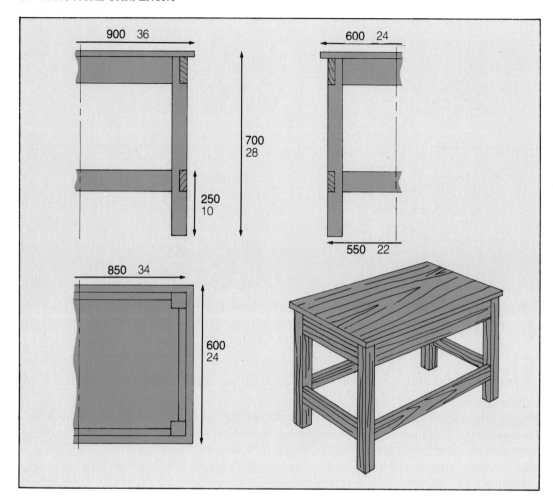

5.2 *Part views may show all you need to draw.*

4 LEGS 700×50×50
2 TOP RAILS 500×100×25
2 TOP RAILS 800×100×25
2 LOWER RAILS 500×75×25
2 LOWER RAILS 800×75×25
1 TOP 920×600×25

5.3 *A cutting list helps you pick from available wood or decide what to order.*

surfaces, vital outside surfaces will be level with each other, even if there are slight discrepancies on the inside when you cut joints. If you do not use the marks, and gauge a joint from one side of one piece and the other side of another piece with which it has to mate, there could be enough difference to spoil the fit. At this stage it will help to number the parts, or otherwise mark them, and also to put the numbers on the drawing.

In anything framed you cannot get the final assembly square in all directions if parts that ought to be the same length are not. A beginner may mark out each piece of wood separately, but a craftsman marks all pieces that have to be of identical lengths together, using a try-square across them all, with a knife where cuts must come and a sharp pencil elsewhere. In the case of the table shown being built here and on pages 170-1, the four legs are marked across

with a little waste left at each end for trimming later (fig. 5.4b). All the rails going one way are similarly marked (fig. 5.4c) and all the rails the other way are marked together. In this case we assume dowel joints, but if tenons were used there would have to be allowance for them.

The marks on the face surface are squared round, on all four sides for the cut ends, and only to the surfaces necessary for joints. For each of these markings the stock of the try-square is put against the face side or edge. All the rails may be cut to length at the marked knife lines. Check that they match each way, and level anywhere necessary.

5.4 Work from a face edge and mark parts that are to be similar together.

DOWELS

The rails shown come level with the outsides of the legs (fig. 5.5a). This makes the use of a dowel drilling guide easier, but if the holes are to be drilled without it, mark across each rail end and its leg together (fig. 5.5b) and letter or number the parts that mate, so that you do not confuse them later. Gauge from the outside face surfaces (fig. 5.5c), and it is a help to push an awl into the crossings where the drill is to enter.

Drill squarely into each part. How far to take a dowel is a matter of experience, but about twice its diameter into each piece is usually enough. A dowel as it goes into a hole is something like a piston in a cylinder, and the wood could split if nothing is done to release surplus air and glue. You can buy dowels prepared with tapered ends and grooves (fig. 5.5d), but if you cut your own from rod, saw a shallow

Note: Measurements in millimetres are given in **bold type**; measurements in inches are given in normal type.

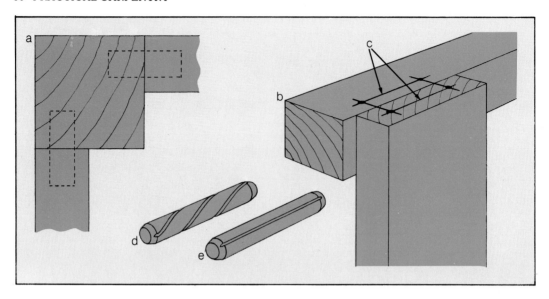

5.5 *For dowels to legs, mark rail and leg together. Grooved dowels allow air and surplus glue to escape.*

groove along each one (fig. 5.5e). Make the holes slightly deeper than you expect the dowel to go, so that there is no risk of the dowel bottoming and preventing the surfaces of the joint from meeting. In this example there are two dowels in each joint. There may be more in larger joints, but never come down to one in a small joint: it would be better in that case to change to two thinner dowels.

The solid wood of a table-top may expand and contract a little and that should be allowed for by using buttons. Plough grooves near the top edge of each top rail (fig. 5.6a). When you add the top later, screw buttons to the top with projecting pieces into the grooves (fig. 5.6b) so that they can slide if the top width varies.

5.6 *Buttons under a solid wood top allow it to expand and contract.*

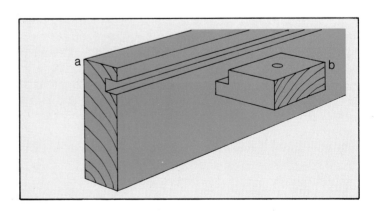

5.7 *(Opposite) Drive and cramp joints tight (a, b), then sight across to check twist (c). Check squareness by comparing diagonals (d, e, f). A weighted board may be needed to hold the assembly true while glue sets (g).*

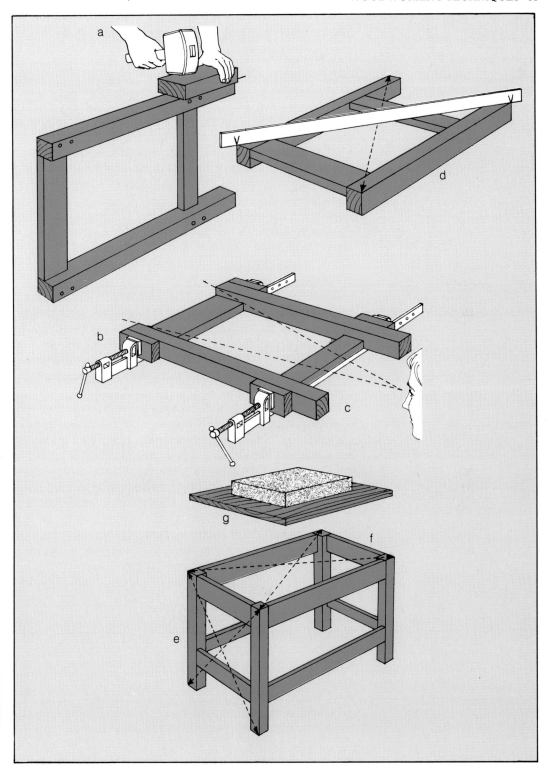

ASSEMBLY OF A FOUR-SIDED FRAMEWORK

Any four-sided framework is best assembled in two stages. In this case opposite long sides come first. Prepare the joints and their dowels with glue, then tap them together, using a mallet or hammer over scrap wood (fig. 5.7a). Remember to check that there is nothing on the bench that can mark the surface underneath. Move to bar cramps, if possible, with scrap pieces to take and spread the pressure (fig. 5.7b). Otherwise use wedges against blocks. Make sure the assembly is level and without twist by sighting across the rails (fig. 5.7c). You can partially check squareness with a try-square against a rail, but it is better to measure diagonals, preferably with a pencil and a light wood rod (fig. 5.7d). There is less risk of error with this than with a rule or tape measure.

Assemble the opposite side in the same way and check that the two assemblies match when brought together with their inner surfaces facing. When the glue has set, remove any surplus and cut the bottoms of the legs to length. The tops of the legs are better left until all the rails are attached and you can make the whole surface fit closely to the table top.

In the second stage, join the rails the other way. You have to square the assembly in two directions before the glue begins to set. Each new side must be checked by measuring diagonals (fig. 5.7e) and you must check squareness as viewed from above (fig. 5.7f). To guard against twist, have the assembly standing on a flat surface so that you can stand back and look at it in several directions. Check diagonals between legs at both rail levels, then sight across to see that rails are parallel with each other and all legs are upright. If there is any tendency to spring out of shape, you can put a board over the top with a weight on it (fig. 5.7g).

MAKING A TABLE-TOP

If the top has to be made up of boards joined together, there must be no risk of them separating later. With modern synthetic resin glues, a simple meeting of two true surfaces may be enough. If the edges are planed very slightly hollow in their lengths and a cramp is used across the centre, the ends will be brought together extra tight. It is at the ends that a joint may try to open after completion.

The edges could be dowelled (fig. 5.8a). Put dowels near the ends, but the others can be quite widely spaced. You

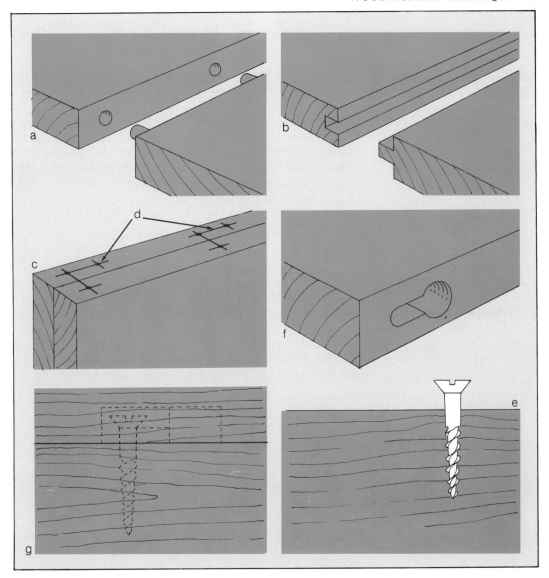

could use tongue and groove joints (fig. 5.8b), but the appearance at the ends would not be acceptable for good quality furniture, although the joint is a good one for other applications.

A good way to strengthen the joint is by secret slot screwing, and this has the advantage of not needing cramps. At fairly wide intervals along the joint mark the edges as if for dowels (fig. 5.8c). On one edge make more marks 18 mm (¾ in) away (fig. 5.8d). Choose fairly stout steel screws – 10 gauge × 25 mm (1 in) should suit this joint. Drill for and drive

5.8 To make up width, boards may be dowelled (a) or tongued and grooved (b). Secret slot screwing will pull and hold parts together (c, d, e, f, g).

the screws into the centre of the edge with single markings, leaving about 6 mm to 9 mm of the screw standing above the surface of the wood (fig. 5.8e). In the other piece drill a hole large enough to clear the screw head at the offset position and the size of the screw neck at the other position, then cut a slot that width to the other hole (fig. 5.8f). Do all this deeper than the extension of the screw-head from the other piece.

Bring the boards together dry and knock one along the other so that the screw heads cut a way along the bottom of the slot (fig. 5.8g). If that is satisfactory, knock the boards back and separate them. Give each screw one-quarter turn. Put glue on the surfaces and knock the boards back together again to complete the joint.

The table-top could have square edges. They could be curved, but a partial curve (fig. 5.9a) looks better than a semi-circle (fig. 5.9b). There could be a graduated curve (fig. 5.9c). If you want the top to look lighter, that curve might be turned over (fig. 5.9d). Various mouldings are possible around the edge, either worked with appropriate planes or with a cutter in a router. A simple step down with a curve (fig. 5.9e) may be all that is needed. If your tool kit is limited, this has the advantage of being possible to cut by first making a rabbet and then rounding with a plane and glasspaper.

5.9 *Edges may be curved to improve the appearance of a table top.*

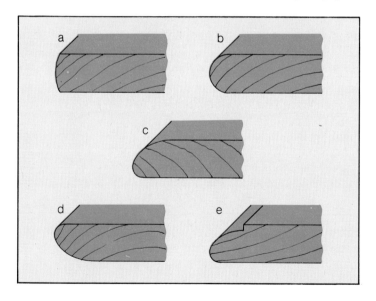

Make a trial assembly of the top to the framework, but it is easier to clean up the wood and finish with stain and polish or varnish if the top is removed until the framework has been completed.

MORTISE AND TENON JOINTS

The most widely used traditional joint is the mortise and tenon, in several variations to suit applications. Some parts that were joined with tenons are now dowelled, but any competent craftsman should be able to cut good mortise and tenon joints. They provide a good glue area and are mechanically strong.

The table with an enclosed shelf and diagonal lower rails (fig. 5.10) shows some applications of the joint. Cut and mark out the parts from the drawing and cutting list. The plywood

5.10 *A table with a shelf and rails uses several versions of the mortise and tenon joint.*

Note: Measurements in millimetres are given in **bold type**; measurements in inches are given in normal type.

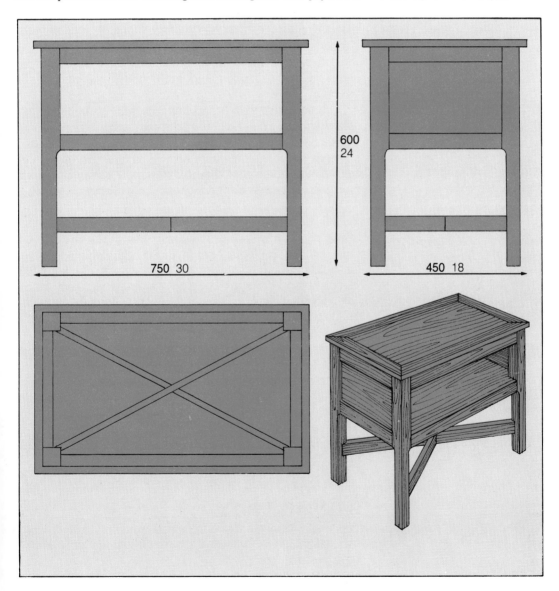

Note: Measurements in millimetres are given in **bold type**; measurements in inches are given in normal type.

CUTTING LIST FOR TABLE SHOWN ON P.91

4 legs	**600** ×	**45** × **45**	24 ×	1¾ ×	1¾
4 rails	**700** ×	**35** × **25**	28 ×	1⅜ ×	1
4 rails	**400** ×	**35** × **25**	16 ×	1⅜ ×	1
2 bottom rails	**850** ×	**35** × **18**	34 ×	1⅜ ×	¾
2 top frames	**800** ×	**65** × **18**	32 ×	2⅝ ×	¾
2 top frames	**475** ×	**65** × **18**	19 ×	2⅝ ×	¾
1 top panel (plywood)	**725** × **400** ×	**9**	29 × 16	×	⅜
1 shelf (plywood)	**750** × **425** ×	**6**	30 × 17	×	¼
2 fillets	**700** ×	**12** × **12**	28 ×	½ ×	½
2 fillets	**400** ×	**12** × **12**	16 ×	½ ×	½

panels are let into grooves in the rails and the tops of the legs, so plough them to suit. Cut back the legs to the bottoms of the grooves (fig. 5.11a) and mark on them the positions of the rails.

It is customary to make tenons one-third of the thickness of the wood if the parts are both the same thickness, but where the rails are narrower than the legs the tenons are stronger if thicker than one-third of the rail thickness. Cut back to the bottoms of the grooves those parts of the rails that will make tenons, and gauge both these pieces (fig. 5.11b) and the legs for the joints. The bottom shelf rails have tenons full depth (fig. 5.11c). At the top, joints cut to full depth would have weak mortises open to the tops of the legs. Instead, the tenons are haunched (fig. 5.11d). For this, the excess length first left on the leg provides a buffer to the risk of the end grain breaking out when the mortise is being cut.

Cut all the upper rails, their joints and the panels. But a trial assembly might wear the wood and loosen the joint. A craftsman does not usually make this sort of trial with mortise and tenon joints, trusting his workmanship.

Check actual sizes in relation to your drawing. Make a full-size plan view of the leg positions and mark on it the diagonal lower rails. This will give you rail lengths and angles. At each leg, cut away to the size of a rail (fig. 5.11e) so that the tenon shoulders will fit against it and the tenons go into the leg (fig. 5.11f).

HALVING JOINTS

Where the diagonal rails cross there must be a halving or half lap joint to keep them at the same level. This is a joint used in many places where parts cross and may even be used at a corner instead of a mortise and tenon in less-

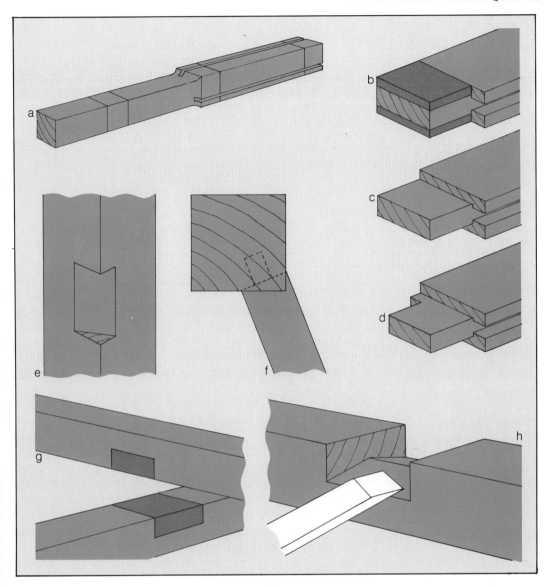

important work. Here the parts cross diagonally, so you have to mark with an adjustable bevel on the surface and square down to lines gauged from the top face edge of both pieces (fig. 5.11g). A common fault in a halving joint is to cut out too much in width or depth. Mark with a knife and cut inside the lines. Pare the bottoms with the chisel sloping upwards a little from each side (fig. 5.11h), and only level the bottom when you are down to the line each side.

The shelf could be rabbeted into the rails, but it is simpler to support the plywood on fillets glued inside the rails (fig.

5.11 *These table legs have thicker grooved tops (a). Tenons are cut in stages (b, c, d). Rail to leg joints are diagonal (e, f).*

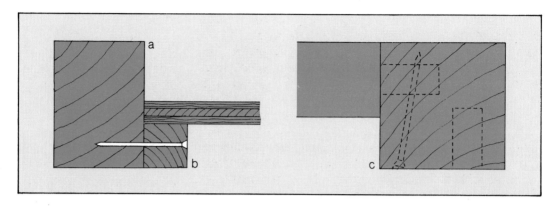

5.12 *The shelf rests on fillets (a), glued and pinned (b). A nail from inside will hold a tenon after a cramp has been removed and while the glue sets.*

5.12a). This makes accurate fitting of the shelf easier after the other parts are assembled. Glue the fillets to the rails before assembly. They could also be screwed, but it should be sufficient to use a few panel pins to keep the strips in place (fig. 5.12b).

Assemble the back and front independently. The plywood panels need only have a small amount of glue near the bottoms of the grooves, so avoiding the problem of cleaning off excess. Cut the plywood to a size that makes an easy fit – it need not fit tightly against the bottoms of the grooves. With mortise and tenon joints you can manage with fewer cramps. When a rail is tight into its leg, drive a thin nail into it from the inside, where it will not show (fig. 5.12c). That will hold the joint close while the glue sets after you have removed the cramp.

When you assemble square parts like this, the diagonal rails have to be brought in at the same time as the two parts come together. The panels will help in squaring. Be careful that the widths across the legs at the bottoms are the same as at the tops. If you have to use a bar cramp across the diagonals, pad outside the legs to avoid damage to the corners.

MITRE JOINTS

The top, in this case, has a frame around a plywood centre. The width of the frame should extend past the inside of the rails (fig. 5.13a). Rabbet the strips, keeping them overlong at this stage. Leave the outside edges square, even if they will eventually be rounded or moulded. This is better for cramping. Mark opposite sides to length together, marking the corners with a mitre square. Something has to be done to hold these wide mitres together, although once the table-top is in position the framework will reinforce the joints.

Dowels could be set across (fig. 5.13b), but that brings problems of cramping. The cramping problem is eased if the dowels are parallel with one edge (fig. 5.13b), but that brings problems of cramping. The cramping problem is eased if the dowels are parallel with one edge (fig. 5.13c), but it is difficult to drill without slipping. Another way is to let in a piece of wood across the joint on the underside (fig. 5.13d), preferably while the joint is held close in a mitre cramp. Similar to this is the use of a corrugated fastener on the underside (fig. 5.13e). These fasteners are normally only associated with the crudest woodwork, but in this case they are justified, as they will not show.

With the frame assembled, carefully cut the plywood panel, which may be faced with a matching veneer. As you plane the panel near the size, make its edge slightly tapered (fig. 5.13f), so that it makes a very close fit as it is pressed in.

5.13 *The top frame comes over the rails and legs (a) and may be strengthened with dowels (b, c) or fasteners below (d, e). Tapering the panel edge makes a close fit (f).*

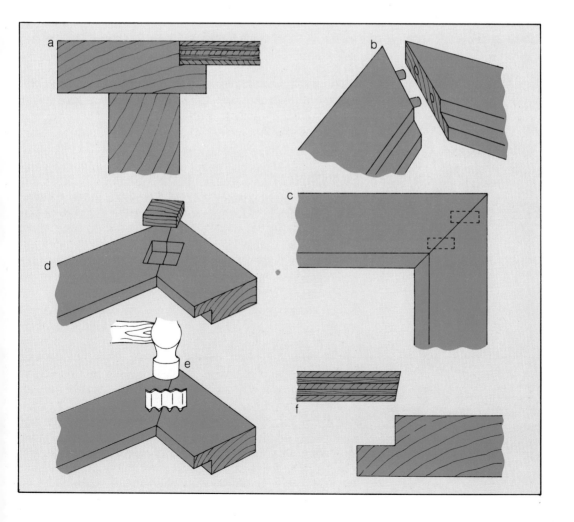

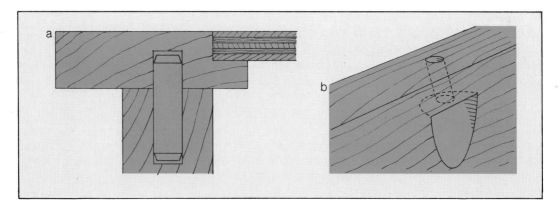

5.14 *The top may be dowelled (a) to the rails, or pockets for screws upwards may be cut (b).*

Use strips of wood along the joints as you press them tight with 'G' cramps.

As there is no problem of expansion and contraction with this type of table-top, it can be fixed down rigidly. You could fix a few dowels along each rail to supplement glue (fig. 5.14a). Another way would be to use pocket screws driven upwards from inside the rails (fig. 5.14b). Drill diagonally downwards into the rails, then chop out enough wood on the inside to admit the screw head. This is a good method of fitting a table or stool top, but as in this case the shelf makes access difficult – except with a short screwdriver – dowels are preferable.

HOUSING OR DADO JOINTS

The common application of a housing joint is in fitting a shelf to the side of a bookcase or something similar. It takes a load across the joint, but the basic form does not offer much resistance to pulling apart. A simple example is a wall bracket to support a vase of flowers (fig. 5.15). The back and shelf could be shaped or decorated in many ways, but this description is mainly concerned with the joints.

The shelf goes into a notch across the back and that is a simple housing joint. Except for cutting its end squarely, there is no special preparation of the shelf. Care is needed to avoid marking or cutting the notch too wide. It may go half through the back, although if that is thick the groove may be comparatively shallower. Use a knife to draw across the surface, and gauge the depth (fig. 5.16a). For hand cutting use a fine backsaw over a bench hook and keep the kerf inside the line. It helps to bevel across the deeply cut knife line with a paring chisel (fig. 5.16b) to keep the saw in position. The waste may be removed entirely with a chisel, but this is the place to use a little hand router to level the

5.15 *A shelf bracket is an example of the use of a housing joint.*

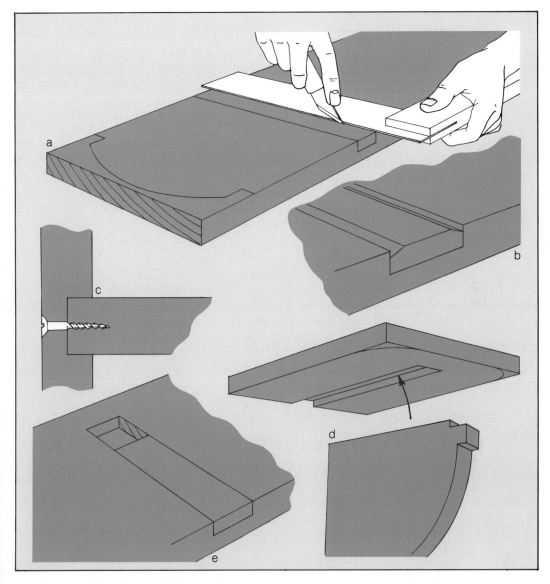

bottom. Use a straight-edge to check that the bottom is level. If it has any high spots away from the edges, the shelf will not bed down tightly.

As the back of the bracket will not show, a few screws can be driven into the shelf end (fig. 5.16c). The support can also be screwed through from the back without notching it in, but there may be a stopped housing joint under the shelf (fig. 5.16d). Its forward end is notched into a groove that does not extend across the full width. For hand cutting, the dado is marked out and the closed end of the groove chopped out with chisels, for a distance of about 25 mm (1 in), but with a

5.16 *Mark a groove across the grain with a knife (a). Paring against the cut forms saw guides (b). Screw the shelf joint from the rear (c). For the stopped housing joint (d), cut the closed end with a chisel to permit saw movement.*

little waste left at the extreme end (fig. 5.16e). This allows you to saw the sides of the groove, using a limited movement of the saw within the cut-out, and then removing the waste as in the simple housing joint. Finally, the end, which has taken knocks from the saw, may be trimmed to size. The support is glued into the groove without screws.

Through housing joints can be cut with a fine radial arm saw or with a circular saw set to a small projection, but the most convenient power tool is a router with a plain cutter, not necessarily as wide as the intended groove. With a piece of wood cramped across as a guide, a groove may be cut either through or stopped. If the cutter is narrower than the final groove you can use a second setting to make up the full width. With a stopped housing joint a chisel must follow the router to square off the end of the groove, or the piece fitting in can be rounded to suit.

Housing joints are used in a block of hanging shelves (fig. 5.17a), which are stiffened by a piece fixed across the top. The layout and assembly are straightforward. The narrower top shelf goes fully into a stopped groove (fig. 5.17b). The other shelves are notched to bring their fronts level with the uprights (fig. 5.17c).

5.17 A block of shelves (a) has two forms of housing joints (b, c), which can be strengthened with screws or nails from below (d).

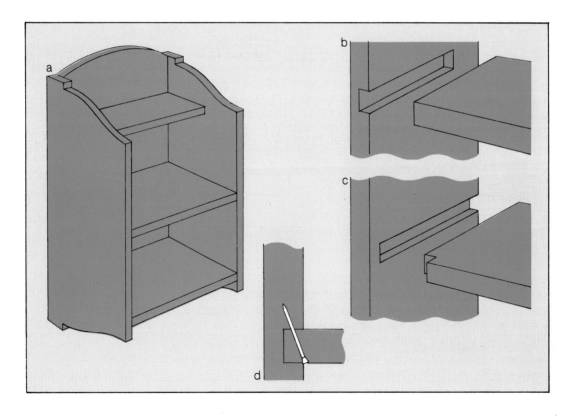

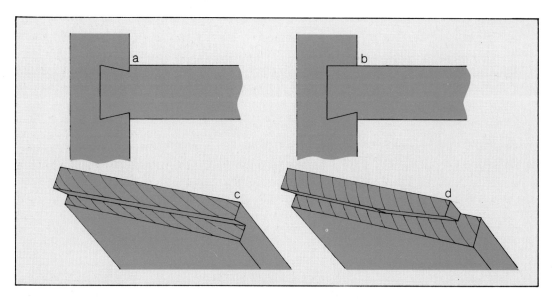

5.18 *Dovetailing (a, b) strengthens a housing joint. Tapering (c, d) makes a tight fit.*

The grooves cannot be very deep, so they do not provide much area for glue, and the strength of the joint is reduced by end grain meeting side grain. The best glued joints come between side grain surfaces: there is not such a good bond between end and side grain, so this housed joint needs the added strength of screws or nails. Driven from outside, they would spoil the appearance of the sides. Instead, thin screws or nails can be driven diagonally upwards from the inside. Two in each joint should be sufficient. If the fastenings are kept close into the angle between the shelf and the side, they will not show much, if at all (fig. 5.17d). The angle of driving should be judged to bring the point out of the end of the shelf at about the centre of the thickness of the side.

Another way of increasing the mechanical strength of the joint is to cut it with a dovetail section, on top and bottom (fig. 5.18a) or on one side only – usually underneath (fig. 5.18b). The shelf must then be slid in from the back. The angle need only be quite slight and can be pared across with a chisel on the shelf, while the groove is angled by tilting the saw or by using a suitable router cutter.

If the shelf is wide, it is difficult to cut a dovetail-shaped housing so that the shelf slides in satisfactorily. Assembly is eased and tightness is ensured if the dovetailed part is tapered (fig. 5.18c). Marking out and cutting must be carefully done, but this makes a very secure joint. With a very wide shelf, getting an even taper is difficult: the dovetail part can be made parallel for perhaps half the width – measuring from the back – and the taper taken forward from there (fig. 5.18d).

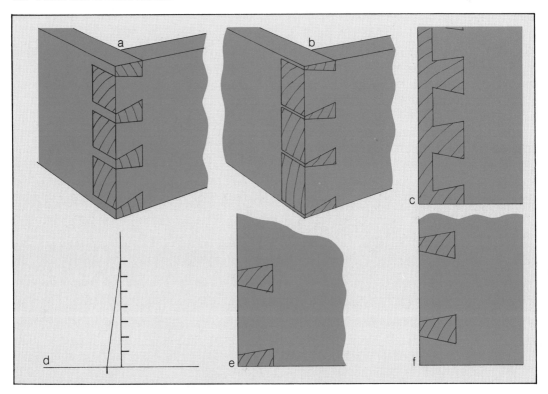

5.19 *Hand-cut dovetails may have wide or narrow pins (a, b). Machine-cut dovetails may have pins and tails the same width (c). The dovetail slope can be drawn (d) for setting an adjustable bevel. There could be either a pin (e) or half a tail (f) at an edge.*

DOVETAIL JOINTS

Carefully-fitted dovetail joints are often regarded as the mark of a craftsman, although there are plenty of other woodworking processes at least equally difficult. Dovetails provide a resistance to pulling apart in one direction and a good strength the other way, due to the ample side grain glue area. Handcut dovetails usually have the tails much wider than the pins between them (fig. 5.19a). At one time cabinetmakers were proud of making joints with exceptionally thin pins (fig. 5.19b), but – except as a display of the craftsman's skill – such joints have no advantages. Dovetails can be cut by machine, but these are mostly stopped and can be recognized by their having the pins and tails the same width (fig. 5.19c). Dovetails are often cut with too great a slope on their sides. About 1 in 7 is reasonable (fig. 5.19d), but the degree of taper may be varied according to the thickness and hardness of the wood, with a wider angle for softer woods.

Haphazard dovetails might be just as strong as evenly-spaced ones, but they look ugly. To avoid this, time has to be spent judging how the parts of a joint should be spaced. In normal construction there are pins at the edges (fig. 5.19e), but sometimes it is better to have half a tail at an edge (fig.

5.19f). There are no rules about proportions of dovetail joints, but having the tails about twice as wide as the thickness of the wood, with pins rather narrower than the thickness, gives reasonable proportions in normal work. There must be modifications, though, to get spacing of pins even within any particular overall width. Once a craftsman tried to hide dovetails, but now well-fitted through dovetails are regarded as decorative features.

A box is a typical example of through dovetailing. Its bottom is of solid wood screwed and glued on (fig. 5.20). The wood section may be about 100 mm (4 in) × 12 mm (½ in) and overall sizes can suit needs without affecting details of the

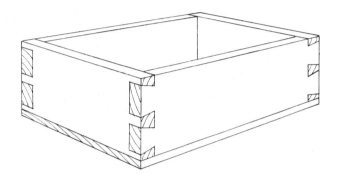

5.20 *Dovetails make strong box corners.*

joints. It is possible to make the parts with tails first or those with pins first. Either method can give good results, but making the tails first permits easier marking of one piece from the other.

The angles can be marked uniformly with a template. Several are on sale, but one can be made of bent metal (fig. 5.21a) or thin pieces of wood (fig. 5.21b). Mark the wood's thickness back from the ends of each piece. There can be a very small amount of excess wood at each end, but too much waste will interfere with cutting the joints. Space the dovetails on one end. Put two pieces together in a vice, and square across (fig. 5.21c), then saw down the sides of the tails and cut in at the sides. Reverse the second piece and use the first as a saw guide for cutting that. Do the same with the fourth end, so that you have cut all tails after marking them on one only, and they will all look the same. In larger work some of the waste can be cut out with a bandsaw. Even in small joints, some waste can be removed with a coping saw, but mainly it has to be chopped and pared out with a bevel-edge chisel, working from each side and always supporting on a flat piece of scrap wood. Careless work can cause the grain to break out. Be careful not to cut below the line and not to leave high spots in the thickness (fig. 5.21d).

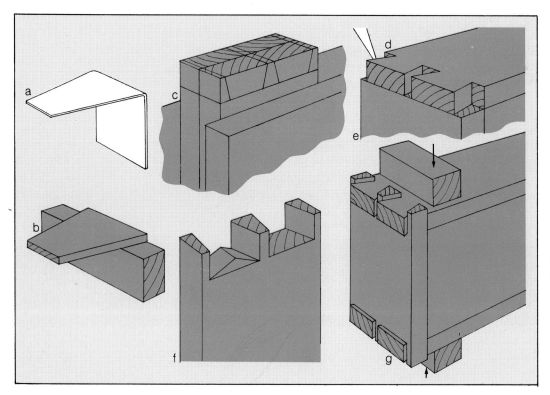

5.21 *A gauge can be made to mark dovetail angles (a, b). Tails can be marked and cut together (c), then pins marked from them (d, e). Cut between the pins (f) and drive joints together with supporting blocks.*

The pins and sockets can be marked with a tail piece held in place while a thinly-pointed pencil or a fine awl is used (fig. 5.21e). Use the base of the cut between the tails as a guide against the other wood – not the outside edge. At this stage it is advisable to mark the two parts of each joint, so that they are kept together. It is very unlikely that you will produce joints that are interchangeable and there is no need for that degree of precision.

Cut down the pins with the saw on the waste sides of the lines you have marked. Some of the waste can be removed with a few diagonal cuts (fig. 5.21f), then the bottoms of the sockets are levelled with chisels. Remember the slopes and be careful not to cut into them when working from the wide sides. As with mortise and tenon joints, trust your workmanship and do not risk wear in the joints by making trial assemblies.

When you assemble, the tails should pull the joints tight in the direction they are cut, but you may have to use cramps squeezing on scrap pieces of wood just inside the actual joint area (fig. 5.21g). Check squareness. Let the glue set, then level the joints by planing outside. Have a sharp finely-set plane and hold it diagonally to the way it is pushed – never let it run out at an end grain corner.

DRAWER CONSTRUCTION

There are ways of making drawers without dovetails, mainly devised to suit mass-production, but all the best drawers have the fronts and sides dovetailed to each other, preferably by hand. As the joint details are not wanted visible on the front, the bottom is usually grooved into the sides and front and a part tail at the bottom can hide this (fig. 5.22a). The front is usually thicker than the sides, so that the tails can be of adequate length. When marking out a joint, avoid going too far into the front, as appearance could be spoiled if the covering wood over the tails gets pierced or cracked.

The front is grooved to take a plywood bottom. The sides can also be grooved (fig. 5.22b) or there may be a separate grooved piece inside (fig. 5.22c). If the drawer slides on a runner and guide in the traditional way, the separate piece gives a greater bearing area along the bottom.

5.22 *Stopped dovetails cover a drawer bottom (a, b, c) with a part tail (d, e). Remove waste with a drill, chisel and saw (f, g, h).*

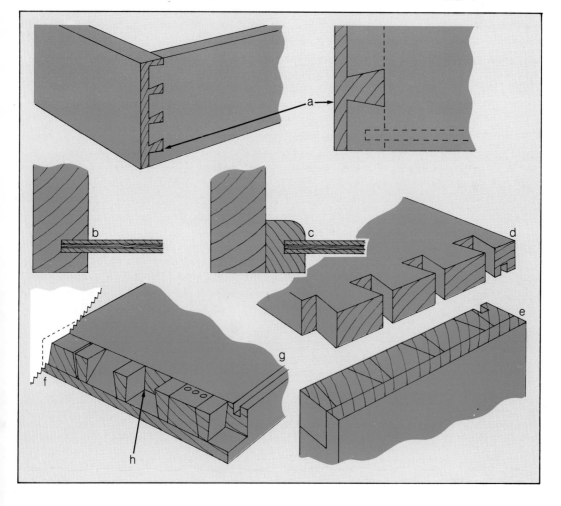

Mark out in a similar way to the through dovetail, but allowing for the stop piece at the front (fig. 5.22d). Cut the tails in the same way as for a through dovetail joint. Mark the other piece from them and square on to the surface (fig. 5.22e). You can saw diagonally inside the marked lines (fig. 5.22f). The rest of the waste has to be removed with chisels, but the work can be eased and the risk of breaking through the front reduced if holes are drilled (fig. 5.22g). Use a depth stop. Hold the wood firmly on flat scrap wood on the bench top, and make cuts across the grain before lengthwise cuts into them. Although bevel-edge chisels will do most of the work, the extreme corners of the sockets are best cleared with a sharp pointed knife (fig. 5.22h), or the inner corners of the tails can be tapered so that they do not bind in these angles.

It is usual for the back of a drawer to reach down only as far as the upper surface of the bottom, which can then be slid into its grooves after the other parts are assembled and held with a few screws driven up into the back. Through dovetails are used at the back (fig. 5.23a), arranged so that

5.23 *A drawer back is fitted above the bottom.*

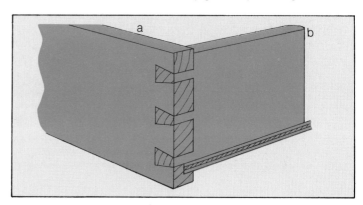

the back stops above the grooves – with its top often kept a little lower than the sides, and rounded (fig. 5.23b). If the drawer has to be adjusted inside the back of its casing, the tails may be left long and finally planed to stop the drawer at the right position. It is important that a drawer should be the same width at the back and front, and be made square, particularly when you check the sides in relation to the front. Any errors mean that the drawer will not run properly nor fit closely at the front.

Older drawers were always made to close flush with the front of their casing and any old furniture examined will be found arranged in this way. Much modern furniture has the drawer front overlapping so that it hides the gaps around the drawer. This greater tolerance is necessary if tedious hand

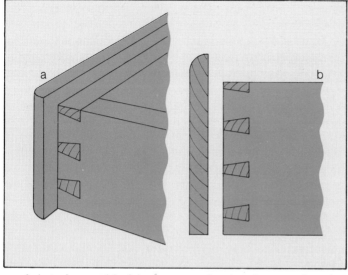

5.24 *An overlapping drawer front may be cut solid or a piece added.*

work is to be avoided in mass-production, but overlapping fronts are now accepted as features of modern design, so may be used in individual pieces of furniture.

The drawer front may be fairly thick and have a rabbet cut so that the joints are set back (fig. 5.24a). This makes a form of stopped dovetail, but because of the overhang, a saw cannot be used on the sockets. An alternative is to make the front in two thicknesses. This is simpler and allows of a neater fit than rabbets, as well as making it possible to use simple through dovetails (fig. 5.24b). The drawer can be made up completely without the false front, allowing any planing or other adjustment to get a good fit. The front can be added as a final step, with glue and screws from inside the drawer.

CHIPBOARD JOINTS

Although veneered chipboard can be treated as wood in many ways, its construction of wood chips in synthetic resin does not permit much detail work – such as the cutting of interlocking joints similar to those used in solid wood. In such uses there is a tendency for corners to break and particles to come away. Because of this and the widespread use of chipboard in mass-production, other techniques and joints have been developed, particularly where chipboard is almost the sole constructional material for a piece of furniture.

Chipboard can be cut to curves by hand or with a bandsaw, but the method of covering edges with self-adhesive strips of matching veneer cannot be relied on for very tight curves. If the curved edge is covered with solid wood, any shape is possible, but where it will be exposed there are limits to the amount of shaping. If specimens of mass-produced furniture are examined, nearly all will be seen to have been designed with far more square-ended parts than would be usual with solid wood. This is due to the need for convenience in manufacture and the limitations of the material for finishing curved edges. A maker of an individual piece of furniture can do better than the manufacturer in including some moderate curves, but edges have to be prepared square across and in a way that permits the use of a hot domestic iron for pressing the strip of veneer on. If the curve blends into straight edges, the strip can be in one piece that can be pulled along the straight parts as well as around the curve to get a close fit.

Probably the best joint for most parts of an individually-made assembly in chipboard uses dowels – 6 mm (¼ in) will suit. There are prepared dowels and drilling jigs available to suit the commonly used thickness of chipboard, but cut rod and measured positions may be preferred by a craftsman (fig. 5.25a).

It is not always easy to get close-fitting corners, so where the design permits one part may extend over another (fig. 5.25b). It may help if you cover the line where they meet with a strip of wood (fig. 5.25c). At a bottom a plinth effect can be made by letting the sides reach the floor and setting a front back a little (fig. 5.25d).

Chipboard will take screws, but a screw cannot be left to cut its own way for part of the depth, as is often done in wood (fig. 5.25e). If that was done in chipboard, the material would crack and expand to spoil the surface appearance. Instead, the core size hole should go further than the screw is expected to (fig. 5.25f). Although ordinary wood screws can be used, there are special screws for the material. They look like self-tapping screws intended for sheet metal, and have threads almost to the head (fig. 5.25g).

If screws have to be used through a surface that will show, they may be counterbored and the holes plugged. Instead of putting a wood plug in the hole, there are plastic plugs with shallow curved heads, supplied in colours to match the veneer, which can be glued in (fig. 5.25h).

Another way of joining chipboard parts is with strips of wood screwed both ways (fig. 5.25j). This is suitable for places where the strips will not show. Inside a cupboard or other places where they are hidden most of the time, they could be cut back a little and bevelled or rounded. Behind a plinth, or other place where they are out of sight, they can

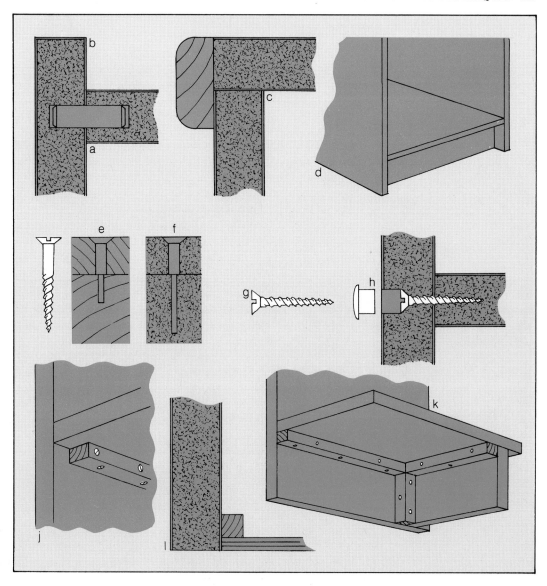

be fixed along all joints (fig. 5.25h). the same idea can be used to hold a plywood or hardboard back in a chipboard cabinet (fig. 5.25l).

There are plastic blocks for screwing in both directions in a similar way to the strips of wood, and others where two mating blocks can be fixed to the two parts and drawn together with a bolt. These are particularly suitable for furniture that has to be taken apart or is supplied in a knock-down form for the customer to put together. They have little value in the building of furniture that will never have to be dismantled.

5.25 Dowelled joints (a, b) can be used with chipboard. Joints may be hidden with wood (c) or set back (d). Screw holes that need go only part way in wood (e) must be full depth in chipboard (f). Special chipboard screws (g) may be sunk and plugged (h). Wood strips can be used to join parts (j, k, l).

WEDGES

A wedge can exert considerable power over a short distance. For a temporary cramp, blocks can be nailed or screwed to a stiff piece of wood, then a wedge driven against a block to tighten an assembly (fig. 5.26a). A single wedge has a tendency to push the parts to one side, but it is possible to give a parallel push with a pair of folding wedges (fig. 5.26b). Both wedges should be cut at the same angle. What the angle is may not be critical. A shallower angled wedge puts on more pressure, but can only move the part being pressed a small amount. With a steeper angle, the movement is more, but the available pressure is less – although it is usually more than enough. To reduce any tendency to move the work sideways, the wedges should be tapped in with alternate blows.

5.26 *A wedge may be driven to apply pressure (a), but a pair of wedges (b) give a parallel action. Wedges may be driven outside a tenon (c), but are better arranged to spread it (d), particularly to give stiffness to a light assembly (see fig. 5.27). Wedges in a stub tenon (e) will spread it as it is driven in (f).*

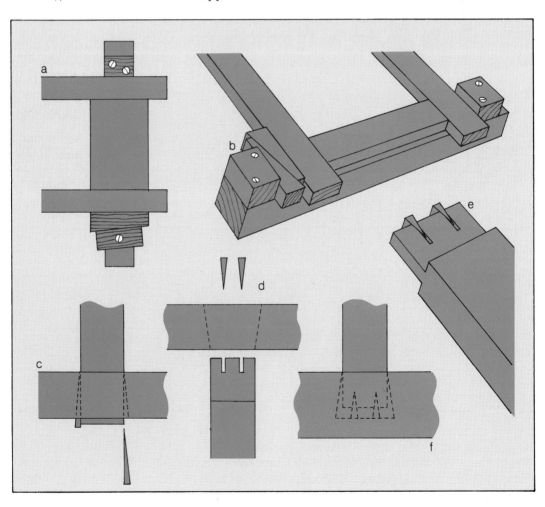

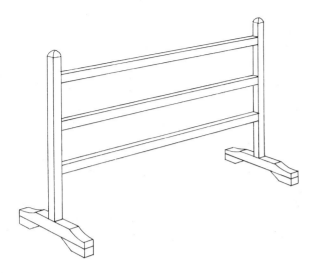

Before the days of reliable waterproof glues many joints were wedged to give them mechanical strength even if they were glued as well. Through tenons may have had wedges driven outside them (fig. 5.26c). This tightens by compressing the tenon, which is not as efficient as spreading it. A better way is to put one or two saw cuts across the end of the tenon before it is driven, with wedges driven into the saw cuts to spread the tenon. This is helped by making the mortise slightly tapered, so that the spread tenon widens and cannot pull out (fig. 5.26d). Even if the parts being assembled are softwood, it helps to use hardwood wedges, to get a better spread. Another way of increasing tightness is to thoroughly dry the wedges in an oven; then they may be expected to absorb moisture from the atmosphere and expand after driving. Have the wedges too long, so that they and the end of the tenon can be cut off and planed level after tightening.

That sort of joint is useful in outdoor carpentry, where the wedge joint stands a good chance of remaining tight whatever the weather does to the woodwork. It is also suitable for an assembly like a light clothes airer, where the wood is of comparatively light section and the maximum stiffness is needed in all the joints to keep the assembly in shape.

There is an ingenious method of spreading the end of a stub tenon with wedges, called 'fox wedging' or 'foxtail wedging'. A stub tenon is one that goes into a mortise that is not cut right through.

Make the joint with the tenon to fit the mortise, but the bottom of the mortise can be widened slightly to allow for the spread of the tenon (fig. 5.26e). Put two saw cuts in the end of the tenon. Make two small wedges of rather wider angles than would be used to spread a tenon in a through mortise. These go in the saw cuts as you assemble the joint, and press against the bottom of the mortise to spread the end of the tenon as the joint is drawn tight (fig. 5.26f). The skill comes in estimating the size of wedges that will give sufficient spread, yet not be so large as to prevent the tenon being pushed in fully.

A reminder of times when furniture often needed to be dismantled and re-assembled is the 'tusk tenon', which uses a wedge for tightening. This is seen in some chairs, but is best-known for the lower rail in refectory, or similar, tables (fig. 5.28). It looks best in oak of fairly stout sections, even if it

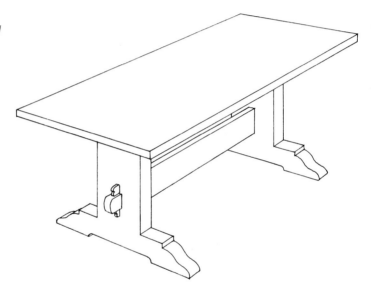

5.28 *A refectory table shows a typical use of a wedged tusk tenon at the end of the lower rail.*

is cut small as in a coffee table or for use in making a stool. The rail may go through the end either horizontally (fig. 5.29a) or on edge (fig. 5.29b), or for a larger table the shoulders may taper at the top and go into a step at the bottom (fig. 5.29d).

For tightening, the hole that takes the wedge is tapered to match the wedge, but it is cut back so that when the joint is driven tight there is still a gap behind the wedge, which is then levering against the table leg surface (fig. 5.29e). When making this joint it is advisable to start with a wedge longer than you expect to need, and then to make a trial assembly and trim the wedge so that it will extend approximately equal amounts above and below the tenon. The ends of the wedge can be decorated (fig. 5.29f).

The other joints in this sort of table could be dowelled, but traditionally they are mortise and tenons. At the tops and

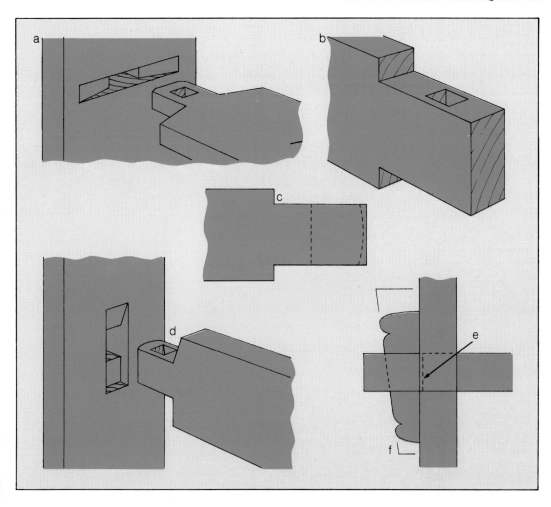

bottoms of the legs there are multiple tenons, with haunches between (fig. 5.30a). It is always easier to cut such joints before doing any shaping to the wood, so that you have flat rectangular stock to use on the bench-top or in a vice.

A central top rail could be fitted, but better support for the table-top would be provided by two rails (fig. 5.30b). A solid wood top should be held with buttons in slots, but for a framed top or one with the main area made of blockboard or plywood, and therefore not liable to expand or contract, dowels could be used.

Another way to tighten a mortise and tenon joint may not seem to be wedging at first glance. A peg or dowel inserted across the joint can be used to tighten it. This is called 'draw-pinning', and was used in timber-framed houses. It can be employed for any assembly in which there is no room for cramping – because of size or obstructions.

5.29 Tusk tenons take several forms, but all go through to be tightened by wedging.

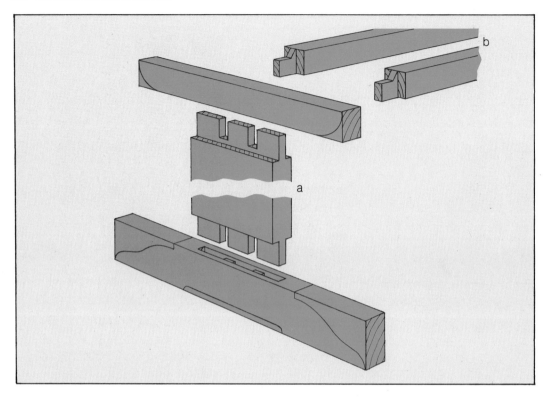

5.30 *Multiple tenons are used on wide boards (a). Two rails come under a table top (b).*

A mortise and tenon is made in the usual way, then a hole for a peg is drilled across the mortise, preferably rather nearer where the tenon shoulder will be than the centre of the wood (fig. 5.31a). The tenon is put dry into the mortise, and the outline of the hole is marked through; then it is withdrawn. Instead of drilling a hole as marked, the drill is entered nearer the shoulder. How far depends on the hardness and strength of the wood and how much further in you want to pull the tenon. As an example, with 50mm (2in) square softwood, the hole could probably be moved 3mm (⅛in) in from the mark (fig. 5.31b).

Into this goes a peg of a diameter to suit the hole, but made too long and tapered for a short distance (fig. 5.31c). When it is driven in, it will pull the tenon tight into the mortise. The tapered part of the dowel goes right through, and the ends are cut off.

NAILED JOINTS

Most people claim to be able to drive nails, but there are differences between work done by an expert or by those of less experience. If wood has to be in a certain position, such as flush with a line, out of sight underneath a board into

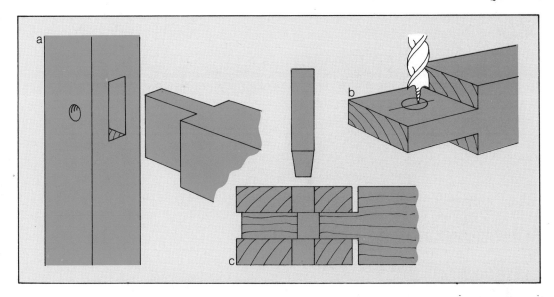

which you want to drive nails, other nails can be entered tilted along the line as a guide (fig. 5.32a) and withdrawn later. In a nailed joint, closer spacing of the nails is needed where the joint is most likely to be pulled open, or as the corner of a box (fig. 5.32b).

A nail holds by squeezing the top piece of wood between its head and the friction of the nail in the lower piece. Tightness of the nail in the upper piece does nothing for strength in the joint, so if the wood is very hard or you are using large nails, a clearance hole in the top piece will aid driving and avoid the risk of a split near an edge.

A nail does not hold as well in end grain as it does when driven across the grain. You can get a better grip in that case by using dovetail nailing (fig. 5.32c).

If a row of nails is to be driven along a batten, there is a risk that if you keep them in a straight line cracks may develop – possibly some time after driving. The nail-heads could be staggered (fig. 5.32d), but the joint can be strengthened by sloping the nails towards the centre as they are driven – another version of dovetail nailing.

A problem when nailing thin parts together is that the lower piece will not take a sufficient length of nail to provide a sure grip, so the nails must be taken through and clenched. It may seem neatest to sink the nail end along the grain (fig. 5.32e), but there is a risk of splitting. It would be stronger to turn over the nail across the grain, but then it is difficult to drive it level and the exposed point could be dangerous. A better way is to bend the end so that you can drive it diagonal to the grain and bury the point. To do this

5.31 *A mortise and tenon joint can be pulled tight by draw pinning with a dowel through offset holes.*

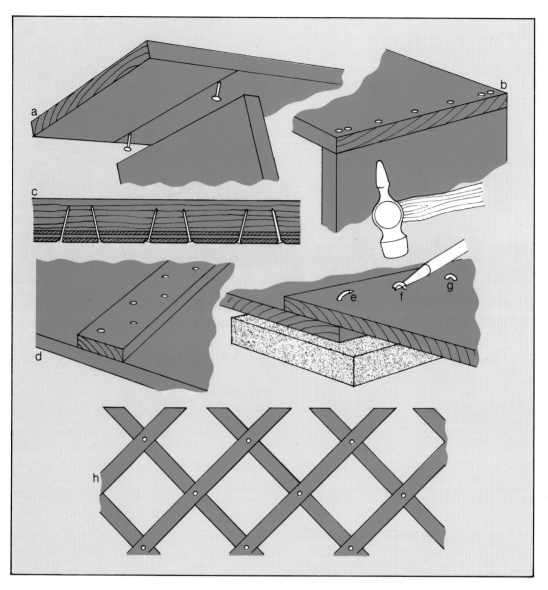

5.32 *Temporary nails locate the parts of a joint (a). Extra end nails (b) or dovetailed nails (c) give increased strength. Staggering nails (d) reduces the risk of splitting. Clenched nails (e, f, g, h) give the effect of rivets.*

drive the nail through, then support the head on an iron block. Hold the end of an awl or other spike against the nail end and hammer it over (fig. 5.32f). Remove the spike and hammer the point into the wood (fig. 5.32g).

Besides joining pieces, as in the overlapping planking of a clinker or clench-built boat, single nails can be used to make pivots in wood toys or at the laps of garden trelliswork (fig. 5.32h).

HINGES

There are now a very large number of ingenious hinges, mostly used for such things as kitchen equipment, with some designed particularly for chipboard. For most general cabinetwork and carpentry in solid wood, butt hinges are still the usual choice. They may be of steel or brass, and in sizes from those for tiny trinket boxes to some much larger than the everyday carpenter is likely to need. The ordinary type are intended to be let into the wood and it is in getting the hinges properly located that many workers go wrong.

A hinge swings on the pin through the knuckle. If there are two or more hinges, the knuckles must be in line. The knuckle must also be clear of the surface, so that the door or lid swings free. If the centre of the pin is below the surface of the wood the hinge is fixed to, the parts will bind on each other.

A butt hinge is made so that it closes with the flaps parallel, but not touching. If you let the flaps in that much, the door clearance will be the same (fig. 5.33a). You can let them in deeper if you want to reduce the clearance. If you cut too deeply the hinge can be packed out with paper or cardboard.

In most cases, it is best to cut the recesses to fit closely around the hinge flaps (fig. 5.33b). Keep them parallel. Hinges are supplied drilled and countersunk to suit a particular gauge of screw. If you do not drive a screw squarely, its head may project slightly above the surface of the flap and could bind against the one opposite – preventing the door

5.33 *A hinge is made to give clearance when closed and let in (a, b, c). For chipboard there are thin hinges (d) that do not have to be let in.*

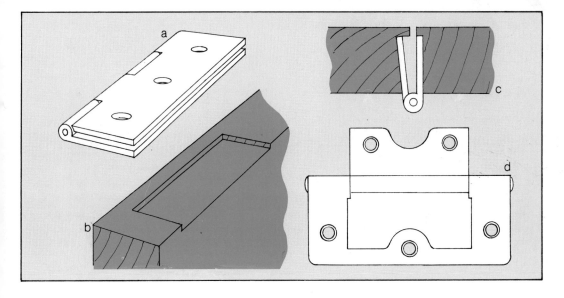

from closing completely. One hinge flap can be let in at an angle to give better screw clearance (fig. 5.33c) without altering the position of the knuckle.

One modern version of the butt hinge was developed mainly for use with chipboard, where cutting recesses cleanly can be difficult. This is made of thin metal, with one flap folding into the other (fig. 5.33d) so that the total thickness is no more than the usual clearance between a cabinet door and its post. There is no cutting of the parts to be hinged, and the hinge can just be screwed straight on.

Gateleg and other tables with hinged flaps can present an ugly joint if a flap is cut square and is hanging down on ordinary hinges (fig. 5.34a). Better tables have rule joints, so named from the similarity of the section of the joint to those in the old two-fold carpenter's rule. For this to work properly special backflap hinges must be used. Most hinges do not open much more than 180°, but a backflap hinge goes back to a right-angle and its holes are countersunk on the outside (fig. 5.34b). The fixed table-top has a moulded edge over which a shaped edge on the flap goes, with the pivot coming within the thickness of the wood (fig. 5.34c and d).

To fit this sort of hinge, draw a side view and about this draw the thickness of the wood, with the hinge flaps let in

5.34 A table flap on an ordinary hinge (a) falls to leave the joint open, but a backflap hinge (b) allows the flap edges to open with a moulded appearance (c, d, e).

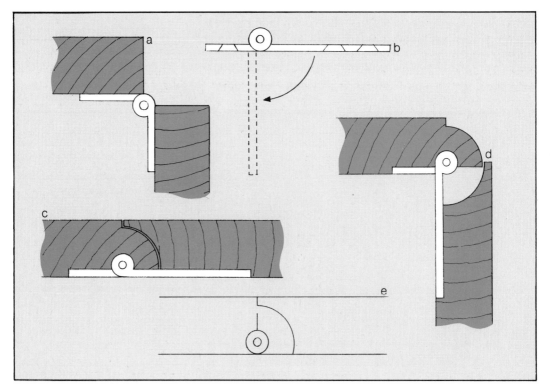

flush. The shaping of the section must be done with the compass point at the centre of the hinge knuckle (fig. 5.34e). Notice that the screw holes in one flap are kept far enough out to clear the hollowed edge of the flap.

Make the rounded edge of the fixed top first, by cutting a rabbet and rounding the part below. A card template of the shape, made from your drawing, is useful for putting over the wood and checking progress. Hollow the other part to match. In the finished joint the rounded fixed part will be visible. When you make trial assemblies, any adjustments should be made in the hollow part.

The outer edges of all parts of the table-top can be moulded in the same way as the flap joint, so that there is a uniform appearance whether the table is closed or open. There should be a hinge fairly close to the end of each joint and at least one elsewhere. If a flap warps, even slightly, the movement of the joint will be affected, but if it is fixed with enough hinges the wood will not warp so easily.

FRAMED DOORS

Besides solid doors, framed doors can be made with ply-wood or glass panels, and these make attractive fronts for cabinets. A plywood panel is usually let into a grooved frame (fig. 5.35a), but a glass panel is put in a rabbeted frame (fig. 5.35b), so it can be replaced – if it gets broken – by removing the fillets. Plywood is sometimes fitted in the same way. The frame is made with the sides carried through and the top and bottom rails tenoned into them, with the top

5.35 *A plywood panel may fit in a groove (a), but glass is better fitted in a rabbet (b). Corner joints must be cut back to allow for grooves (c).*

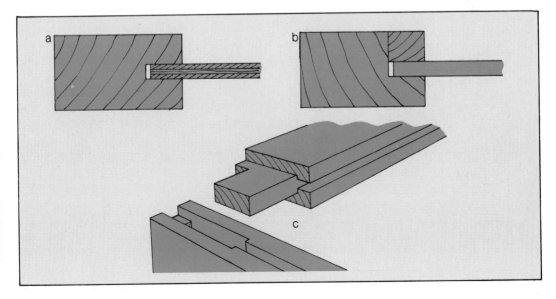

rail and the sides the same width and the bottom rail wider. Strength depends on the corner joints and these should be haunched mortise and tenons.

For a plywood panel in grooves, prepare the wood and keep the sides overlength. In most furniture doors the joints have stub tenons (those that do not go right through), but many room doors and others where appearance is less important may have the tenons taken through and wedged.

Mark out the sides with the positions of the rails and extra length left at each end. For the rails the important length to measure is between the shoulders, then allow more for the tenons and cut away the groove. Cut back the tenons to the bottoms of the grooves and gauge around the tenons and along the mortises – always working from the face sides, which will be at the front. Cut the waste from the sides of the tenons, which then have to be haunched (fig. 5.35c).

Make a haunch on the tenon as deep as the groove in the other piece and far enough from the edge to reduce the risk of the end grain beside the mortise breaking out, but not so far that the tenon is weakened by being made too narrow.

How far the tenon goes into the other piece depends on the wood sizes, but the deeper the tenon goes, the stronger it should be.

It is unwise to plan a mortise so deep that there is a risk of breaking through. About three-quarters of the thickness of the wood should be about right. Cut out the mortise and the socket for the haunch (fig. 5.35d).

The panel need not reach the bottoms of the grooves, but there should not be much clearance. Then, when you have squared up the assembly, the glued panel will help to keep it in shape. Join top and bottom rails to one side, then slide in the panel and add the second side. Cramp up and get the assembly square and without twist, then leave it for the glue to set. The horns projecting at the corners can be cut off if you are fitting the door soon, otherwise they offer protection if the door will be left about and could get knocked at the corners. House doors are often supplied with horns on for this reason.

For a glass panel in a rabbeted door, the construction is very similar except for the tenons having to be given stepped shoulders. Work to the front sizes, but then mark the depth of the rabbet for the shoulder at the back of each joint (fig. 5.36a). It is usual to arrange for the thickness of the mortise and tenon to come inside the rabbet, even if that puts them off centre. It is possible to cut into the front part, but it is easier to make the joint a neat one if it is set inside the rabbet.

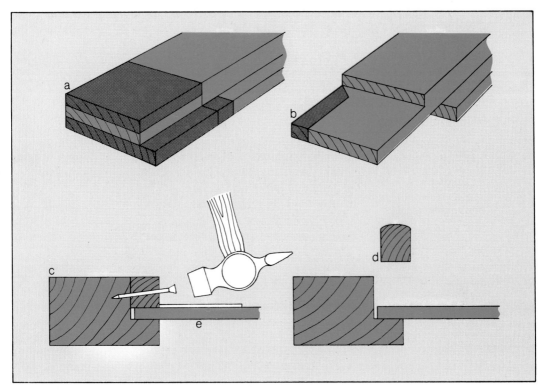

There has to be a haunch, which could be the same as the sort described for the grooved frame, but it is possible to cut it sloping so that it does not show on the outside (fig. 5.36b). Assembly is the same as for the grooved frame, except that the glass panel does not go in until later. It may help to keep the frame square while the glue sets if a piece of scrap plywood or hardboard is fitted in temporarily.

When the glass is fitted, the fillets may have rectangular section and should come to the same level as the frame (fig. 5.36c). They could have their exposed edge rounded (fig. 5.36d). Where these pieces meet they should be mitred, but the first pieces put in could overlap instead. In any case, make the fillets full in the length so that they bow slightly and can be forced down as they are nailed. Use thin panel pins and have them driven already almost through the fillets before these are sprung in. It helps if you angle the pins slightly. Put a piece of stout cardboard against the glass and slide your hammer on it (fig. 5.36e). Only a few pins are needed. Too many may make it difficult to lever out the wood if you have to make a repair.

To avoid damaging the glass, cut the frame to size, prepare it for hinges and handles and make a trial assembly in its frame, all before putting in the glass. You may also find it

5.36 *The shoulders of a tenon are stepped (a) over a rabbet. A haunch may be sloped (b). The fillet over glass may be flush or rounded (c, d). Card can be used to protect glass from the hammer when nailing (e).*

worthwhile staining and polishing the wood first. To avoid reflections in the framing, the insides of the fillets and the rabbets could be stained or painted a flat black.

Corners of both sorts of door are sometimes dowelled, but this is not as strong as tenoning and is really an expedient for mass-production. A craftsman-made door should have mortise and tenon joints.

CLOSE CORNER JOINTS

There are many assemblies in which the corner post or leg is fairly thin in relation to the parts to be joined to it, meeting it from two directions. This means that joints of sufficient depth to be strong will overlap or meet. Care is needed to accommodate them so that the amount cut away does not weaken the corner piece too much.

An example is a stool frame intended for seating with rush or seagrass (fig. 5.37). The tops of the legs extend above the

5.37 *A stool frame intended to be covered with rush is an example of an assembly where rail joints have to meet inside each leg.*

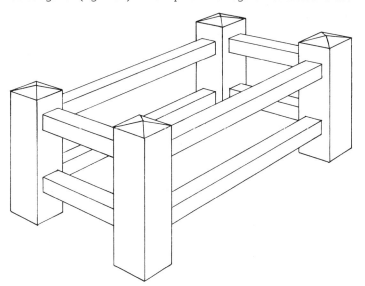

top rails, so the tenons do not need to be haunched, but to ensure sufficient length in the tenons they are taken into the leg far enough to meet with a mitre (fig. 5.38a). Square the bottoms of the meeting mortises, but cut the ends of the tenons short so that they do not actually meet. There is no need for precision in cutting the mitres, but get them reasonably close to 45°.

At the lower rails there could be a similar joint, but it is usually possible to arrange the rail heights different in the two directions (fig. 5.38b). That allows the tenons to go further without mitres. You can deal with dowels or turned rods

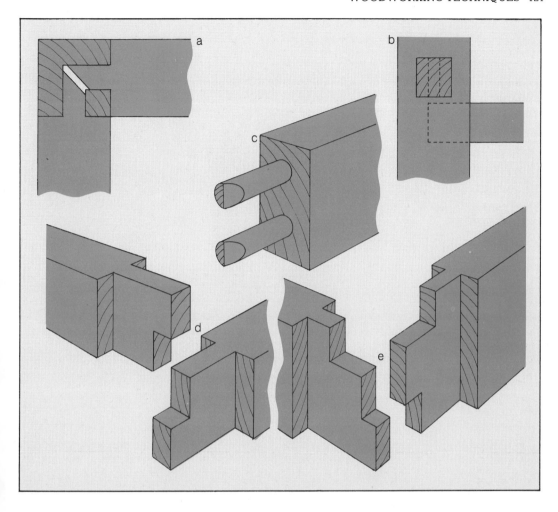

in a similar way, either mitring completely or partially (fig. 5.38c). If you use turned rails without shoulders, pencil on them where the leg surface should come in order to get the correct penetration. Otherwise you may find when you check that the legs are parallel with each other by measuring across at top and bottom, that much more of the rail goes in at one end than at the other.

There are ways of notching tenons into each other instead of mitring. Notches could be used with the stool rails (fig. 5.38d), but they are more appropriate to deeper rails, such as may be used for an upholstered stool or the top rails of a table. In that case part of the tenon is made like a haunch and the other part goes full depth. This cuts less out of the leg when mortising, so there is more solid wood left to provide strength than there would be if full tenons were mitred (fig. 5.38e).

5.38 *Rail tenons can meet with a mitre (a) if they cannot be arranged at different levels (b). Dowel ends may have to be mitred (c). Instead of a mitre, tenons can be cut to step over each other (d, e).*

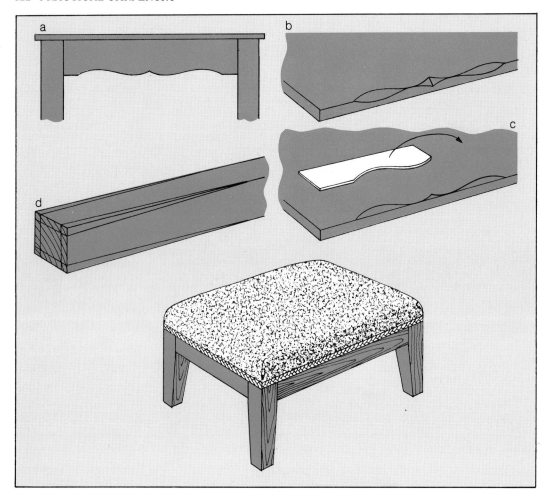

5.39 *Rail edges may be fully shaped (a) or bevelled (b, c). Legs may be tapered (d).*

LEG AND RAIL SHAPES

In modern furniture there is less use of decoration than there was in years gone by. Some Victorian furniture is so covered with decoration that it seems the craftsman wanted to avoid leaving any plain wood visible. However, modern furniture benefits from some departure from straight lines and angular corners. The general effect, though, is of plainness: much of the beauty comes from the overall shape and the grain pattern.

The lower edges of top rails or other rails under shelves of a cabinet can be shaped. One way is to cut curves with a bandsaw and clean the edges with spokeshaves or *Surform* tools (fig. 5.39a). Another way is to leave the edge basically flat and straight, but work the curves diagonal to the edge (fig. 5.39b). If this is a part that comes below the normal sight line, the visual effect is as good as the cut right across and may be easier to work, if you do not have a bandsaw. In both cases the curves must be symmetrical and centrally located, so make a half template with card (fig. 5.39c) and turn it over.

If there is much extension of a leg below the lowest horizontal member, it looks better tapered. There could be a taper all round, down to a square on the end (fig. 5.39d). The taper might come only on the inner surfaces (fig. 5.39e), leaving the outer corner straight, and this appearance may be favoured. A slender taper looks graceful, but remember to leave enough bearing surface at the bottom – small ends may mark carpets.

Another method of lightening the appearance of a rail or leg is to use wagon bevelling, which gets its name from the practice of wheelwrights, who used their drawknife to make this form of decoration on nearly all otherwise square edges of wagon parts.

In its simplest form this is a stopped bevel or chamfer (fig. 5.40a). To mark it out use a notched piece of wood and a pencil (fig. 5.40b). Mark the ends on each surface at 45°. You can cut diagonally across with a saw at each end, but leave bevelling the ends until later, or they may become damaged. If you have to work by hand, pare with a chisel to the pencil lines. If the work is long enough, pare only towards the ends and get the middle to size with a plane (fig. 5.40c). You may want to level the bevel with abrasive paper wrapped around a block of wood, but be careful not to give it a round cross-section. When you are satisfied with the centre part, pare down the ends carefully (fig. 5.40d). The effect of wagon bevelling depends on clean accurate cuts.

If you have a router with a suitable 45° cutter the bevels can be cut accurately and quickly. That will leave rounded ends (fig. 5.40e), but you can convert them to the angled ends with a chisel.

On some legs the wagon bevelling may be at the outside corner only and carried to the floor (fig. 5.40f). On some tables it may be satisfactory to carry that outside bevel right through to the top, but it looks better in most cases if you leave something square above the bevel.

A long piece of wagon bevelling may be broken and a simple notch put between (fig. 5.40g). That can also be done at the end of any wagon bevelling and is effective on the lower edge of a rail, where the legs have wagon bevelling all round between upper and lower rails. Wagon bevels can be put all round square and rectangular lower rails but if the wood starts with a fairly small section already, be sure you are not weakening it too much. Remember that with a chair, stool or table, someone may push a foot hard against a rail,

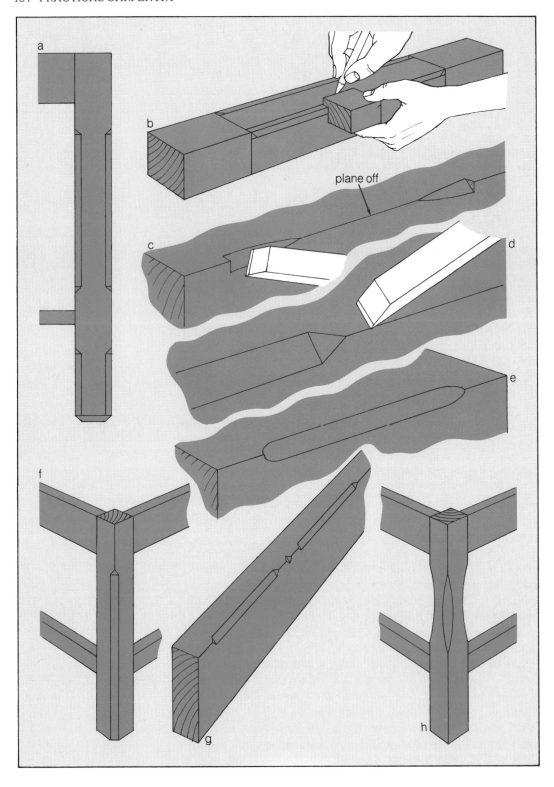

plane off

or tilt the assembly on to two legs – putting a considerable load on the rails serving as bracing.

A simple alternative to basic wagon bevelling is to use curved hollows, which are much quicker to do and look quite effective when used, for example, to reduce a leg section between upper and lower rails (fig. 5.40h). With a little practice you can do the work between pencil marks without further marking out, using spokeshaves or curved *Surform* tools. Matching hollows may be worked along rail edges.

5.40 *(Opposite)* Wagon bevelling decorates square edges.

Cabriole Legs

In the eighteenth century there developed a fashion for cabriole legs on tables and chairs and the design is still used. The name refers to a leg with a pronounced knee and foot extending diagonally from the corner. In some antique examples there is elaborate carving in the length of the leg and many legs finish in the form of a claw holding a ball. In modern furniture it is more usual to use clean sweeps to the curves and finish the foot just as a rounded form. The design may be referred to as Queen Anne, but it was widely used during later reigns (fig. 5.41). In a chair, only the front legs are made in this way, while the rear legs curve to give support, but are otherwise plain.

Some cabriole legs extended outside the line of an imaginary containing square section, with the result that either much solid wood was cut to waste or pieces had to be glued on and shaped. But appearance may be spoiled by a glue

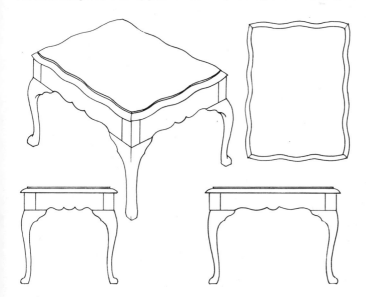

5.41 *Cabriole legs are a special form found in antique and reproduction furniture, as shown in this Queen Anne table.*

line and by the difference in grains. In a modern leg it is better to keep the curves moderate, so that they may be cut from solid wood, except for wings – which may be added at the top. The leg, wing and rail can then all make a matched system of outlines (fig. 5.42a).

The example shown is coffee-table size and the plan of the shaped part of a leg all comes within a square of about 70 mm (2¾ in) (fig. 5.42b). As there will be four legs to be marked with curves in both directions, start with a template of the outline. Use this to mark the shape on the wood (fig. 5.42c). Saw the outline in one direction (fig. 5.42d). This will remove some of the marking out in one direction, and – as you gain experience – you may omit the second marks until later. But if you are cutting with a handsaw it is helpful to put the scrap pieces back for the second cuts, to give you flat surfaces to work through the saw. They may be lightly nailed back or held with adhesive tape. This leaves you with a leg of rectangular section, but with the curves correctly outlined (fig. 5.42e). Make sure each leg finishes with the cuts as true as possible. Get the top part true and straight. It is advisable, if legs are to match, to do the same work to each leg in turn, before moving on to the next stage.

The rest of the shaping is mainly done by eye as you take off the angles with spokeshave, *Surform* tool, planes and abrasive paper. When sections are nearing completion you can make them even and remove tool marks by pulling a strip of abrasive paper or cloth around them, but you must finally get rid of the cross-wise scratches with lengthwise sanding. The foot should finish round in section, and this section continues up the slender part above the foot. But, as you shape progressively further up the leg, it should be allowed to get more angular and with rounded corners. This brings the shape to blend into the square top and leaves flat surfaces for the wings to be attached (fig. 5.42f).

Usually the rails have to be tenoned into the leg; then the wings blend into them (fig. 5.42g). If the wings are dowelled into the legs before assembly, they can be glued to the rails as they are fitted.

If the legs are to be used to make a coffee table, the top could be a plain rectangle with moulded edges, but to carry through the Queen Anne theme it should be scalloped or given a pie crust edge (fig. 5.42h). This needs careful marking out. You have to get the sets of curves to divide neatly into the length of the side both ways. You might make the curves slightly different one way from the other, but it helps if you start with the top design and modify it to take an exact number of curves each way, then make the other parts to

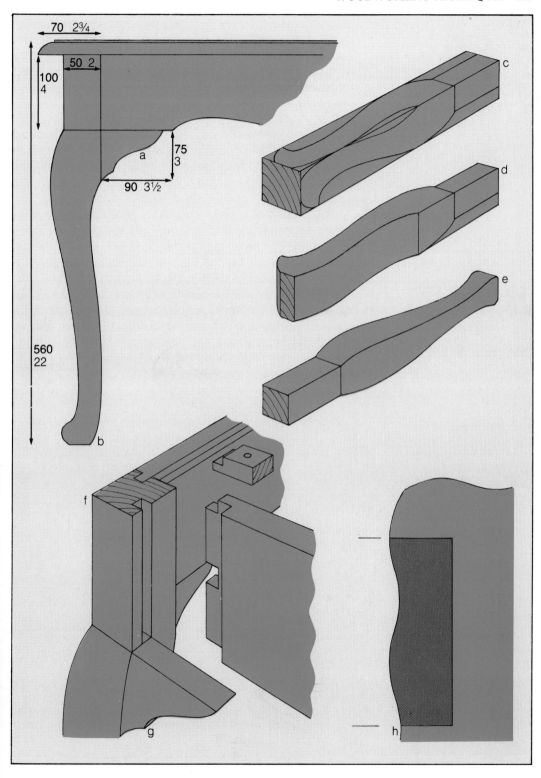

70 2¾

50 2

100
4

a

75
3

90 3½

560
22

b

c

d

e

f

g

h

match, instead of trying to plan the edge-shape after making the underframing. Make a template of a series of curves and use that to move around and get the shapes matching. Moulding such a shape is difficult and tedious by hand. Once the outline has been cut truly, a moulding cutter in a router can quickly and accurately finish the edges.

There is an angular variation on the cabriole leg that has possibilities in small things, like footstools, but might not look satisfactory in larger assemblies. The effect is of a tapered leg with a foot, but with no curves (fig. 5.43a). Only the two outer surfaces are shaped. The inner corner remains square.

Start with a piece of square section, and mark the outline on one face (fig. 5.43b). Saw down into the angle and taper towards the cut. Bevel the bottom of the foot. Mark the shape the other way on what you have just cut (fig. 5.43c). This allows you to keep a flat surface downwards. Taper the other way, taking care to match the shapes. It is usual to do the shaping only below the rails, but you can include lower rails behind the tapered part, as the inner surfaces are flat. With these legs and the full cabriole ones, it is easier to cut most mortise and other joints while you are still handling a square section of wood, before you start shaping.

5.43 *A simplified version of a cabriole leg is suitable for stools.*

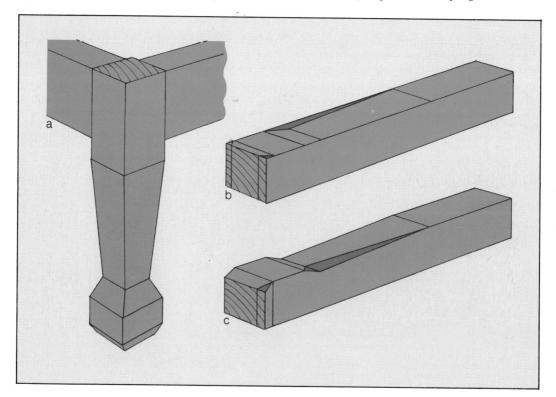

HANDLES

A vast range of handles, made of metal and plastic, is available for drawers and doors. If you are making reproduction furniture there are brass and other sets of handles, hinges, escutcheons and other things that will make your work look authentic. Of course, a plastic fitting would not be appropriate, although there are some with metallic finishes that would be difficult to identify.

It is easy to spoil the appearance of a piece of furniture with a wrong handle, but a safe choice in nearly all circumstances is a wooden handle. You could choose a handle made entirely of wood, or you might prefer one of wood mounted over a plastic or metal plate. Surfaces tend to get soiled round handles, so some sort of guard there may be a good thing. It could also show off the handle, which might not be very apparent otherwise.

Handles can often be worked in a strip, sufficiently long for all the handles needed. This also helps if you are planing the shape – it is easier to work accurately along a good length than to work on a short piece. It also helps if you make the handle on the edge of a wider piece of wood. That gives you something to grip in a vice and you can cut

5.44 *Drawer and door handles can be made from wood.*

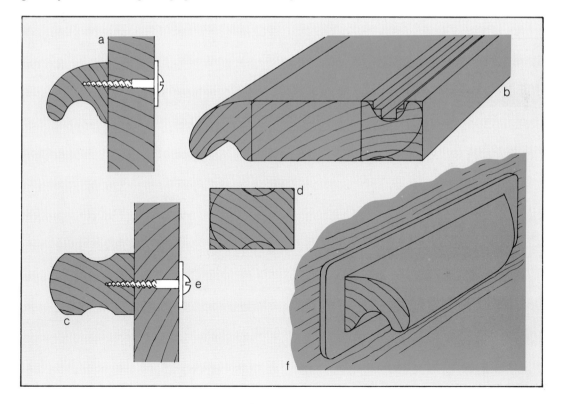

through after you have made the section of handle. You could shape handles on opposite sides of the same piece.

A drawer handle needs a good lip to get your fingers under (fig. 5.44a). Its section can be made by hollowing, either with a router cutter or a plane. You can also get the shape by ploughing some of the waste away, following with coarse abrasive paper over a shaped wood block. The outside can be shaped with ordinary planes (fig. 5.44b).

A door handle may be made in a similar way (fig. 5.44c). Make two hollows in the sides to provide a grip, then round off the front surface before cutting it away from the wider piece (fig. 5.44d).

Handles of this sort would be cut to length and left with square ends in mass-production. For individual work we can improve the handles by rounding the ends. Both sorts of handles can be held with wood screws driven from the other side, but put the screws through large washers (fig. 5.44e). This is advisable even if you glue a handle on, as a pull sometimes puts on a considerable load.

A piece of metal or plastic may be sandwiched between the handle and the door or drawer (fig. 5.44f). Plated brass or translucent black plastic sheeting may be felt to give an air of quality with polished wood. In some cases the backing may be a piece of contrasting veneer stuck on. Even with a more utilitarian item, such as a workshop cabinet or outdoor furniture, a thin piece of wood or plywood can be fixed under a handle.

The two types of handle described are only examples. It is possible to spend considerable time shaping and carving handles to suit particular situations. Commercially-produced handles, often in plastic, can give you ideas for your own wooden ones.

Chapter 6
APPLYING TECHNIQUES

Carpentry, cabinetmaking, joinery, or whatever term is applied to any particular branch of woodworking, is concerned with making things. The work in producing the required results usually involves the application of many basic functions and techniques, which then have to be altered to match each other. Quite often adaptations have to be made, to suit the materials available, and sometimes one technique has to be worked in with another so that both differ a little from their basic form. It is in the combination of techniques that much of the interest and skill of woodworking comes in. Parts have to be joined so that joints have adequate strength, but these may have to be linked together and altered to suit circumstances.

With experience comes the ability to plan construction so that you know what stages are best made and assembled first. You learn to think ahead and do certain work in anticipation of a later need, at a point in your progress when the particular operation is more easily attended to. If, for example, a large number of holes have to be drilled, you mark them out and drill them all at one stage, rather than deal with them only when other work shows that they are needed. Besides enabling you to do better work more efficiently, you will find this makes progress more rapid. If what you are making is for sale, this is an important consideration. Your time is usually the most expensive part of a project.

This thinking ahead is important. You should know the move after the next. Not only that, you should know the sequence of moves right through to the end. It can be very frustrating and time-wasting to reach a point where, for instance, you need screws of a particular size and discover you do not have them. This also applies to wood. For most things you should have all the wood you need before you start, otherwise you may tackle part of a job and then find you cannot get matching wood later, or the stock sizes available are not what you expected: you might have adapted the design to use what was in fact available if you had known when you started. If there are metal fittings involved, it helps to get them quite early in the project so that the wood can be prepared to suit.

For most things you make, it is easier to work on the bench on individual pieces of wood than to wait until later and try to do the same process on a part that has been fixed to other pieces to form part of an assembly. All the joints in a particular piece should be cut in the single piece of wood, recesses may be made for hinges, prefabricate every piece as far as it is possible to go before joining it to anything else. Sometimes you may not be able to cut a joint or do some other preparation until parts of the assembly have been brought together, but even then you can do some marking out and possibly some preliminary cuts that will simplify the work later. You may even sand some surfaces, that would be difficult to get at after assembly, but do not use abrasive until after you have done all the cutting, as minute particles of grit embedded in the wood will blunt cutting tools.

Before starting any new project, check over the wood you have. It is a natural material and is far from uniform, but most of it can be used. A piece with a knot or other flaw near an edge might be built in so that the imperfection is hidden. Mark such a piece and arrange its face side and edge accordingly. You may even be able to use a piece of which part is undersize, by keeping that part away from the visible surfaces and cutting adjoining parts to suit. You only need to get into the loft of an old house or turn over a piece of old furniture to see how pieces that did not quite come up to size or had irregular surfaces were used in ways that made these things unimportant. It is not suggested that wood should be deliberately used unprepared where it does not show. But it is possible to do perfectly good work, by arranging wood at the preliminary planning stage so that the less-perfect parts will be hidden – provided, of course, that they will still function adequately.

This is not a book of projects, but this chapter shows various things to make using the techniques already described. Their purpose is to illustrate constructional and other techniques, but it is hoped that the designs will also have some appeal. There are cutting lists and information on making the projects, as well as details of the special techniques involved, but most individual craftsmen tend to modify published designs to suit their own ideas – and this is normally satisfactory: that is what makes them individual craftsmen.

TWIN PEDESTAL COFFEE TABLE

As shown (fig. 6.1) this table has two turned pillars as legs. Turned parts always give a light appearance, but a similar table could be made with square legs, possibly with wagon bevelling or other edge decoration. The curved feet might then be changed to a more angular outline to be more in keeping with the angular decoration of the legs.

The sizes (fig. 6.2 and cutting list) specify a table for use beside an armchair, intended for one person. It would be possible to increase the top area, but be careful to keep the spread of the feet ends to somewhere near the same spacing as the corners of the top, for the sake of stability. The design might be adapted to be a stand for a pot plant, but if it is taken much higher be careful to give the feet sufficient spread to prevent tipping.

The table should be made of the same hardwood throughout, although it could have an interesting appearance with the pillars in a wood of very different colour to the other parts. Whether the top can be made in one piece, or must be made up by edge gluing, depends on the wood.

Prepare wood for the pillars truly square before turning. You should not need to do anything to their surfaces after turning. There are a great many possible designs to use for the turned parts. One is shown (fig. 6.3a). What is important is, having turned one pillar, to get the other one to match. Leave a little excess wood at the ends at this stage.

At the top of each pillar the joint is an open mortise and tenon, or 'bridle' (fig. 6.3b). Cut this to be a good push fit before shaping the tapered ends, and make sure it finishes squarely. There are at least two ways of joining the feet to the legs. They can be dowelled, or you can use a dovetailed housing joint. In both cases the joint should be cramped, yet the outside curves are unsuitable for normal cramping. To allow for this, projections are left to provide square cramping faces on each leg (fig. 6.3c); these are cut off later.

Make a hardboard template (fig. 6.3d), so that the legs can be marked identically. The alternative is to make one leg and use that as a template for the others, but a hardboard or thin plywood template is more convenient.

Draw the final shape across the projecting ends, and clean up the edges of the feet as far as possible before assembly. The feet will be strongest if their grain is diagonal (fig. 6.3e). In particular, see that the flat under the foot and the flat against the pillar are square to each other and square across.

For a dowelled joint, mark the feet and pillar together in

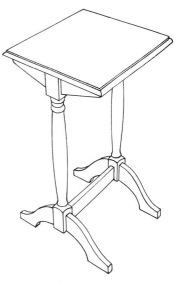

6.1 *A coffee table on twin turned legs has a light appearance.*

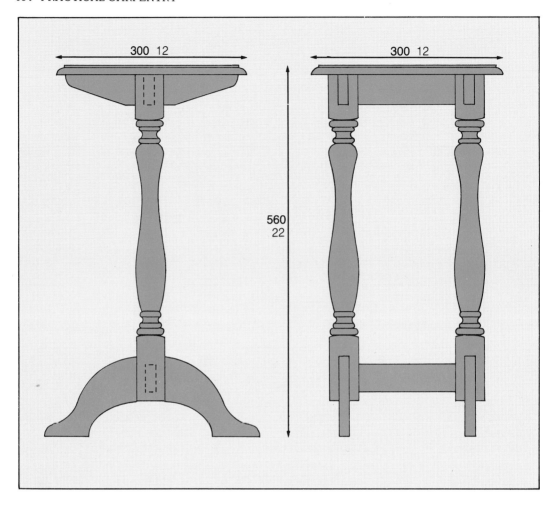

6.2 *Sizes of a twin pedestal coffee table.*

Note: Measurements in millimetres are given in **bold type**; measurements in inches are given in normal type.

CUTTING LIST FOR TWIN PEDESTAL COFFEE TABLE

2 pillars	**500** × **35** × **35**	20 × 1⅜ × 1⅜
4 feet	**230** × **80** × **18**	9 × 3⅛ × ¾
2 rails	**225** × **35** × **18**	8¾ × 1⅜ × ¾
1 top	**300** × **300** × **15**	12 × 12 × ⅝
2 rails	**275** × **35** × **18**	11 × 1⅜ × ¾

each position (fig. 6.3f). Cut the bottom and top of each pillar to length, then glue and cramp on the feet (fig. 6.3g). Check one assembly over the other. When this glue has set, glue in the top crossbars with cramps pinching the joints. Check that the two assemblies match as a pair. Cut off the projections on the feet and smooth the edges. Remove any surplus glue and sand the wood.

If the legs are to be housed, the joint can have a parallel

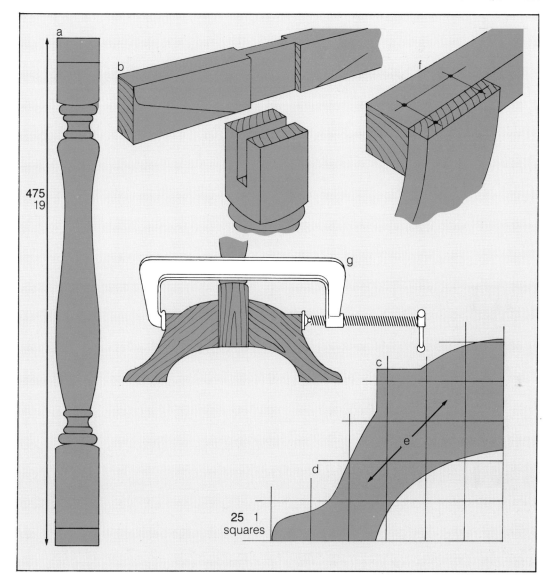

475
19

25 1
squares

dovetail section or be tapered for pressing in from the bottom of the pillar (fig. 6.4a). To avoid a gap showing, the top of each leg joint is cut back to a shortened groove (fig. 6.4b). An accurately-cut joint should pull itself tight, but it is still advisable to cut the projections on the legs and use cramps until the glue has set.

The rails between the ends are the same, and dowelled (fig. 6.5a). There is little strain on the dowels, and it should be sufficient to bore holes for them less than halfway into the pillars. Check squareness when you assemble, particularly across the feet. Have the assembly standing on a level sur-

6.3 *Suggested shapes for legs (a), top (b) and feet (d). A temporary projection in each foot (c) allows the dowelled joints to be cramped (f,g).*

Note: Measurements in millimetres are given in **bold type**; measurements in inches are given in normal type.

6.4 *Feet could be housed to the legs.*

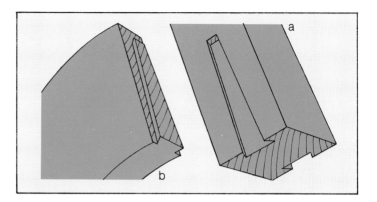

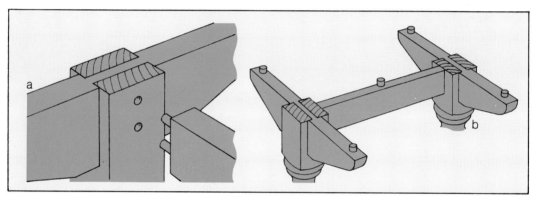

6.5 *Rails and top are dowelled.*

face. Stand back and look at it to see that it stands upright.

The top is straightforward and can have moulded edges. Put the inverted framework against the underside of the top and mark its outline when it is symmetrically positioned. Glue will hold the top on, but this may be supplemented with dowels – five should be enough (fig. 6.5b). They need be set only 6 mm (¼ in) or so into the top.

UPHOLSTERED STOOL

Stools of various sorts are always useful in the home. They are easier to make than chairs, but those of suitable height can be pressed into use at a table when there is a crowd for a meal. A stool is usually made with square corners, but a chair more often has very few right-angles in it. The seat of a stool or chair may be of plain wood, woven cane, rush or seagrass, but the most comfortable top is upholstered. At one time upholstery was rather complicated and something of a trade secret, but with modern materials a stool or chair is easily dealt with.

This stool (fig. 6.6) is of a size for general seating, or it could be used in front of a dressing table or at a piano. It is

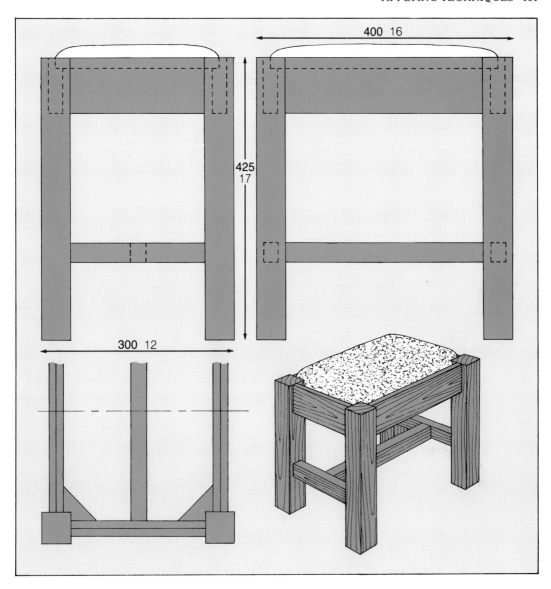

CUTTING LIST FOR UPHOLSTERED STOOL

4 legs	450 ×	35 × 35	18 ×	1⅜ ×	1⅜
2 rails	400 ×	75 × 25	16 ×	3 ×	1
2 rails	300 ×	75 × 25	12 ×	3 ×	1
1 rail	400 ×	25 × 19	16 ×	1 ×	¾
2 rails	300 ×	25 × 19	12 ×	1 ×	¾
1 top (plywood)	400 × 300 × 12		16 × 12 ×		½
4 brackets	100 ×	50 × 19	4 ×	2 ×	¾

6.6 *Sizes of an upholstered stool.*

Note: Measurements in millimetres are given in **bold type**; measurements in inches are given in normal type.

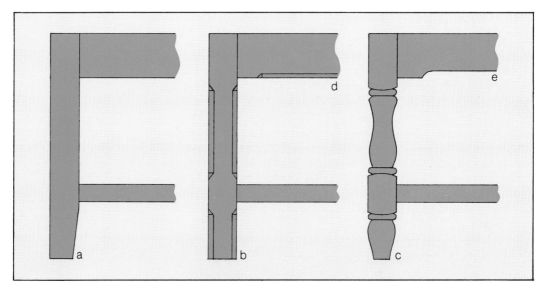

6.7 Alternative ways of shaping stool legs and rails.

always advisable to make a stool longer one way than the other. Anyone sitting will then choose the long way. You can then provide back-to-front stiffening with lower rails, but so that there is leg room you can put a single central rail across from side to side. If a stool is square, the sitter may use it either way and you need to put four rails lower down; they do not allow the sitter's legs to be swung under the seat. The top is made to lift out, so that it can be upholstered as a separate unit.

The stool shown has square legs. The part below the bottom rail could be tapered all round or just on the insides (fig. 6.7a), there could be wagon bevelling on the outer corners only or all round (fig. 6.7b). The parts of the legs between and below the rails could be turned (fig. 6.7c). If the legs are wagon bevelled, the lower outer edges of the top rails should be also (fig. 6.7d). In other cases they could be cut back (fig. 6.7e) or shaped.

Rabbet the top rails (fig. 6.8a). Their joints to the legs could be dowels (fig. 6.8b), but they would be stronger with mortise and tenon joints (fig. 6.8c). The rabbets keep the tenons far enough down the legs to make haunches at the top unnecessary. Even if dowels are used for the top rails, tenons should be used for the lower end rails as they are stronger, particularly if the user tries to tilt the stool onto two legs.

The bottom central rail can be joined to the end rails with a horizontal stub tenon (fig. 6.8d). Cut the mortise as deep as possible. Another way of getting adequate strength there is to take the tenon through, but to let it project with a rounded end (fig. 6.8e) as decoration, instead of planing it level. Cut the mortises in the end rails, but it may be advisable to leave cutting the central rail to length until after the end rails and legs are put together.

Make up the two ends as matching pairs. Leave some excess length on the tops of the legs, to be levelled off after complete assembly. If the bottoms are square, chamfer them slightly all round to reduce the area and harshness of marking of carpets.

Add the lengthwise rails, being careful to get the distances between the shoulders of the bottom rail correct, so that the whole assembly stands squarely. A thin screw can be driven upwards through each of the joints, if you think it necessary.

At the top, the brackets in the corners help to stiffen the stool as well as providing additional support for the upholstered top. Their sides should be square to each other, but do not make a close fit against the leg (fig. 6.8f). This allows you to put in screws square to the sloping edge, and they will pull the bracket towards the corner to make the fit as tight as possible. Arrange these corner brackets level with the rabbets.

6.8 *Rails may be dowelled or tenoned (a,b,c,d,e). Corner blocks provide stiffness (f).*

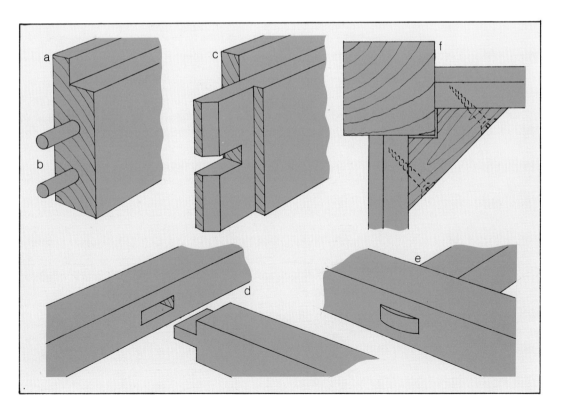

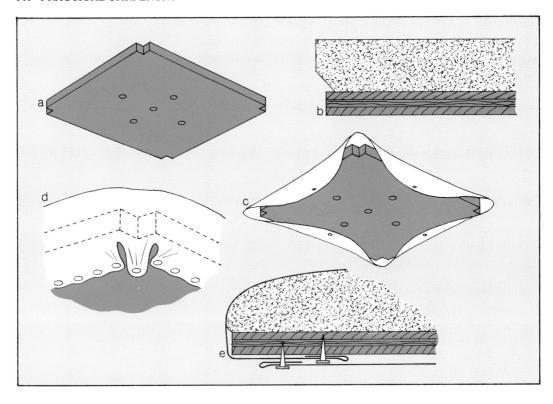

6.9 *The upholstered top is pulled over a wood base and the covering is tacked below.*

The top is a piece of plywood. Its overall size has to be made so that the finished seat will push into the rabbets. To allow for this, wrap the covering cloth over and try length and width with this additional thickness. If you find the plywood is finally too small, you can pack an edge with a strip of thin cardboard under the cloth. Take the sharpness off the plywood edges. Drill a few holes in the central area (fig. 6.9a). They are to let air in and out of the filling in use.

The padding is plastic or rubber foam. It should not be more than 50 mm (2 in) thick, and half that might be enough for comfort. Over this goes a piece of cloth, which may have to be chosen to match other furniture. Plastic-coated fabric can give a leatherlike look. That or closely-woven cloth can go directly over the foam, but with a more open weave it is better to put a piece of light loosely-woven plain cloth over the padding first. So that the foam will make rounded edges, cut it slightly bigger than the plywood and bevel its underside all round (fig. 6.9b). This can be done by slicing with a knife, a process which may be helped by lubricating with water.

Fix the cloth with 9 mm (⅜ in) tacks. Stretch the cloth over near the centre of each side at first (fig. 6.9c), then work along the sides from there, keeping the tacks in line and putting on an even tension. How far apart to space the tacks to get a neat effect depends on the cloth and the filling, but 25 mm (1 in) will probably be about right.

At each corner the cloth has to be pulled into the hollow to fit around the leg. Pull diagonally and tack there (fig. 6.9d), then fold any surplus cloth and tack that, if it is thin and flexible. Thicker covering may need darts cut out to let the underside settle flat. Trim surplus cloth evenly inside the lines of tacks all round.

That will probably be all you need to do, but for a neater underside a piece of plain cloth can be tacked on, with its edges turned in (fig. 6.9e). If you plan to do this, keep the first lines of tacks further in from the edge of the seat, so that there is room for another line through the underneath cloth, which is folded back on itself before tacking.

DINING CHAIR

A dining or side chair looks a simple thing until its shape and many angles are examined. It has developed from a stool with a back to something designed to provide support and comfort without being as form-fitting as an upholstered lounge chair. There are not many right-angles in it, and the joints are quite small in relation to the loads they have to carry, yet most of these chairs stand up to a considerable amount of use, and abuse, over quite a long period.

In front view it is usual for the legs to be square to the floor and the seat, with the back often continuing straight up above the back legs, but in side view the front legs may slope, the seat may not be parallel with the floor, and the back legs extend on the floor for stability, then continue in a curve to form the back. When viewed from above the seat is narrower at the back than at the front, and the cross-members of the back are curved. Lower rails may be arranged in several ways and are not always parallel with the floor. All of this makes chairmaking into something different from the usual run of cabinetmaking or carpentry, yet if it is tackled in steps there is no reason why the amateur with a reasonable amount of practical experience should not be able to make satisfactory chairs.

It is usual to consider making four or six chairs at a time, rather than a single piece. If all are tackled together, the total time expended may seem considerable – but it takes less time overall than if you made the chairs one at a time, and they are more likely to finish as exact matches.

The chair shown (fig. 6.10) has a hollowed lift-out uphol-

6.10 *A dining chair is an example of basic construction adapted to an assembly that has to provide comfort for the human body.*

stered seat, which is slightly higher at the front than at the back. The basic chair has a single central splat in the back, and square front legs (fig. 6.11). There could be a number of narrower splats, or the central one could be fretted or carved. The front legs might be carved, wagon bevelled or turned. The back legs are best left untreated. Much depends on the wood chosen. A hardwood with an interesting prominent grain pattern would suit a plain design, while a plainer wood could be turned or carved.

It will help if certain parts of the chair are drawn to full size. Draw half a plan view of the seat to give you the sizes and angles of the side rails and their joints. A side view will give the shape of a back leg, and the seat may come about 30 mm (⁹⁄₁₆ in) higher at the front than at the back. The front leg is square to it, so it slopes back from the floor.

Mark out the pair of back legs (fig. 6.12a) and cut the front curves, but leave the rear edges straight until after the joints have been cut. Prepare the front legs a little over-length. The two side seat rails have rabbets to support the seat (fig. 6.12b), but the front and back rails are without rabbets, although they are hollowed across (fig. 6.12c). Shape the front rail and use it to mark the curve on the shorter back

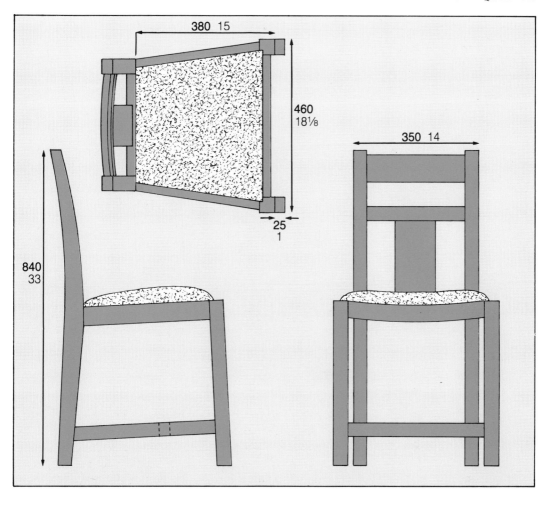

6.11 *Suggested sizes for a dining chair.*

Note: Measurements in millimetres are given in **bold type**; measurements in inches are given in normal type.

CUTTING LIST FOR DINING CHAIR

2 back legs	**850 × 90 × 35**	34 × 3½ × 1⅜
2 front legs	**470 × 45 × 45**	18½ × 1¾ × 1¾
2 seat rails	**400 × 45 × 35**	16 × 1¾ × 1⅜
1 front seat rail	**470 × 75 × 25**	18½ × 3 × 1
1 back seat rail	**360 × 60 × 25**	14⅛ × 2¼ × 1
1 back top rail	**360 × 50 × 40**	14⅛ × 2 × 1⁹⁄₁₆
1 back lower rail	**360 × 40 × 40**	14⅛ × 1⁹⁄₁₆ × 1⁹⁄₁₆
1 back splat	**300 × 750 × 12**	12 × 30 × ½
2 seat sides	**380 × 40 × 25**	15 × 1⁹⁄₁₆ × 1
1 seat back	**330 × 40 × 35**	13 × 1⁹⁄₁₆ × 1⅜
1 seat front	**460 × 40 × 40**	18⅛ × 1⁹⁄₁₆ × 1⁹⁄₁₆
4 corner blocks	**75 × 50 × 20**	3 × 2 × ¹³⁄₁₆
3 bottom rails	**460 × 30 × 15**	18⅛ × 1¼ × ⅝

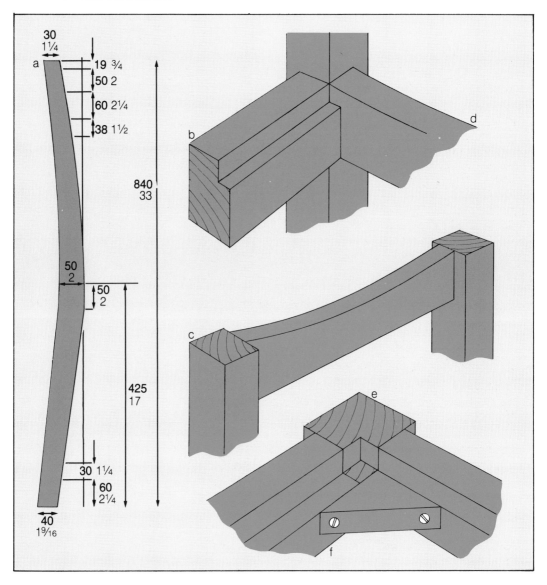

6.12 *Sizes of the rear legs control most other dimensions (a). Rails are notched and shaped (b,c,d,e). A corner block makes a seat support (f).*

Note: Measurements in millimetres are given in **bold type**; measurements in inches are given in normal type.

rail. Tenon the back seat rail into the leg so that its inner surface is level with the leg surface (fig. 6.12d). At the front legs, allow for cutting in to take the seat (fig. 6.12e). The front legs are square to the crosswise rail, when viewed from above, so the shoulders of the tenons on the side rails must be cut across at a suitable slight angle.

Dowels are sometimes used for the rails around the seat, but tenons are stronger. When the chair is assembled, notch the tops of the front legs down to the size of the rabbets and screw in corner blocks level with the rabbets (fig. 6.12f). Where they meet the hollowed front and back rails, keep

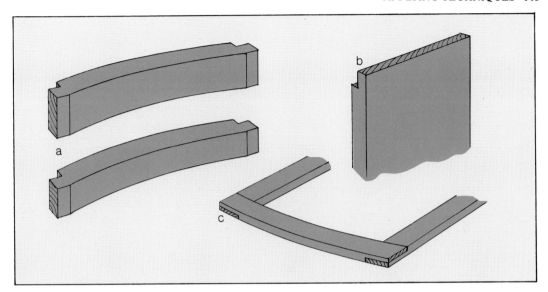

their surfaces parallel with the curved rails. The corner blocks act as seat supports as well as strengtheners.

6.13 *The chair back and seat parts are curved.*

The lower rails are tenoned to the legs. Their shoulders have to be angled a little in both directions if they are to make close fits. Mortises for the centre rail can be prepared, but it may be best to leave cutting the centre rail to length until you have made a trial assembly of the other parts.

At the back, the two rails are cut to curves about 12 mm (½ in) deep. These curves and those of the seat rails could be drawn round a steel rule sprung to shape. The ends of the curved rails must be cut square for tenons (fig. 6.13a). The central splat goes into one of these and into the top of the rear seat rail. If barefaced tenons are used (fig. 6.13b), only the shoulder at the rear has to be cut to match the hollowed seat rail.

Assemble the back and front parts as units first, and let their glue set. When the side rails are added, have the chair standing on a flat surface and check symmetry as viewed from above. Compare diagonals. If the corner blocks are prepared to the angles from your full-size drawing, they will pull the chair into shape. Bring in the bottom crosswise rail at the same time as the other rails are put in, otherwise it cannot be added.

The seat frame is made up of pieces finished to about 75 mm (3 in) by 15 mm (⅝ in), but as the front and back are curved, they have to be cut from thicker wood. Joints at the corners may be halved (fig. 6.13c). The overall size of the seat frame must allow for upholstering and the thickness of the wrapped cloth, so that the seat fits tight in its frame.

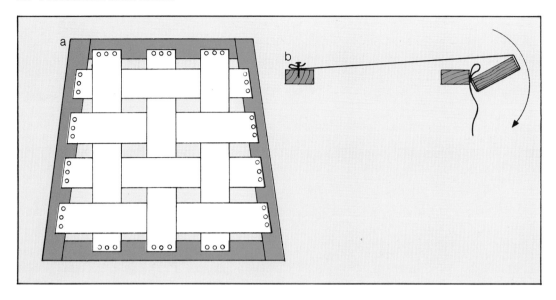

6.14 *The chair seat is supported on webbing stretched across the frame.*

Thin plywood could be used, sprung to the curve of the seat, but it would be more comfortable to have webbing under the padding. Webbing is about 50 mm (2 in) wide and may be of cloth or reinforced rubber. Either can be used, arranged so that the gaps between strips are not as wide as the webbing. A pattern is made up with the webbing interwoven (fig. 6.14a). Fix the webbing with tacks a short distance in from one side. Turn the end back on itself. Three tacks there will probably be enough. At the other side the webbing has to be strained. There are special webbing strainers, but you can use a short length of wood to lever against the frame (fig. 6.14b). Put in two or three tacks, then cut off the webbing with enough to turn back over and tack again. With rubber webbing you can tack without turning over either end. Try to get the same amount of tension on each piece of webbing. If you mark at the edge when the first piece is unstrained, then note how far the mark moves, that will give you a guide to the load to put on subsequent pieces.

From this point the fitting of padding and covering is the same as for the stool, except that the corners are not hollowed to allow for the legs, so they are easier to deal with.

BEDSIDE CABINET

This is an example of carcase construction (fig. 6.15), with a fitted drawer and a cupboard with a door. The main parts are intended to be made of solid wood, but it would be possible to frame plywood for the sides and make a top with plywood framed round in a similar way to that described on p.94 for a table-top. The sizes (fig. 6.16 and cutting list) will make a compact table. They could be increased, but if the

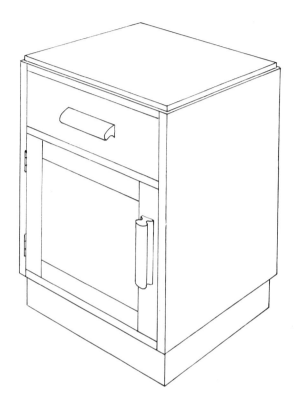

6.15 *A bedside cabinet is an example of carcase, door and drawer construction.*

CUTTING LIST FOR BEDSIDE CABINET

2 sides	660 × 300 × 18	26	× 12	×	¾		
1 top	380 × 300 × 18	15	× 12	×	¾		
5 rails	380 × 40 × 18	15	× 1⁹⁄₁₆	×	¾		
6 rails	300 × 18 × 18	12	× ¾	×	¾		
2 plinths	380 × 75 × 18	15	× 3	×	¾		
2 plinths	300 × 75 × 18	12	× 3	×	¾		
2 door frames	430 × 50 × 25	17	× 2	× 1			
2 door frames	360 × 50 × 25	14	× 2	× 1			
1 door panel (plywood)	400 × 300 × 6	16	× 12	×	¼		
1 bottom (plywood)	360 × 300 × 6	14⅛	× 12	×	¼		
2 handles	150 × 25 × 18	6	× 1	×	¾		
1 drawer front	360 × 150 × 18	14⅛	× 6	×	¾		
2 drawer sides	300 × 150 × 12	12	× 6	×	½		
1 drawer back	360 × 150 × 12	14⅛	× 6	×	½		
1 drawer bottom (plywood)	360 × 300 × 6	14⅛	× 12	×	¼		

Note: Measurements in millimetres are given in **bold type**; measurements in inches are given in normal type.

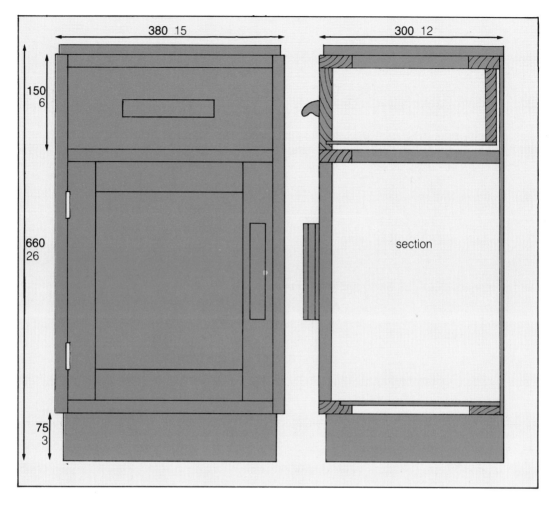

6.16 *Sizes of a bedside cabinet.*

Note: Measurements in millimetres are given in **bold type**; measurements in inches are given in normal type.

cabinet is made wider, be careful to avoid having a drawer very wide in relation to its back-to-front depth. That might cause sticking, due to its trying to wobble as it is moved out or in.

Make a pair of sides and mark on them where the other parts will come. At the top edge there are two rails across at back and front, and they should be dovetailed to the sides (fig. 6.17a). When the top of the cabinet is put on it will be set back about 3 mm (⅛ in) at sides and front, so keep the dovetail far enough back for its details to be covered. At the bottom, the main area inside is plywood, resting on rail at the back and rabbeted into a front rail, with strips set across underneath as side support (fig. 6.17b). The two rails may be dovetailed into sides, but the support strips can be screwed on.

Between the drawer and the cupboard comes a front

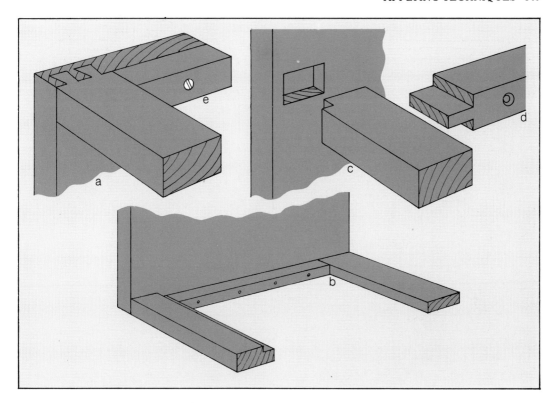

stretcher or rail, which can be housed into the sides (fig. 6.17c). Mark out all the crosspieces together so that the distances between shoulders are the same.

In the cabinet shown, the space between the drawer and the cupboard is open and there is no need for a rail across the back below the drawer. But if you prefer to close that space, there will have to be a rail at the back; then the parts are grooved to take a thin plywood panel.

The drawer bottom has to rest on runners. These are side strips which continue the level of the front stretcher and they may be glued and screwed on. So that they maintain the level without risk of movement, put small tenons at their end (fig. 6.17d). At the top, the drawer has to be prevented from tilting as it is pulled out, and the piece of wood that does this is called a kicker (fig. 6.17e). It will also be used to take screws driven upwards into the top.

The back can be of thin plywood set in side rabbets, made with the solid outside part thick enough for the back to be hidden by the top when it is fitted. The edges of the back piece will not show at top and bottom, so they can be glued and nailed or screwed in place as one of the last steps of assembly. You may be glad to leave the back off, so that you

6.17 *Constructional details of the bedside cabinet.*

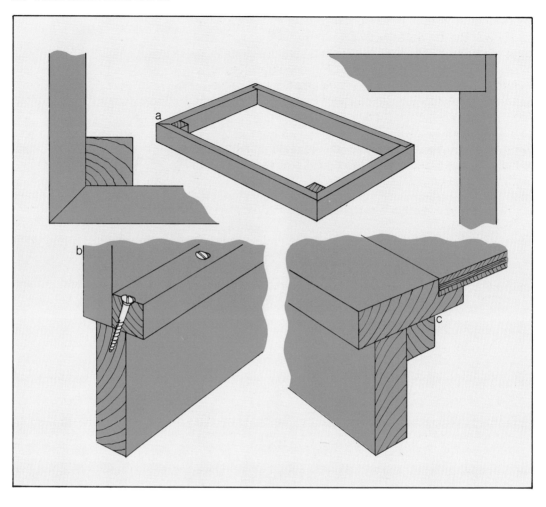

6.18 *Details of the plinth for the bedside cabinet.*

can see internal parts better as you work on them.

With the sides and all the crosspieces prepared, assemble the carcase, but do not finally fit the bottom plywood, although it can be cut and tried. Square the assembly in the usual way. Pay particular attention to where the drawer will fit, checking that the parts are square and that the spaces between runners and kickers are parallel.

The plinth is made up as a separate assembly (fig. 6.18a). The front corners are mitred, but the back ones can be simple laps or rabbets, both with reinforcing blocks inside. Make the plinth level with the back, but set in 12mm (½in) at the sides and front. At the sides and back, attach it with screws set downwards (fig. 6.18b), but at the front – to avoid screw heads spoiling the appearance inside the cupboard – fix a strip underneath with screws pointing both ways (fig. 6.18c). Alternatively, you can glue in the plywood bottom.

The door is mortise and tenoned as already described on pp.117-20. The frame edges around the panel could have wagon bevels, stopped in the usual way, or you could take them to the corners with rounded ends (fig. 6.19a). This feature is particularly suitable for cutting the bevels with a router. Two 50 mm (2 in) hinges may be used, allowing the door to swing whichever way is most convenient for the user. The handle shown is a wooden one, screwed on from the back. It should be located above the middle of the door, so that it is easy to reach from the bed. A magnetic or spring catch would be better than any fastener that requires a hand

6.19 *Constructional details of door, shelf and drawer of the bedside cabinet.*

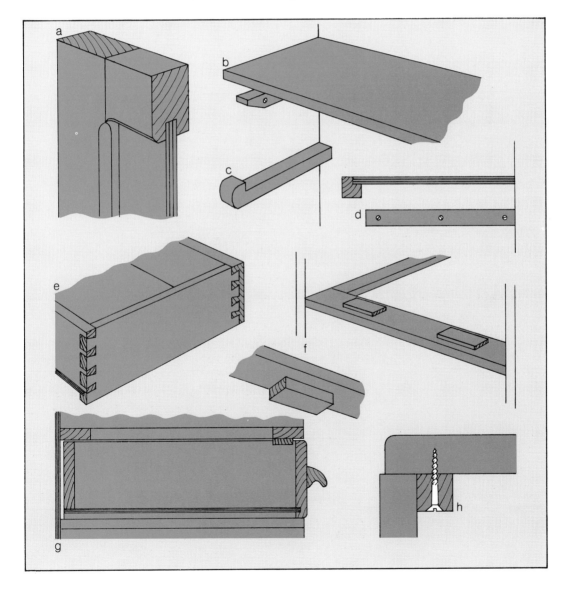

movement before it is released. The catch may act as a door stop, but if it does not small blocks can be fixed inside, either at side or at top and bottom.

There could be a shelf inside. As with any shelving, consider the sight line. You might get maximum capacity in the cupboard by making a shelf that came out as far as the door, but because you look downwards into the cupboard, almost everything below the shelf will be out of sight. You must consider whether that matters. If you want to pack in as much as possible, it may not. Otherwise, it is better to set the front edge back and accept a narrower shelf.

Usually it is an advantage to make the shelf removable. In its simplest form the shelf is a piece of solid wood resting on a support, which is set back a little (fig. 6.19b). The shelf can be prevented from sliding forwards by putting a lip on the supports (fig. 6.19c). You can economize on materials by making the shelf of plywood with a solid wood front (fig. 6.19d), with the support hidden. If you want to fix the shelf, it can be screwed to this.

The drawer is a straightforward assembly (fig. 6.19e), with stopped dovetails at the front and through dovetails at the back. You can make it reach almost to the back, but it would be unwise to rely on the back of the cabinet acting as a drawer stop. Instead, gauge back the thickness of the drawer front on the top of the stretcher and put two stops there (fig. 6.19f). You could use a long one, fixed right across the width, instead. But do not rely on just a small central one, as that would not be sufficiently positive and the drawer might settle slighty askew. Obviously, the stops must be thin enough not to show under the drawer bottom.

If you want to prevent the drawer being accidently pulled right out there can be a stop at the top, but you need to make the back of the drawer as deep as the sides, instead of cutting down, as is often done. Put a stop under the top rail, very similar to those on the stretcher, but arranged so that the drawer back meets it when still a little way inside the cabinet (fig. 6.19g). With the natural tendency of the drawer to fall as it is pulled out, this will restrict its movement just before it comes out, but if you want to remove the drawer, tilting it upwards should free it. You may have to round the undersides of the sides at the back of the stop to permit this, if the drawer is a very close fit.

When you polish or otherwise apply a finish to the cabinet, it is usual to leave most of the drawer parts untreated, polishing just the front and a short distance back along the sides. A new drawer often sticks. It needs lubrication, but do not use any form of oil. Instead, rub along the runners with beeswax or candlegrease, which gets results without being messy and without soaking into the wood and swelling it.

Make the top carefully to give a parallel and equal margin over the front and sides of the carcase. At the rear it covers the plywood back. Round its top edges slightly, and attach it with glue and screws set upwards (fig. 6.19h). Fit the back to complete assembly.

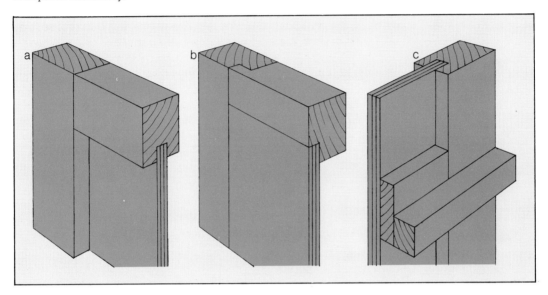

If the sides are to be framed plywood instead of solid wood, they could – like the door – have grooved parts (fig. 6.20a), or the plywood could be fixed flush with the frame in rabbets (fig. 6.20b). With synthetic resin glue and proper cramping, the plywood joint in that type of framing can be relied on without nails or screws through the plywood. With both types the main joints to other parts can be the same as for solid wood sides, but you have to allow for the recessed plywood where the drawer comes. At the drawer bottom level put a strip behind each runner to act as a side guide for the drawer (fig. 6.20c). At the top the frame will come low enough below the kicker to act as a guide there.

6.20 *If panelled sides are used, plywood may go in a groove (a) or a rabbet (b). Drawer runners will have to be packed out (c).*

THREE-LEGGED STAND

A tripod will stand firmly on almost any surface. Anything with four legs may rock if the floor is not level. That is the main reason why three-legged pieces of furniture are made, apart from the attraction of their appearance. Arranging three symmetrically-placed feet brings special problems of layout. There are also some problems of design. It does not look right to put a square top above three legs. The top should usually be hexagonal or round. A triangular top would have corners too acute for normal use. Three separate legs cannot conveniently have square tops if they are to have rails between them: it would be better to make them round or hexagonal, to take mortise and tenon joints. Even then there is difficulty in cutting joints that are strong enough. The alternative is a central pillar with three feet and a basic design is shown here (fig. 6.21), to be made without the use of a lathe. A turned version follows on pp. 157-61.

In laying out a three-legged design a plan view is most important (fig. 6.22). The three feet should extend outside the area of the top to ensure stability. How much they need to extend depends on the size and weight of the stand. A tall stand ought to have a greater spread of feet than a short stand. The feet are at 120° to each other – that being one-third of the 360° of a circle. The easiest way to set this out is by stepping off the radius around the circumference of a circle (fig. 6.23a) and then joining alternate points to the centre.

The first thing to make is the hexagonal pillar. To look right, all six faces must be exactly the same width. Draw a hexagon the size you want, and prepare a piece of wood with its thickness the distance across the flats and its width the distance across the points. On the end of this draw the hexagon and continue the corner lines along the wood. A notched block and a pencil (fig. 6.23b) will do this without leaving the scratches a gauge would. If you have a circular saw and a planer with tilting fences you make your cuts close to the lines, otherwise use a hand plane all the way. Check the widths of the faces and make any adjustments with a finely-set plane.

Make a template for the three feet (fig. 6.23c). Mark and cut them with a projection for cramping, to be cut off after gluing. The bottom of the pillar may be cut square or it could project a little to an obtuse point. Mark around for the dowel holes, with matching markings on the feet (fig. 6.23d). When you drill for the dowels into the pillar, let them run into each other, leaving room for maximum penetration of the dowels.

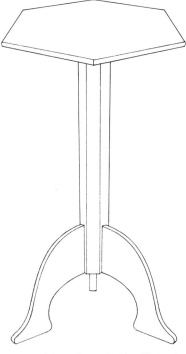

6.21 *A three-legged table will stand level on any surface.*

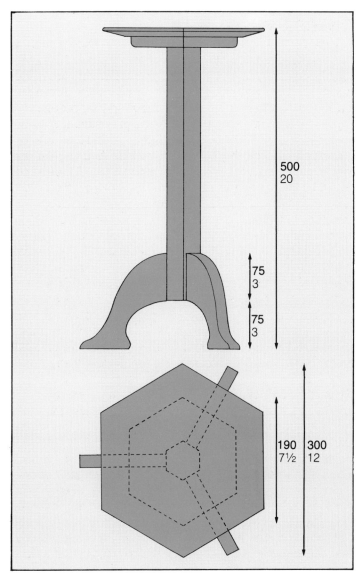

6.22 *Suggested sizes for a three-legged stand.*

Note: Measurements in millimetres are given in **bold type**; measurements in inches are given in normal type.

CUTTING LIST FOR THREE-LEGGED STAND WITH HEXAGONAL PILLAR

1 pillar	**425 × 50 × 45**	17 × 2 × 1¾
1 top	**300 × 300 × 17**	12 × 12 × ¹¹⁄₁₆
1 top	**190 × 190 × 17**	7½ × 7½ × ¹¹⁄₁₆
3 legs	**220 × 90 × 19**	8½ × 3½ × ¾

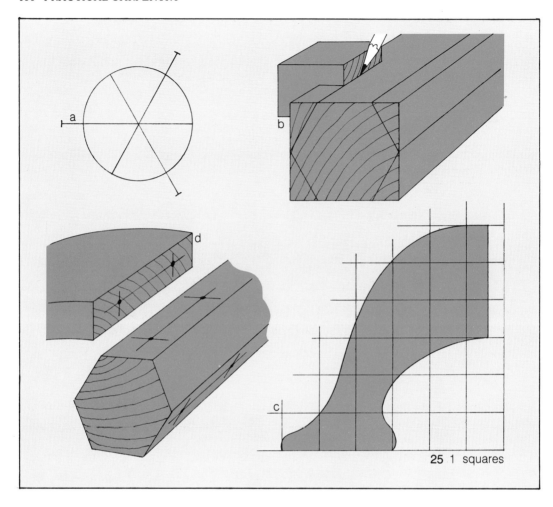

25 1 squares

6.23 *Stepping off a radius will give equal spacing (a). Mark the pillar section (b) and attach the feet (c) to it with dowels (d).*

Bore the holes in the feet slightly too deep for their dowels. Then, when you assemble, get the dowels tightly into the pillar before pressing on the feet. It will be easier to glue and cramp the feet one at a time, but be careful that there is not a build-up of hardened glue in adjoining empty holes.

At the top there is a piece of solid wood, reinforced below by another with its grain set crosswise. Mark and cut both hexagons (fig. 6.24a). Thin edges of the top piece equally all round, by tapering from below (fig. 6.24b) and round the edge section. Some of these tables or stands have carved top surfaces, but if most of the top will be covered by a plant pot, there may not be much point in this. One simple decoration can be made with a carver's 'V' tool or 'veiner', following two concentric hexagons (fig. 6.24c) or two interlocked triangles (fig. 6.24d).

The block under the top provides attachment to the pillar.

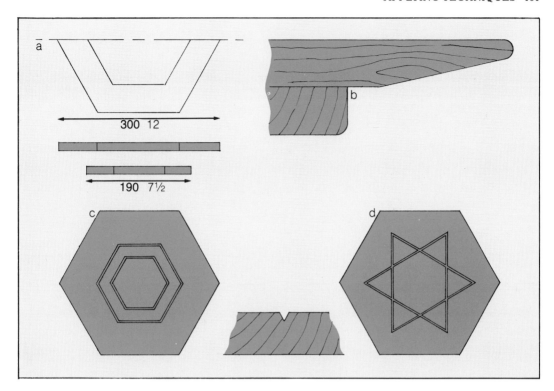

Find the centre of the end of the pillar by joining corners, then drill there for a dowel. Drill the centre of the top block in the same way. Join the parts by gluing in a dowel. Cut the top of the dowel level and invert the stand over the inverted top and glue it on, with three screws or dowels set upwards, if you think they are necessary.

Take care that the top is put on squarely to the pillar in all directions, then put the stand on a level surface and measure the height of the edges of the top all round. If necessary make adjustments by planing the bottom of a foot.

6.24 *The top rests on another piece below (a). Its edge may be thinned (b) and incised cuts used to decorate the surface (c,d).*

Note: Measurements in millimetres are given in **bold type**; measurements in inches are given in normal type.

TURNED THREE-LEGGED TABLE

Except for the feet, all the parts of this table or stand are made on a lathe (fig. 6.25). The suggested sizes (fig. 6.26) make a small table that can be put beside a chair, or used as a plant stand. There is a similarity in general form to the previous stand, but there are additional problems in arranging the three feet around the round pillar. Turn the pillar with a dowel at the top and a parallel part at the bottom, keeping that part as large a diameter as you reasonably can in relation to the proportions of the other parts, so as to leave ample wood for cutting joints (fig. 6.27a).

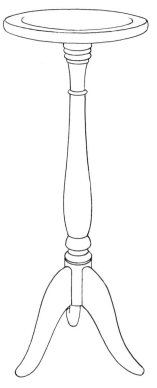

6.25 *This three-legged table has all parts except the feet turned on a lathe.*

6.26 *Sizes of a turned three-legged table.*

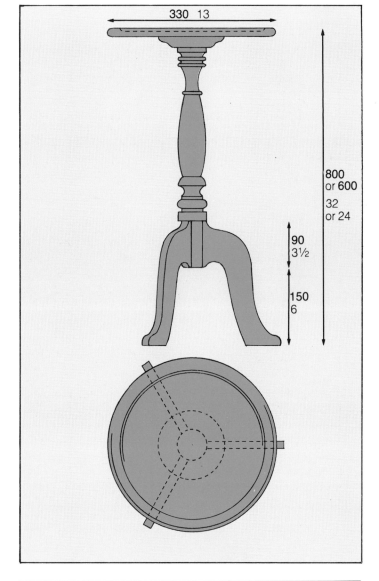

Note: Measurements in millimetres are given in **bold type**; measurements in inches are given in normal type.

CUTTING LIST FOR TURNED THREE-LEGGED TABLE

1 pillar	**630 or 430 × 75 × 75**	25 or 17 × 3 × 3
1 top	**350 × 350 × 20**	14 × 14 × $^{13}/_{16}$
1 support	**175 × 175 × 25**	7 × 7 × 1
3 legs	**175 × 60 × 19**	7 × 2¼ × ¾

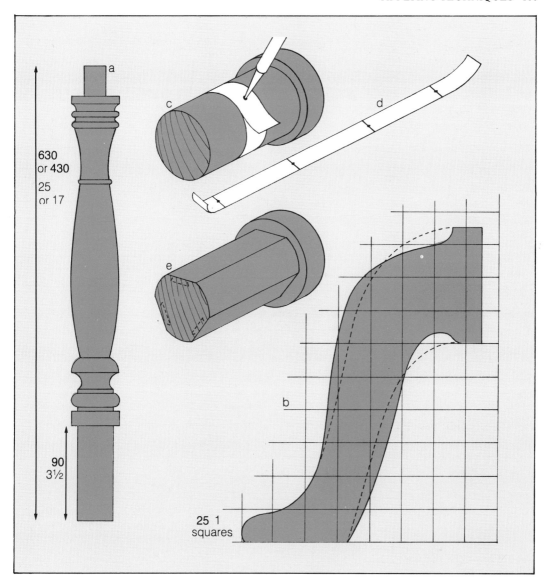

As with the previous stand, make sure you give the feet a sufficient spread on the floor to provide stability. The feet could be generally similar to those of the other stand or you might include some additional shaping (fig. 6.27b). There could be dowels, but tapered dovetailed housings are what is suggested.

You can find where to place the feet on the parallel part of the pillar by drawing a circle of the same diameter as the pillar and stepping off the radius, so that you can project along the cylinder. Another practical way is to wrap a strip of paper around the cylinder so that it overlaps, then prick

6.27 *The pillar (a) can be divided into three for the feet (b) with a strip of paper (c,d,e).*

Note: Measurements in millimetres are given in **bold type**; measurements in inches are given in normal type.

through the two thicknesses (fig. 6.27c). Open the paper out. The distance between the pricked holes is the circumference. Divide this distance into three (fig. 6.27d). Put the paper back around the cylinder and mark through the three positions.

At the three positions cut flats the same widths as the thicknesses of the feet (fig. 6.27e). These are the places where you mark and cut the dovetailed housing joints. As with the previous dowelled joints, fit and cramp each foot separately, checking the symmetrical arrangement as you go.

The top shown is turned with a lip at the edge (fig. 6.28a). Its size and that of the whole table may be determined by the largest diameter that can be swung in your lathe or the size of an available piece of wood. Before you remove the top from the lathe, hold a pencil against the underside of the revolving wood to draw a circle of the size of the support piece, so as to indicate its location.

Turn the support piece with a taper towards its edge and with a central hole to suit the dowel on the pillar (fig. 6.28b). Cramp and glue the support piece to the top, with their grains crossing. Cut the dowel on the pillar so that it is slightly shorter than the depth of the hole, then glue the pillar to the top. Check squareness and see that the finished table stands upright. Turning ensures parallel and square parts. Where the pillar comes against the top support piece it helps in getting a close and true fit if the shoulder is slightly undercut towards the dowel (fig. 6.28c), so that its outside comes close to the underside of the support piece.

*6.28 *The table top has a lip (a) and fits over a support (b) with a hole for a dowel with a slightly undercut shoulder (c). If a leather inlay is to be fitted, turn a suitable recess (d).*

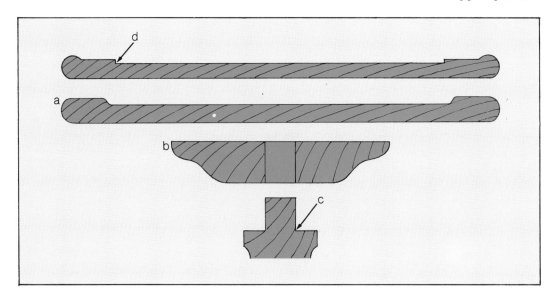

In its traditional form, this table had a piece of leather glued in the top. That is still possible, but it is probably better to use a plastic-coated fabric of the type that looks like leather, holding it down with a contact adhesive. To accommodate it, turn a recess of suitable depth (fig. 6.28d). Be careful that it is flat across, as unevenness will show through.

BUILT-IN TABLE

While most furniture is free-standing, some items can be built-in, with advantages of rigidity and economy of space. Furniture attached to a wall makes more use of available space and is firmly there with no risk of its being knocked over. Against this, it is necessary to be sure that what you are planning will suit your needs and not obstruct something else, as a piece of built-in furniture may be difficult to re-move without leaving marked or damaged walls.

It is possible to build comparatively narrow things, like bookshelves (which would be unstable if free-standing), up to the ceiling, with attachments to the wall. Corners and recesses do not normally get full use and something built-in will occupy them without interfering with other furniture or movement above a room. Shelves or tables can be fixed in such spaces.

Surprisingly, many houses are built with room corners not square and walls not upright. The errors may be slight and do not matter for normal purposes, but if you just make something to go in a corner and assume it is square both ways, you may be faced with gaps that should not be there.

Suppose you want to make a table top a close fit in the corner of a room. Mark the height it is to come on the walls. Measure two distances from the corner along these lines – not necessarily the final size of the table – then measure diagonally between the marked points (fig. 6.29a). You might measure with an expanding tape rule, but it is difficult to make such measurements accurate. It is better to mea-sure the diagonal with two overlapping pieces of wood, pre-ferably tapered at the ends (fig. 6.29b). You can pencil on them the positions of overlap or cramp them together to transfer the measurement.

Make similar measurements on your wood for the table-top, and you can draw a line to be cut that will match the room corner (fig. 6.29c). The front of the table should be parallel to the back and the end square to it. Never repeat an inaccurate angle away from the place where you have to fit to it. Anything built-in should be squared properly where

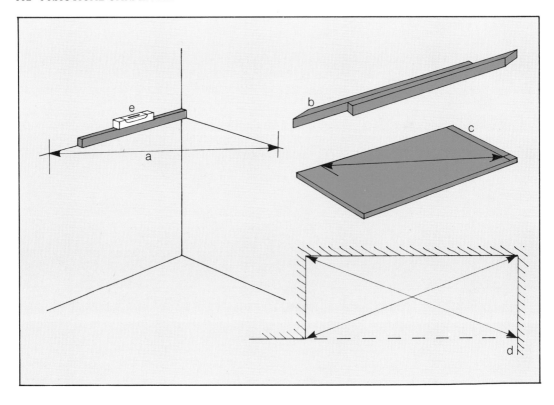

6.29 *For a corner table, check the angle and repeat it on the wood (a,b,c). In a recess, measure both ways (d).*

it is not in contact with the wall. For instance, you might have to cut an edge of an upright at an angle to suit an uneven wall in an old house, but the other side of the upright, which may be a doorway, should be vertical. It would be wrong to make a door out of square so that its post comes parallel with a sloping wall.

Another good place for a table-top is in a recess. Here you have the problem of checking two angles. With only one corner it is possible to fit by trial and error, but with an enclosed space your first fitting is probably the last. If the recess happens to be narrower at the front than the back, you cannot just put a squared piece of wood in and get it right. Instead you have to mark the height of the table-top on the walls and measure diagonals both ways (fig. 6.29d), then transfer the sizes to the wood.

Fortunately, floors are usually horizontal, even if wall corners are out of plumb or not square to each other, but it may be advisable to check with a spirit level that a line parallel with the floor is accurate (fig. 6.29e), before assuming you can use it as a datum.

Some prefabricated built-in furniture is sold almost like free-standing furniture, but if you are making a particular

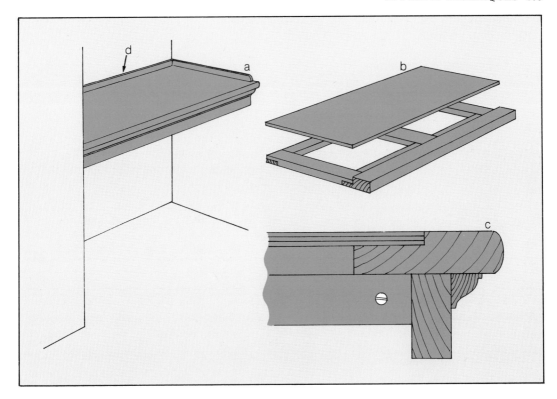

6.30 *A table in a recess may be built up (a,b,c). Strips (d) protect the wall.*

piece you can use the walls as supports and parts of the whole thing. There may be no need to include separate backs and sides. You then get the maximum capacity by going right to the walls. A simple example is a table-top in a recess, where there is no need for legs or framing, except at the front (fig. 6.30a).

Mark where the top is to come. It may be solid wood, or framed plywood, or it could be chipboard. Only the front edge needs a special finish. A plywood top might have a solid wood front edge, or if it is a kitchen working surface it could have one of the plastic or metal edgings intended for it – something that might not be acceptable in a desk or other table in a living room.

The front edge may need stiffening and some moulding could be attached (fig. 6.30c) to give an appearance of solidity. Screw supports to the walls, to be hidden by the front. There is no need for close fitting corners in the supports, but make sure that top surfaces are level with each other and that the opposite supports are trued with a spirit level – so that the top will not be forced into a twist.

Even with careful marking out, you may not get the top a very close fit at the edges, particularly if the plastering is uneven, and it is worth putting strips around (fig. 6.30d). They should be mitred in the corners and rounded at the front. If the table will be used for things that might damage the wall covering, the strips could be quite deep.

A curtain rail could be mounted behind the front rail, so that a curtain can hide whatever is stored behind it. This is suitable for toys, vacuum cleaners and other things that have to be moved along the floor, as there is no step up – as there would be for a cupboard.

A corner table is simpler to fit, but you have to provide a leg (fig. 6.31a). Mark the table level on the wall and get the corner angle correct, as before. The table leg should get enough stiffness from the rails under the table-top. Lower rails would be inappropriate. Make the rails in the usual way, but it will add stability if you deepen their joints. So that there is enough knee room, the front rail should be cut away

6.31 *A corner table needs a leg (a) strengthened with brackets (b) and secured to the floor with a cut-off screw (c).*

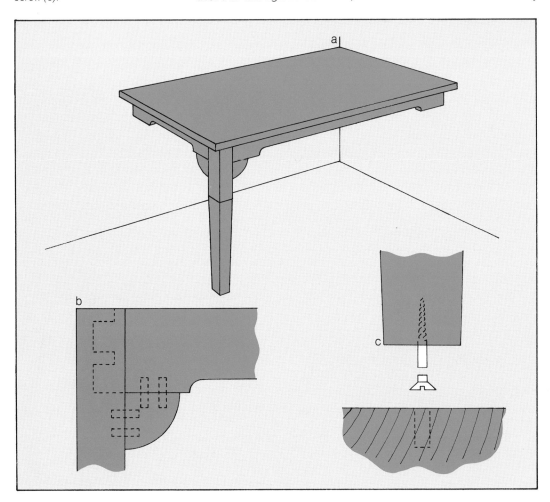

and an additional small bracket could be included (fig. 6.31b), glued and dowelled to the rail and the leg. The end rail does not have to be cut away, but for the sake of appearance it could be treated in the same way.

The leg might be left square, tapered or turned, as you prefer or to match other furniture. It is liable to be kicked or knocked with other furniture. As the top is fixed to the walls, the leg might be fixed to the floor. An inconspicuous way of doing this is with a long screw driven partly into the bottom of the leg. Its head is cut off, and it acts like a thin metal dowel into a hole in the floor (fig. 6.31c).

A drawer might be a useful addition to either table. If the top is made without a front rail, the drawer could hang from it. It might be made like other drawers already described, or a simple one could be a tray with a hollowed front to provide a grip (fig. 6.32a). This would be suitable for tools, so

6.32 *A drawer (a) may hang on runners (b,c) or it can go through a rail (d) with a frame behind (e,f).*

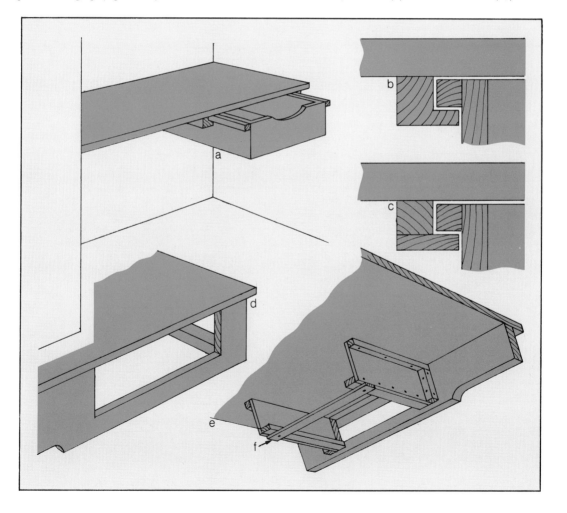

that the whole thing could be lifted on to the work surface. For hanging, square strips are fixed to the top edges of the sides, then combined runners and guides put under the top. These could be rabbeted solid pieces (fig. 6.32b) or built up (fig. 6.32c).

If there is a front rail, it may be deepened so that it can be cut out for the drawers (fig. 6.32d). Strips have to be fixed under the top to carry runners (fig. 6.32e). They need not be solid wood, and it may be better to use thin plywood with strips attached to screw into the top and the rail. If the top is very wide you may not want the drawer to reach fully to the back, so the sides need not go all the way. So that they do not twist at the back, put a strip across below (fig. 6.32f). The drawer could be made in the usual way and may have a false front to overlap the opening in the rail: the front then acts as a stop. Otherwise you must put blocks on the runners to stop the back of the drawer.

CORNER FITMENTS

A table, cupboard or other fitment across a corner will use space that is not otherwise occupied in many rooms. However, a simple triangle does not produce as much useful space as you may need (fig. 6.33a), so it can be increased by squaring from the wall at each side (fig. 6.33b). A simple corner table or shelf made in this way is often used to support a television set. The direction of viewing should be considered. The shelf does not have to be at 45° but can be cut to suit (fig. 6.33c).

6.33 *In a corner a triangle (a) can have its area increased (b) and need not be symmetrical (c). Support rails can be straight (d) or follow the outline (e).*

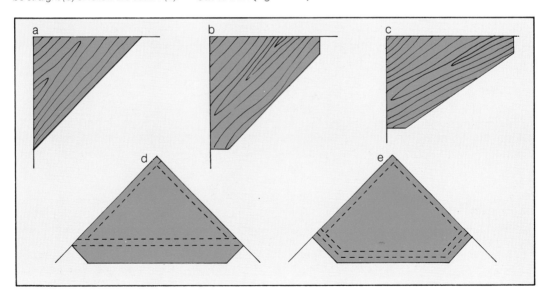

If the angled corners do not project much, the supporting rail can go straight across underneath (fig. 6.33d), but otherwise the rail can follow the outline with mitred joints (fig. 6.33e) and possibly a curtain hanging underneath. The lower part could be made into a cupboard in a similar way to the hanging cupboard described below.

A corner cupboard shows how the triangulated shape can be dealt with. The example (fig. 6.34) could be made with a glass front as a display cabinet or with a closed front as a medicine cabinet in a bathroom. A larger version might be built over a lower cupboard, the two reaching almost from floor to ceiling. There are some attractive antique cabinets of this type, but their basic construction is the same.

The shape of top and bottom controls the other sizes. Check the angle of the corner of the room with an adjustable bevel and use that, rather than a try-square, to mark out the shape; make a full-size drawing of this (fig. 6.35a).

Make the two sides, which should be of similar shape and size, except that one overlaps the other in the corner (fig. 6.35b). In the corner they will be screwed and glued, but they will probably have to be rounded to suit the plaster on the wall. Top and bottom go into housings or dados cut right across the wood, but the shelf is set in stopped grooves. The top and bottom pieces should have their grain parallel with the front. Make them to fit into the grooves, but with the fronts extending enough to cover the upright pieces and allow a little overhang (fig. 6.35c).

If the door is hinged directly to one of the upright pieces at the side, this must be cut to an acute angle and this does not allow very long screws in the hinges (fig. 6.35d). It is better to mitre narrow pieces inside them, so that the door meets a square edge (fig. 6.35e). Glue these pieces together and glue the uprights to the sides when you assemble. If you think something more than glue is necessary you could use secret slot screws or a tongue and grooved joint (fig. 6.35f).

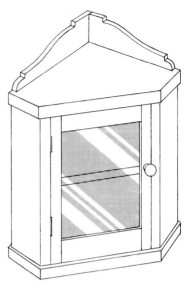

6.34 *A corner cupboard shows how a basically triangular shape can be made more roomy.*

CUTTING LIST FOR CORNER CUPBOARD

2 backs	650 × 300 × 12	26 × 12	× ½
1 top	500 × 350 × 15	20 × 14	× ⅝
1 bottom	500 × 350 × 15	20 × 14	× ⅝
2 sides	500 × 110 × 15	20 × 4½	× ⅝
2 door posts	500 × 30 × 15	20 × 1¼	× ⅝
1 shelf	300 × 300 × 12	12 × 12	× ½
2 door sides	500 × 40 × 15	20 × 1⁹⁄₁₆	× ⅝
1 door rail	250 × 40 × 15	10 × 1⁹⁄₁₆	× ⅝
1 door rail	250 × 50 × 15	10 × 2	× ⅝

Note: Measurements in millimetres are given in **bold type**; measurements in inches are given in normal type.

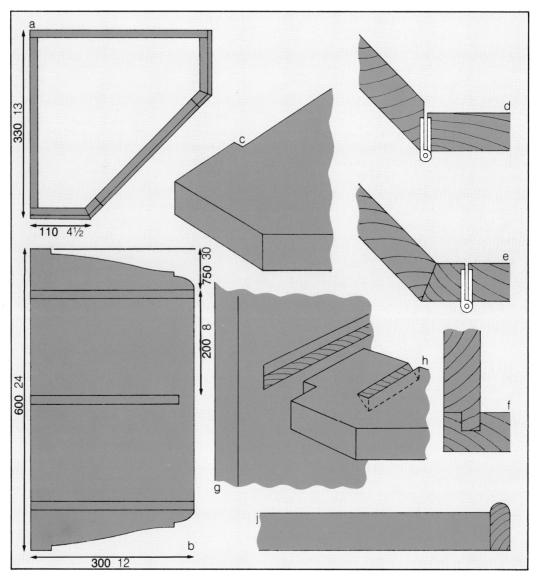

6.35 *Constructional details of a corner cupboard.*

Note: Measurements in millimetres are given in **bold type**; measurements in inches are given in normal type.

The shelf may be cut with its front straight across, or be shaped in a similar way to the top, but cut back far enough to clear the door (fig. 6.35g). If you are to stand plates or other things on edge, you might want to cut grooves parallel with the sides (fig. 6.35h). In any case, a lip on the shelf may be desirable (fig. 6.35j).

Assemble the cupboard before making the door. The shelf must go in before joining the sides. It can be screwed from behind as the screw heads will not show. If the sides are made first, they set the shape before sliding in top and bottom, which can be adjusted, if necessary. The general assembly should come square automatically, but check that the door opening is parallel.

Make the door with a plywood panel set in grooves or a glass panel in a rabbet. The inner front edges may be chamfered to lighten appearance and reduce any tendency to catch dust on the bottom edge. Hinge to whichever side will be most convenient. The door stop could be a small block on the edge of the shelf, if that comes near the door, or you could fix blocks inside top and bottom. If the door is to be locked, the key may serve also as a handle for pulling the door open. Otherwise, fit a small knob or handle, with a spring or magnetic catch.

MAGAZINE TABLE

A fairly light table with storage below its top can be moved about singlehanded and can be used for sewing equipment, as a coffee table, or something to be taken outdoors as a chairside tea table. But its basic use will probably be as a small side table with storage space for magazines and

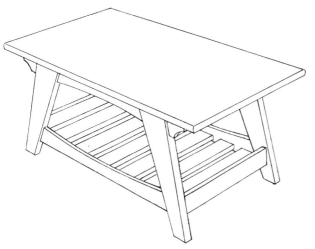

6.36 *A magazine table has storage below and the many parts all contribute to the strength of the whole assembly.*

books. The table shown is of a moderate size, but the method of construction can be used for tables smaller or much larger (fig. 6.36). The dimensions shown (fig. 6.37) give a proportion that looks right. If they are altered, be careful to avoid too square an outline. The sloping legs look best with a table that is much longer than it is wide.

Make the underframing first, but decide on the type of top you will fix to it as you have to prepare for fitting. There are some suggestions later. Construction is a mixture of bridle, housing and dowelled joints. The bottom shelf is shown as made up of a number of slats set across the width. This is

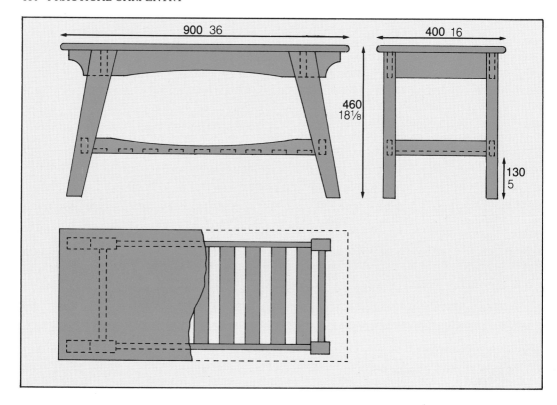

6.37 *Sizes of a magazine table.*

Note: Measurements in millimetres are given in **bold type**; measurements in inches are given in normal type.

CUTTING LIST FOR MAGAZINE TABLE

1 top	**1000 × 400 × 20**	40 × 12 × ¾
4 legs	**500 × 75 × 30**	20 × 3 × 1¼
2 top rails	**1000 × 75 × 20**	40 × 3 × ¾
2 top rails	**400 × 75 × 20**	16 × 3 × ¾
2 bottom rails	**1000 × 50 × 20**	40 × 2 × ¾
2 bottom rails	**400 × 50 × 20**	16 × 2 × ¾
9 slats	**400 × 50 × 20**	16 × 2 × ¾

easy to clean and looks smart. Alternatively, you could have a plywood bottom let into grooves in the rails. The first assemblies are the two long sides, which are then joined with the shorter crosspieces, with the top being added last.

There is no need to draw the table to full size, except for one end elevation, to show the slope of the leg (fig. 6.38a). Although the legs taper, the part that forms the joint with the top rail must have parallel sides (fig. 6.38b). If the taper was allowed to follow through, the joint could not be pushed together. The outer edge of each leg is straight, but the top of the other edge is cut parallel to it. Cut all four legs to shape, leaving a little excess length at the top.

Make the two long rails, but cut their joints before trimming the ends to shape (fig. 6.38c). The table looks best if the undersides of these rails have a hollow ending a short distance in from the legs. About 12mm (½in) of hollow should be enough, and you can draw this by springing a lath so that it passes through the points and getting a helper to mark round it with a pencil (fig. 6.38d).

Your full-size drawing of an end will show you the angle for cutting the lower rail joints and this will provide a guide to length in relation to the top rail. But it is advisable to mark the joints on the legs and rail, then make a trial assembly of the top bridle joints and check the lower rail lengths before cutting them and their joints. The tenons fitted into the legs can be quite short (fig. 6.38e), otherwise you will have difficulty springing them in. Hollows on the lower edges of the top rail and similar hollows on the top edges of the lower

6.38 *Constructional details of a magazine table.*

Note: Measurements in millimetres are given in **bold type**; measurements in inches are given in normal type.

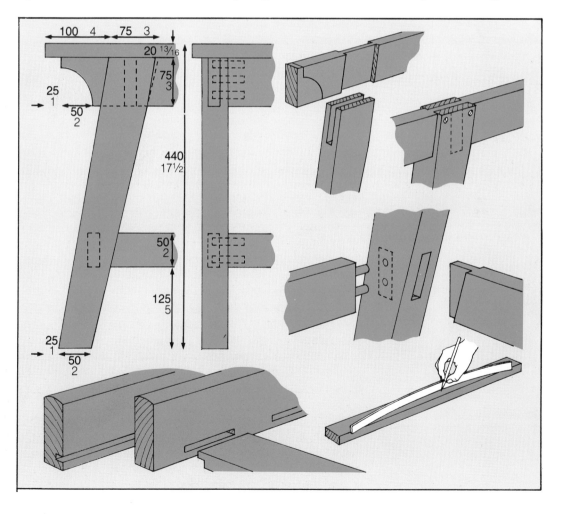

rails, with rounded edges on all hollowed parts, will prevent anyone reaching in from touching a sharp edge.

If the tray bottom is to be plywood, plough a groove to suit in the lower rails (fig. 6.38f). The simplest way to deal with a slat bottom would be to use a long groove and space the slats in it, but that would leave sections of groove showing between the slats. It would look better to cut out only where the slats come (fig. 6.38g). If you have a drill press, much of the waste can be removed with a drill, leaving only a little cleaning out to be done with chisels, or the slats can be rounded to match.

The crosswise rails at the bottom have dowelled joints into the legs (fig. 6.38h). Set the dowels as deep as possible into the legs without risking breaking through. They provide crosswise stiffness in the assembly. The slats are cut to come level with the bottoms of the long rails and their ends have barefaced tenons into the slots (fig. 6.38j). If the tray is to have a plywood bottom, groove the end rails and notch across the corners of the legs to join the grooves when the plywood is put in.

When you assemble the pair of long sides, the bridle joints can be reinforced with screws driven from the inside (fig. 6.38k) where they will not show. Leave marking and drilling the legs for dowels until after assembly.

The simplest top is a single piece of solid wood (fig. 6.39a) held with buttons in grooved rails. You may have to make up the width with two or three pieces glued together. A development of this is making the top of laminations of quite narrow pieces to form what may be called 'butcher-block' furniture. The strips should be square, or not much wider than they are deep (fig. 6.39b). With a good synthetic resin glue there should be no need for dowels or secret screws in the joints, but there may be difficulty in getting the whole top assembly true and flat if you try to glue all pieces at the same time. It is better to glue pieces in pairs or groups of three. When that glue has set, join further in pairs of groups until you have the full width made up. If you pull the parts together with sash or bar cramps, put weights on scrap wood over newspaper on top to prevent the parts bowing upwards under pressure. Newspaper prevents the wood on top sticking and can be easily scraped off afterwards.

The top could be framed plywood, but looks better and is more suitable for assembly to the framing if the end pieces are wide enough to come over the rails and the mitres are cut to suit (fig. 6.39c). As that top will not expand and contract it can be attached with dowels or pocket screws.

The top could be faced thick plywood or chipboard with

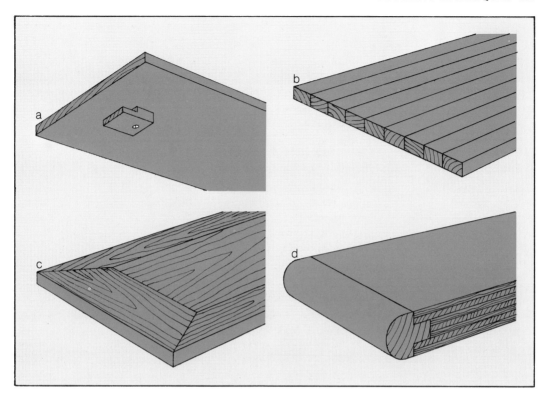

the edges covered with solid wood glued on with tongue and groove joints (fig. 6.39d). This could be an occasion when you veneer a pattern on the surface yourself. It is possible to buy panels already veneered in a decorative pattern, but then the standard panel will settle the size you make the rest of the table.

6.39 *The table top may be solid wood (a), strips glued (b), framed plywood (c), or chipboard or thick plywood (d).*

PARK BENCH

Outdoor furniture varies from the crudest hammer and nail construction with natural logs and branches, to things made with joints comparable to indoor furniture, using planed wood of good quality. Between these extremes are assemblies made from slabs of sawn wood joined with tusk tenons and wedges, with other parts nailed on, but without planing or much attempt at a quality finish. Much depends on the purpose of the furniture, but for good quality garden furniture that is to stay outside all through the year and is expected to have a long life, it pays to choose a durable wood and unite the parts with suitable joints. The ideal wood is teak. Oak is almost as durable. But both woods are expensive, and it is possible to use softwood that has been im-

6.40 *A park or garden bench shows how a properly-jointed construction can make a strong and attractive piece of outdoor furniture.*

6.41 *Overall sizes of a park bench.*

Note: Measurements in millimetres are given in **bold type**; measurements in inches are given in normal type.

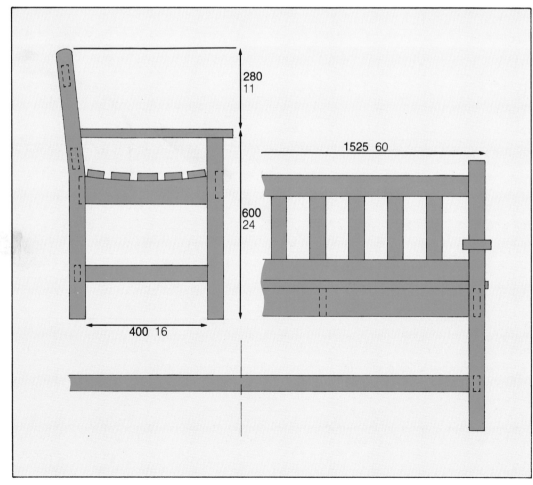

pregnated with preservative. Almost any available wood might be used, if the furniture is moved under cover in bad weather.

Most outdoor furniture is for sitting on. It may be separate seats, just a form or something more elaborate with arms and a back. The most popular arrangement is a bench, and the example (fig. 6.40) is shaped to give reasonable comfort without padding for up to three people (fig. 6.41). The seat is made of slats arranged on a curve and the back is inclined.

The front legs are 45 mm (1¾ in) square (fig. 6.42a) and the back legs match with a bent section cut from a wider piece (fig. 6.42b), so that their lower parts are upright and the upper parts give the slope of the back. The bend comes just above seat level and should include a light curve. Mark the front legs together to get the seat and bottom rail joints level. Do the same with the back legs.

Stub tenons are used for nearly all joints (fig. 6.42c). They might be just glued, but it is better to drill across for dowels through them, with the holes offset for draw-pinning (see p. 111) if you are unable to cramp any parts.

Mark the seat and lower rails together, so that the distances between the tenon shoulders are the same (fig. 6.42d). The top of the seat rails should be hollowed to about 50 mm (2 in) thick with smooth matching curves. When the two intermediate supports are made they should have matching curves. Cut the mortise for the bottom and seat rails at each end.

Make the arm rests (fig. 6.42e). For most of their length their sides are parallel to each other, except for tapering to the rear legs, where they are tenoned. At the front there is not much thickness for tenons. You could dowel or screw down into the leg tops. If tenons are used, it is better to use twin ones to get maximum glue area (fig. 6.42f).

Prepare the lengthwise parts, making sure that all the

CUTTING LIST FOR PARK BENCH

	mm	inches
2 front legs	600 × 45 × 45	24 × 1¾ × 1¾
2 rear legs	875 × 90 × 45	35 × 3½ × 1¾
2 bottom rails	525 × 45 × 18	21 × 1¾ × ¾
4 seat rails	525 × 75 × 22	21 × 3 × ⅞
2 arms	600 × 90 × 22	24 × 3½ × ⅞
2 seat rails	1600 × 75 × 30	63 × 3 × 1¼
2 bottom rails	1600 × 45 × 22	63 × 1¾ × ⅞
2 back rails	1600 × 75 × 22	63 × 3 × ⅞
11 back slats	350 × 50 × 12	14 × 2 × ½
5 seat slats	1600 × 50 × 19	63 × 2 × ¾

Note: Measurements in millimetres are given in **bold type**; measurements in inches are given in normal type.

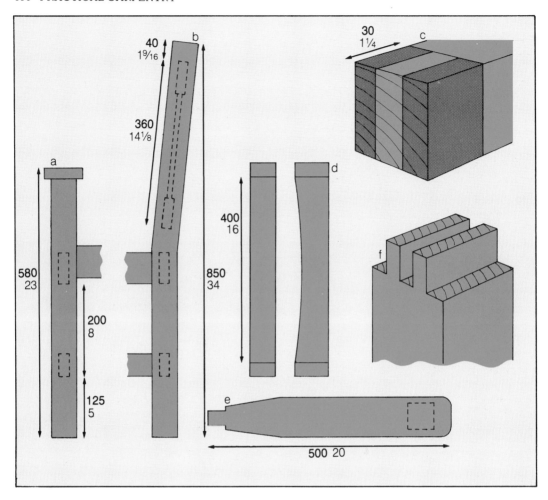

6.42 *Sizes of parts of a park bench.*

Note: Measurements in millimetres are given in **bold type**; measurements in inches are given in normal type.

distances between shoulders are the same (fig. 6.43a). The front seat rail comes almost level with the front of the legs. It can have a barefaced tenon, and its front edges can be curved for comfort (fig. 6.43b). The seat back rail also comes near the fronts of the rear legs, but it does not have to be rounded. It has to take the ends of the intermediate seat supports.

Make the top and bottom back rails the same, with tenons set into the upper parts of the back legs (fig. 6.43c). Space the slats evenly along the back. Put the mortises centrally in the rails, but shoulder the tenons on the thin slats on one side only (fig. 6.43d). Make up the back assembly, checking that it is square by measuring diagonals. This assembly settles the squareness of the whole bench.

Make up the pair of ends squarely, ensuring that they match each other. The arms and the seat should finish parallel with the floor and square to the legs. Use a single dowel through joints or two smaller ones set diagonally (fig. 6.43e). Assemble the lengthwise parts to the ends with the legs standing on a level surface. Make sure the assembly is square when viewed from above.

The seat slats go through the end frames for a short distance, and they need two intermediate supports. Make the supports to fit between back and front rails, where they can be screwed (fig. 6.43f). You could tenon or dowel them during earlier assembly, but screws should be enough. Notice that the intermediate supports come below the front rail edge, as that must line up with the tops of the slats. Use a long straight edged piece of wood to check that the hollows of the ends and the supports are level.

Well round the top edges of the slats. Space them evenly, with a central screw at each crossing, with the space between the front rail and the next slat about the same as the space between the other slats.

Take the sharpness off exposed edges that come near sitters. The bottoms of the legs have end grain exposed and they could absorb water. The ends could be sealed with waterproof glue, or you could nail on squares of wood about 25 mm (1 in) thick to overlap a little all round to form feet.

6.43 *Rails and seat parts of a park bench.*

Note: Measurements in millimetres are given in **bold type**; measurements in inches are given in normal type.

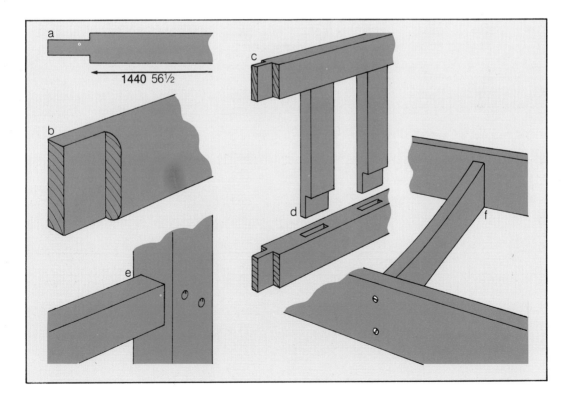

Chapter 7
FINISHING

Most things made of wood have to be given a protective coating that may also improve appearance. Leaving many woods bare would result in them deteriorating, becoming worn, and absorbing dirt or moisture. A few woods can be left untreated. Teak and oak are sometimes left bare in exterior work. Some of the resinous softwoods will stand up to the weather without protection. For most purposes, particularly for indoor furniture, some sort of applied finish should be regarded as normal. Besides the protective coat the wood may also be altered in colour by staining. Most finishes are sufficiently transparent for details of the wood to show through. If an opaque finish is required the wood may be painted.

The quality of any finish depends to a large extent on the state of the wood surface underneath. You cannot expect an applied finish to hide a surface that is rough or contains flaws. The finish follows whatever is underneath and may even make it look worse. Consequently, you have to consider the final appearance while still working on the wood.

The first step towards the finish is planing. If the wood has been machine-planed, you should follow with hand planing to remove the ridges across the grain left from the rotating cutters. Sanding would not have the same effect. Power planing tends to bend up minute ends of wood fibres and sanding may do the same, while hand planing should cut them off – assuming that the plane is sharp. In many hardwoods the grain, which is one of the attractions, does not plane smoothly in any direction. In that case, follow the plane with a cabinet scraper. Scrape all over, as well as over the uneven part, so as to maintain a flat surface.

Follow by sanding. Do not use a disc sander and limit the use of a belt sander to narrow parts. An orbital sander may be used on broader surfaces. But if planing and scraping have been thorough, you can go straight on to hand sanding. In any case it is best to do the final sanding by hand.

There are several abrasive papers available, but for wood the usual ones are glass or garnet, with the particles held to the backing with glue. Some glues used are not waterproof and they absorb moisture from the atmosphere. This weakens them, so that the grit comes away rapidly. It helps if you heat the paper before use, to drive off moisture, in order to get longer use from it. There are different systems of grading abrasive papers. Sometimes there is a number indicating the size of grit, but the usual method of grading papers uses 'F2' (fine 2), 'M2' (middle 2) and 'S2' (strong 2) for average general-purpose papers. A woodworker should not need anything coarser than that, but finer grades go down to 1½, 1, 0 and many further 0s, such as 3/0 (sometimes referred to as 'three nought').

Abrasive paper comes in sheets that can conveniently be torn into four (fig. 7.1a) and then wrapped round a block (fig. 7.1b). Cork is the traditional sanding block material, but wood faced with rubber or plastic is just as good.

If you need to sand across the grain, make sure further rubbing with the grain removes any of those scratches. A clear finish tends to emphasize scratches that might not have been obvious in the bare wood. It is unlikely that you will need to use paper coarser than F2 and that may be all that is needed, but if you follow with one or more finer ones, brush off any loose particles of the coarser grit before following with finer paper, otherwise you may drag it along and spoil the surface.

With some woods, particularly the open-grained types, there will be some tiny bent fibres left after sanding. When you apply a liquid finish they will stand up and leave a roughness on the surface. You can reduce this problem by wetting the wood after sanding. This lifts any small fibres. Let the wood dry and sand again to remove them.

Consider finishing as you approach assembly. Some parts, such as lower chair and table rails, will be easier to sand before assembly, provided that you are careful not to damage them or get excess glue on them later.

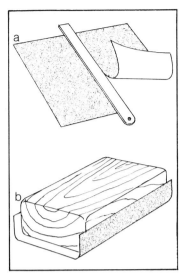

7.1 *Abrasive paper may be torn into convenient sizes (a). For flat surfaces it is wrapped around a block (b).*

FLAWS

Ideally, all the wood you use is perfect, but wood is a natural material and you may have to accept some slight flaws. Some irregularities of grain may be regarded as decorative.

A knot breaking the surface in softwood may exude resin for some time after the wood is cut, and that would cause unevenness and softness of any finish applied over it. Brush one or two coats of shellac in methylated spirits over the knot. Shellac can be bought ready made up as French polish, but a thicker mixture is preferable. This treatment is important under paint. Some clear finishes may act as their own sealers.

Cracks and holes, or even badly-fitting joints, can be disguised with stopping. There are prepared putty-like stoppings to press in with a knife. Some are coloured and intended to be used before staining. Not all stoppings will take stain and finish the same colour as the surrounding wood. Leave a stopping slightly above the hole, so that you can sand it level when it has hardened.

Plastic wood is rather more than a stopping. To a limited extent you can use it to build up something like a part that has splintered away and work it to shape to match the wood.

Do not be tempted to fill a flaw with glue. In anything much wider than close contact, the hardened glue crazes as it hardens, becoming full of tiny cracks that remove its strength. If you want to provide strength as well as filling, mix sawdust with glue to make quite a dense putty – which you press into the hole. The sawdust prevents crazing. However, such a mixture – or plain glue – will not take stain.

FILLERS

All wood is porous, but in most cases the tiny cells cannot normally be seen. In other woods the effect is to make gaps between the grain lines. The most obvious example is oak. A liquid finish sinks into these gaps and even after many coats there is still a mass of hollows. Such wood needs filling before finishing, but how much is needed varies according to the wood.

Fillers are related to stoppings. Some are fairly thick pastes, others are softer, while others are quite liquid. As a guide to the need for fillers: oak, chestnut, elm and ash all need a paste, rubbed hard across the grain to make it penetrate, and then the cloth is rubbed along the grain and the surface left for a day before sanding lightly. Mahogany varies, but most of it and walnut and sapele need a medium filler. The closer-grained hardwoods, such as beech, sycamore and birch can have a liquid filler brushed on. Some specimens of those, together with ebony, holly and many of the pines and spruces do not need filling. Hardboard is very absorbent and needs its own liquid filler.

STAINING

Most furniture is stained, but it does not have to be. Many woods are attractive if left in their natural colours. Some woods are so regularly stained that many users regard the stained finish as natural. Oak is usually made browner. Mahogany has its redness intensified. It is possible to stain one wood to look the same colour as another, but the grain pattern will not be changed, so it is still obvious to anyone who knows grain that the basic wood is not genuine. However, you may have to mix woods in a piece of furniture, and staining will match them. A plywood panel can be matched to the surrounding wood with stain.

A stain changes the colour of wood without obscuring the grain. Paint hides the grain details. A stain penetrates the wood. Paint remains on the surface. Varnish and other clear finishes remain mostly on the surface, like paint. There are varnish stains, where the colour is in the varnish. They are best avoided. If the surface wears, the colour as well as the gloss goes. With separate stain the colour is retained in the wood.

A stain consists of a pigment in a solvent. The solvent may be water, oil or spirit (alcohol or methylated spirit). The solvent affects drying time. Spirit stains are quickest to dry, water stains are slowest to dry – and cheapest – but oil stains will go on evenly and are most popular. A quick-drying stain is difficult to apply evenly. So spirit should be used only for narrow parts or touching up damaged wood.

Oil stains are sometimes sold as wood dyes and are available in a large range of shades, mostly browns and red/browns or combinations, and given names that bear little relation to the woods they are used on. Brush oil stain all over a surface quickly, getting a good coverage. It should soak in evenly without brush marks. Any excess can be wiped off with a cloth. With any staining, start at the least important parts. This usually means the underneath, turning the work about until you finish with the top. Face towards a light. Look for runs from one surface on to another. Wipe them off. End grain soaks up more than surface grain. Wipe end grain with a cloth before it gets darker than the surface grain. Very open end grain may be partially sealed with thin glue sanded level, but that is not easy to get right.

Wood with an oil stain that has dried will look darker than when it was first applied. You can put on a second coat if you want a darker effect, but do this with care as there is no satisfactory way of lightening wood that has come out too dark.

Water stain usually comes as a powder to be dissolved in hot water. You can make up a concentrated solution and thin it as needed. You get a more even effect by brushing on two thin coats than by applying one thick coat. Go all over a piece of furniture with one application, so that it is all wet at once – splashes of stain on a dry surface are difficult to remove. Water stain tends to lift the grain, so feel for roughness after one coat. You may have to sand lightly before a second coat.

Oil and water do not mix, so do not try to mix stains. You might use an oil stain after a water stain that has thoroughly dried, but you cannot use water stain over an oil stain. Water stain is not always effective on oily or resinous wood. Try some on a scrap piece.

Spirit stain may come in liquid form or it may be a coloured powder to dissolve in methylated spirit. Besides the usual wood colours, also obtainable in the other stains, there are brighter colours, such as red, yellow and green, that may have uses for colouring veneers for marquetry. Spirit stain can be sprayed to give an even effect, but it is very difficult to brush over a large area smoothly. The stain dries very rapidly, but you should always try to add new stain against a wet edge. Bringing it against a dry stain will leave a line, so spirit stain is more successful on a strip narrower than the brush width, which can be covered in one stroke.

In repair work spirit stain may sometimes be used, even where there is polish or other finish over the original stain, as it can penetrate some of them.

There are some chemical treatments of wood that you should know about, but are unlikely to use. Much older oak furniture was 'fumed' – meaning exposed to ammonia fumes in a cabinet. This makes a rich dark brown colour different from anything that can be obtained with stains. Permanganate of potash is a chemical bought as crystals, to be dissolved in water. When brushed on many woods it turns them brown. This is a safe chemical to handle, but you need to experiment with scrap pieces of wood to see the effect on them. For most staining needs today it is best to use oil stain or wood dye.

POLISHES

There are several ways of putting a protective film over wood. Most finishes have a gloss, which may be quite high or anything less – down to a matt surface. Some gloss is usually desirable. The film has to stand up to wear in normal use, so it has to be fairly hard. A snag with a very hard film is that it is also brittle and may crack. The wood base on which the finish is put is also liable to expand and contract slightly, so there should be some flexibility in the film.

It is often desirable that a finish should withstand heat and moisture. Many of the traditional finishes will not, but there have been many developments in recent years, so synthetic finishes can be obtained with very good resistance to liquids of all sorts, as well as to heat and abrasion. Not all of these treatments are suitable for household furniture, where some traditional finishes still have a place.

Some of the finish on much old furniture is the patina of age. Animal or vegetable fats may have been rubbed in, and there may have been later polishing with oil or wax, but the quality of the present finish is mainly due to handling. Natural fats from the skin and the rubbing of clothing all helped to produce the finish. Obviously getting a finish in that way is no use today. The nearest similar modern treatment uses oil or wax polishes, either directly on the bare wood or over another finish used as a base.

Oil and wax polishes

Polishing with linseed oil is a slow process. Close-grained hardwoods, such as mahogany, respond better than oak and elm or other open-grained woods. However, these coarser woods are oil-polished. Much old oak church furniture has not had any treatment except oil. Linseed oil can be thinned with a little turpentine. Heat it by standing it in a container of hot water. Direct heating would burn the oil.

Put plenty of oil onto the wood, and let it soak in. Rub it hard with a cloth so that oil fills the grain. Wipe off any surplus. After a few days, do this again. To produce a lustre, rub the surface hard with a piece of coarse cloth, such as sacking. It is the heat generated by friction that produces the shine. It helps to wrap the cloth around a brick when working on a flat surface. Leave the work for a few days and do it again, and repeat for as long as necessary to get the desired results.

That is how it was done in more leisurely days. You can speed the process by mixing a little varnish with the linseed oil and turpentine mixture. As much as half varnish may be used for the first two coats. They will seal the wood and prevent too much oil soaking in. Later coats should have less varnish. No oil finish lasts indefinitely and you must be prepared to give further treatments at intervals, which may be quite long ones.

A modern varnish and oil mixture is sold as teak oil or tung oil. Follow the maker's instructions, but it is normally applied and rubbed in the way just described. If what you are making is a reproduction of something that was oil polished, you must use a similar treatment. If not, one of the other finishes may be preferable.

Treating with linseed oil is a good way of protecting outside woodwork. Thinned warm oil will soak in. There is no need to attempt to shine the finish. If time can be spared to treat wood in this way then let it dry, coats of varnish can then be applied. Much outdoor varnished wood deteriorates after long exposure to the weather and the finish becomes white, due to moisture soaking into the wood below the varnish. Oil in the wood prevents or delays this and helps the varnish to keep its appearance longer.

Wax polishing is probably at least as old as oil polishing. The original wax may have been beeswax, but that is rather soft and most modern wax polishes are mixtures. Many paste polishes sold for reviving the finish on furniture are basically wax. Carnauba is the hardest wax used – it is always mixed with beeswax, paraffin wax and ceresine, using turpentine as a solvent. It would be unwise to attempt to mix your own wax polish. It is better to buy prepared furniture wax polishes.

Wax polishing could start from the bare wood in the same way as oil polishing, but it would be at least as long a process. Part of the oil treatment involves forcing oil into the pores of the wood, but wax polishing keeps more to the surface; so it helps if you seal the wood first. The grain should be filled, then the wood given one or two coats of varnish, which can be lightly sanded smooth before a wax finish is added.

You have to build up wax on the wood before you can polish it, so at first you concentrate on making a layer of hardened wax. It can be lightly rubbed on with a cloth, working in a circular manner and then along the grain. Leave it for ten minutes or so, then rub lightly with a cloth again. Leave it for at least an hour, then go through the process again. You will probably have to repeat the action many more times before you finally achieve that mellow shine associated with wax. Further polishing may be done at longer intervals – say several weeks – as the sheen builds up and becomes more permanent.

Power cannot really take the place of hard work. You can use a powered buffing head driven by an electric drill, but keep it moving and experiment with the amount of pressure. Too enthusiastic power buffing may lift off the wax. Hand work will be needed to get an even shine.

Today, wax is probably best regarded as something for reviving other polished finishes rather than as a first polish in its own right. You can get a good finish by giving wood several coats of varnish, which is then rubbed matt and finished with wax. An alternative to abrasive paper is pumice powder on a cloth, used in a similar way to applying polish. Some so-called non-scratch domestic scouring powders can be used in this way. If you use powder, make sure it is all removed before polishing. A vacuum cleaner is better than a brush. A tack rag (from a varnish shop) will lift dust as it is wiped over a surface.

Not all furniture revivers are wax. Some may be suitable for use over an existing synthetic finish, as applied by spray to mass-production furniture, but they are not always suitable for more traditional finishes. Read the instructions. Some floor polishes are unsuitable for furniture.

French Polish

Since the days of Chippendale and the great cabinetmakers, much furniture has been French polished. It is a smooth finish with a high sheen, which has been considered superior to any other gloss finish. It is a technique involving a fair amount of effort and it requires skill. You have to be patient. The finish is not very durable. Many liquids, including water, will harm it. A hot cup stood on it will leave a ring. Consequently, care has to be taken with French polished furniture, using mats and other protections. Older pianos are examples of the high polish obtainable with this method of finishing.

French polishing is done with shellac dissolved in methylated spirit. Shellac comes from India in the form of flakes. You can dissolve your own or buy French polish already prepared. If you can buy it concentrated, you may thin it with more spirit, as you need it, but most suppliers only have the one concentration ready for use.

Normal shellac has a transparent orange colour, which is suitable for all woods except those of very light colour. If light woods are to be kept as light as possible, bleached or white shellac may be used. Bleached shellac does not have a very long life in store. It has even less resistance to dampness than orange shellac. Some methylated spirit contains resin, which makes it unsuitable for use in French polish, so it is usually better to buy the mixture described as French polish than to mix your own with spirit you are uncertain of.

Shellac *can* be brushed on like paint or varnish, but with spirit as a solvent it dries quickly and it is difficult to get an even result, with the same problem as spirit stains. An advantage of quick-drying is that you can put on coats at fairly close intervals, probably five or more in a day. For the best brushed result, sand lightly between coats. Hard shellac sands as a white powder. If it does not, you are sanding

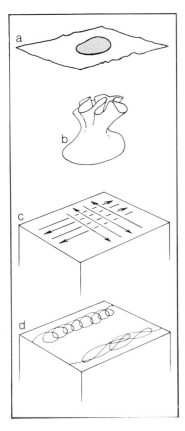

7.2 *The rubber for French polishing is made with a pad of cottonwool and a piece of cotton cloth (a), wrapped and squeezed to force out polish (b). Straight strokes on the surface (c) are followed by circular ones (d).*

too soon. Besides abrasive paper you can use fine steel wool or pumice powder on a cloth. In all cases, make sure there are no particles left when you put on another coat.

Brushed shellac may be the treatment chosen for the inside of a cabinet when the outside is French polished, but brushed shellac is not as good as modern varnish for normal appearance and protection of the outsides of furniture. It is no use for exterior purposes, as damp weather will be certain to destroy it.

French polishing is a rubbing process with a pad that lets out small quantities of polish. The pad should be of cotton wool, wrapped in a piece of old cotton cloth. This must be old cloth, so that it is free of fluff and lint. The size of the pad should be comfortable to grip, possibly 75 mm (3 in) across, wrapped in a piece of cloth about 200 mm (8 in) square (fig. 7.2a). To make the pad, draw the cloth up around the cotton wool and twist it (fig. 7.2b). The pad will be soaked in polish, which will harden if left to dry, and then have to be discarded, but it can be made to last some time if it is kept in an airtight jar.

It is important that the wood surface is as near perfect as possible. More than any other method of finishing, French polish shows up flaws and minor imperfections. The three stages in polishing are called bodying-in, building-up and spiriting out. Bodying-in is the process of putting a coating of shellac on the wood, to be brought to a gloss later. The final polish is dependent on there being a good layer of shellac to work on.

Sprinkle shellac mixture on the pad and wrap the cloth round it so that the liquid oozes through. Rub across the grain and then with it (fig. 7.2c). Cover every part of the surface, including the corners, and keep the pad moving – never lift off the pad from the surface being polished, only raise it as it goes over an edge. Change to a circular or figure-eight action (fig. 7.2d) and continue rubbing lightly until all the polish in the pad has been used up. Let the surface harden – it does not take long – then repeat the bodying-in process with a newly-charged pad.

In all the polishing stages concentrate on the edges and particularly the corners. The body of the panel will then probably be taken care of in the process. Look at the surface and check that it has an even coating of dry shellac. Use more polish on the pad as often as necessary to body-in to a regular overall protective coat. Do not worry about the shine, or lack of it, at this stage. Leave the work for a day. For all polishing it is best to be in a room that is as dust-free as possible. Store the work in the same room. It helps if the work can be done in a comfortable temperature. You cannot polish successfully in cold conditions.

After the day's break, you can start the building-up process. Examine the surface in a good light and use fine abrasive to remove any unevenness, but avoid taking off too much shellac. Make sure there is no dust left, then recharge the pad with shellac mixture and go over the surface again. If the pad tends to stick, put one, or no more than two drops of linseed oil on the outside of the pad. At this stage there should not be very much polish on the pad. If the pad leaves an obviously wet streak across the wood as it is used, it has too much polish. If a shiny streak is showing you may have put on too much oil, which can only be removed by further polishing. You can test the pad on a piece of paper. If you press the pad onto it, any oil will make a mark. If there is no mark, you can add another drop of oil to the outside of the pad. Continue rubbing in the same way, with a fully-charged pad and occasional drops of linseed oil.

Work evenly all over and be particularly careful not to lift the pad anywhere except after it has cleared an edge. Similarly, make sure the pad is in motion when you bring it into contact with the surface. Never just put it down at the centre of the work before starting to move it. In this way you build up a good layer of shellac. Pause between coats. Finally, as a further treatment, go all over with the pad charged with polish diluted with about an equal amount of spirit, then leave the work for half a day, at least. You may see smears, but they do not matter at this stage.

For spiriting-out, use a new pad with a double thickness of cloth. Dampen this with a little spirit and leave it in an airtight container for a short time so that the pad becomes equally soaked. Go over the surface with quite light strokes to remove smears. Do not press hard or use too much spirit, as that may dissolve the surface shellac. Change to another dry pad and go over the surface with a circular motion and then in straight lines along the grain to burnish the wood. Leave it for a few days for the polish to harden fully.

French polishing is obviously a method for dealing with fairly large areas. You might deal with mouldings and narrow strips by working lengthwise, but for many parts that are shaped or pierced the polish must be brushed on. You must judge the amount of polish put on to be about the same as that applied with a pad to adjoining flat parts and be careful to avoid letting brushed polish make marks on pad-polished areas.

As can be seen, French polishing is a lengthy and tedious process – and so not very well suited to modern needs – but it has long been the established method of finishing good furniture and may still be employed on individual pieces of furniture to distinguish them from the products of factories, where this labour-intensive technique would not be economic.

PAINT

Most people are familiar with using paint. For carpentry it is only used on a small amount of furniture. It may be better if some items intended for children are brightly painted, but in most other cases it is more satisfying to let the wood show through.

Paint has uses in structural woodwork, on boats and on much exterior construction. Paints have changed considerably in recent years. Most of the important constituents are synthetic, giving much better all-round qualities than some of the natural materials previously used. Modern paints are easier to apply and should retain their colour better. Not all makes of paint are the same, and some may not be compatible with others, so it is advisable to buy paint of one make for the various coats to be applied to a new job.

There is available a kind of paint that dries with a very hard waterproof coat. It comes in two parts, to be mixed just before use. In practice it is not a good choice for general woodworking, although it has uses – for example, on boats. For most things it is better to use the normal single-part paints.

Wood should be prepared for paint in the same way as for other finishes, except that you do not need to bother much about colour: a stopping in a crack or hole may be a different colour from the wood. What is important is that the surface is level. Paint makers supply comprehensive instructions for using their products. Follow them, but in general there are three stages when you start from bare wood; priming, undercoat and topcoat.

The primer may not be the same colour as the other coats. It is a thin paint that penetrates the wood to provide a grip in the pores and a surface that other coats will bond to. If the first coat does not disguise the grain marking adequately, you may need to apply two coats of primer.

Undercoat provides the body in the paint. It is in a colour compatible with the final coat, but probably a different shade. It dries with a matt surface. If you want to build up more paint skin, this is the stage where you do it, not at the top coat stage. Sand the undercoat if necessary, preferably using 'wet-and-dry' abrasive paper. This is like glasspaper, but the grit is bonded with a waterproof glue and you can use it wet to pick up particles of dust. Get the final undercoat as free of flaws as possible. You cannot level out ridges at the top coat stage.

The top coat is usually, but not necessarily, glossy. One coat over the base provided by the undercoats produces the final finish. Glossy paint tends to be more durable than most paints made with a matt or semi-glossy finish, so if there is no special reason for choosing anything else, choose glossy paint.

Use a good brush. The best are described as 'varnish' brushes, although they are just as much used for paint. Your brush should be as wide as can be comfortably employed on the surfaces. Check whether the paint makers advise stirring. Some must not be stirred as this causes bubbles that dry as marks on the surface. Spread the paint well. On a broad surface you can work across to get an even distribution, then finish with strokes along the grain. When you recharge the brush, spread the paint again, then make your final strokes along the grain back towards the previously painted part and lift the brush as it goes over the edge. In that way you can avoid brush marks.

So far as possible work on a horizontal surface. Turn the work around to bring each surface to the top. If it is a structure that cannot be moved, vertical brush strokes on upright parts will give a smoother result than horizontal ones, finishing off with upward strokes over wet paint above. If you have to brush across a vertical surface, make sure the paint is spread well or you will get 'curtains', which are runs due to too much paint forming ridges as it dries. The only treatment if this happens is to let the curtain fully harden, then sand it level and paint again.

Varnish

Varnish can be thought of as a clear paint. It is used in a very similar way and is always brushed. Varnishes have been used for a very long time to give wood a clear glossy surface. For nearly all that time they have been made from natural resins and lacs mixed with oil and other liquids that serve as thinners and driers. Some of these traditional varnishes are still available, but most varnishes now offered are partly or completely synthetic – and superior in many ways.

Natural varnishes needed precise conditions to be maintained during application. They had to be applied in the warm, and the atmosphere needed to be dry. Cold and damp would stop the varnish drying fully. They took a long time to set, during which they would often collect dust. Temperature and dampness are not quite as critical with most modern varnishes, and they dry in about four hours, becoming dust-free in a much shorter time. Old varnishes dried only by evaporation. Synthetic varnish uses chemical reaction as well as evaporation to provide the setting action.

There are two-part varnishes that make a very hard skin – so hard that some abrasives will not touch it. This is waterproof and resistant to many liquids. Besides its use on boats, this varnish gives protection to bar tops and similar surfaces, but for general use the one-part varnishes are easier to apply and their slight flexibility when set allows for movement in the wood below. A hard two-part varnish might crack with wood movement.

Carefully brushed varnish can give a good finish to furniture. Its resistance to abrasion, heat and moisture is much better than that of most other finishes. The best grade of varnish is sold as 'boat varnish'. Use that for furniture and anything else important. It has a slight orange colour. All layers of varnish are the same: you do not have to buy the equivalent of primer, undercoat and top coat. It may help if you thin the first coat, for better penetration. The maker's instructions tell you what thinner to use.

The number of coats applied depends on the quality of finish wanted. For normal work the first coat soaks in, the next coat forms a protective layer with a slight gloss, then a third coat finishes with a reasonable gloss that may be acceptable for some things. However, it is possible to sand each coat and continue sanding a great many coats. Some coachbuilders want up to eighteen coats or more to get a brilliant smooth high gloss. For furniture, three or four coats should be enough. A good finish can be obtained if the top coat is lightly sanded and then wax polish is applied.

Although synthetic varnish is more tolerant, it is still advisable to observe some of the conditions applicable to natural varnishes if you are to get the best results. Vacuum clean the room as dust-free as possible. Avoid draughts. The wood and the varnish should be over 18 °C (65 °F), so do not move the work in from the cold just before varnishing. Do not stir modern varnish or the resulting bubbles will dry on the surface as rough spots. It usually helps if you make the varnish more fluid by standing the can in hot water. Do not heat it excessively. Be careful of grease on the wood. Sweaty hands may mark the surface enough to affect the varnish finish.

A varnish brush should never be used for anything other than applying varnish. It may be stored in solvent between coats, but it is better to suspend it in varnish, ideally in a sealed container (fig. 7.3). With an open container a skin may form on the varnish. After use clean brushes thoroughly. For varnishing you must have very flexible bristles. An old brush with partly hardened varnish trapped will mark the surface. With good varnish and a soft brush it is easy to put on a coat that dries without brush marks.

Read the maker's instructions about brushing. Some varnish may be spread and worked out like paint, but others have to be 'flowed on' – that is, applied with the minimum of brushing. Spread with the grain and do not go back over for further spreading. Lift the brush off before it has become exhausted. Going over a part too often may suddenly lift the varnish and leave a rough surface. If that happens you must let it dry, then sand it smooth and varnish again.

The makers will indicate drying times. The surface must be hard before you rub down with steel wool, pumice powder or abrasive paper. Get each coat smooth before applying the next. With some synthetic varnish the makers specify a maximum as well as a minium period between coats. These are not sanded and are really intended for protection of boats and exterior woodwork, where the finest finish is not so important. They are not for use on furniture.

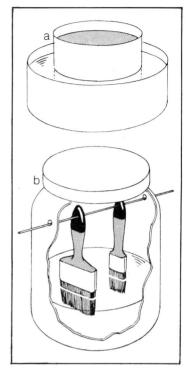

7.3 Cold varnish may be made more fluid by standing the can in hot water (a). Brushes should be stored in solvent or varnish (b).

Spraying

You will have to decide if spraying is the right finish for an individual piece of craftwork. It is the method used today in mass-production where large quantities of furniture can be dealt with as a batch. Spraying suits those circumstances, but might be regarded as unsuitable for a single piece, where there would be much time spent in setting up and clearing away after the job. Of course, spray equipment was not available when much of the earlier fine furniture was made, but there is still a feeling that good cabinetmaking is better finished in other ways.

Some traditional finishes may be thinned and sprayed, but most furniture manufactured today is finished with a special lacquer that leaves a glossy surface not very different from French polish or varnish. The solvent in some lacquers will attack other finishes, so do not use such sprays over or near them.

Spraying requires practice. Runs and curtains can occur and you may not get an even finish. It is unwise to try to spray furniture with the simple equipment sold for amateur touching up of cars. Efficient spraying equipment for furniture is fairly bulky.

SPECIAL EFFECTS

There was once a fashion for limed oak furniture. This used a white deposit in the open grain of the wood. Lime was probably never used, but there are special white pastes for filling the grain. Thick flat white paint can be used. Brush or wipe the material across the grain in all directions and remove the surplus. When it has dried, any surplus is better scraped away than sanded, as that would blur the edges of the filler. You can then apply bleached shellac or pale varnish, so that the filler still looks nearly white.

Furniture is sometimes antiqued by shading its stain to give the effect of wear. This can be done at the staining stage, especially with oil stain. Immediately after applying the stain, wipe parts that are to be lighter. High spots and open areas are normally lighter. You might want the framing of a panel dark and the edges of the panel itself graduated towards a lighter centre. Do not aim at geometric precision. Although the centre lightening may be elliptical, let there be some unevenness as it blends into the darker parts.

In good individual work it is advisable to avoid some of the things used in mass-production furniture, such as 'carvings' that are embossed, flock spraying and special paint effects. The beauty of an individual piece of furniture is in the display of mainly hand craftsmanship, followed by a finish that emphasizes it.

Chapter 8
MAINTENANCE

Much of the quality of work produced by a craftsman is due to the efficient maintenance of his equipment – in particular the sharpness of his cutting tools. Too often, a less-experienced worker puts off sharpening a tool until its bluntness is very obvious. Meanwhile the quality of his work has deteriorated, as a blunt tool tears the surface of the wood instead of cutting it. An experienced craftsman does not begrudge time spent on sharpening. He knows that frequent touching-up of edges will ensure the best possible cuts, and that getting accurate results quickly will be that much easier. There is also the question of safety – there is more risk of hurting yourself while forcing a blunt cutting tool than in handling a sharp one.

Besides tools that need sharpening, there are others that may function in almost any state, but there is a psychological effect to consider. You will feel more inclined to make your best efforts with, for instance, a try square that is clean and polished than with one that is rusty and covered with blobs of glue. Where there are calibrations to consider, as on a steel rule, the risk of error will be reduced if the steel is kept clean. Fortunately, the arrival of good stainless steel has made it easier to keep such tools clean. Where you have to deal with rust or discolouring, fine emery cloth and oil will clean the tool and leave a surface that will remain clean a reasonable length of time. There are not so many wooden tools in use today. At one time a new wooden plane had its mouth sealed with putty and linseed oil poured in and replenished until it exuded from the end grain. We can learn from that. If you are putting a wooden tool away for a period, coat it with linseed oil so that some of it soaks in. A wooden-soled plane soaked in linseed oil certainly performed very well.

SHARPENING EDGE TOOLS
A cutting edge is really a wedge section. The more acute the angle the sharper can be the edge. The edge of a razor is an example of an extremely fine-angled wedge, but it has

little strength. If you tried to work wood with a razor, it would not last long. The angle has to be increased to provide strength. How much depends on the purpose. An axe needs a less acute angle than a chisel. For the majority of wood-working bench tools, the cutting angle is between 25° and 35°. It is the angle between the faces meeting at the edge that counts. The surfaces of a knife blade may be parallel with each other, or nearly so, but the angle at the edge, where its sides meet, should be around 25° for woodworking (fig. 8.1a). It might be finer for cutting paper or other light work.

A plane iron (still called 'iron' although made completely of steel) is fairly thin in modern metal planes and the cutting angle is constant right across its full width (fig. 8.1b). Older plane irons and most chisels are thicker, and it is more convenient to remove much of the metal by grinding at an acute angle and then putting on the sharpening bevel (fig. 8.1c).

An edge is sharp if there is no thickness between the two surfaces when they meet. Perfection may be impossible, but when sharpening try to get as close to it as possible. Apart from knowing that an edge is blunt from the difficulty of cutting with it, you can often see the bluntness as a reflecting line if you look across a blade with a light at the far side. Whenever you sharpen, you briefly rub one or both faces until they meet again.

Sharpening is done with an abrasive stone lubricated with oil, although some workers outside England use water stones. The oil should be quite thin, or it will hold the steel

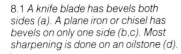
8.1 *A knife blade has bevels both sides (a). A plane iron or chisel has bevels on only one side (b,c). Most sharpening is done on an oilstone (d).*

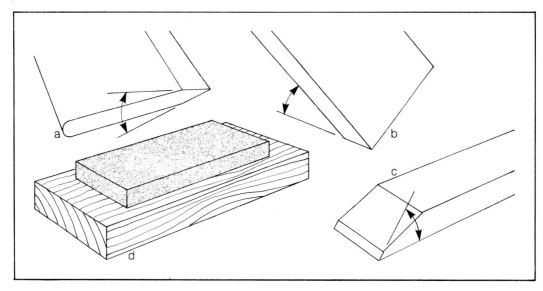

off the stone and prevent sharpening. Light lubricating oil or paraffin will do. For plane irons and chisels the tool is rubbed on the stone, so there is an advantage in having fairly large stones – 200 mm (8 in) × 50 mm (2 in) × 25 mm (1 in) is satisfactory. Each should be mounted in a box or a hollowed block of wood (fig. 8.1d), preferably with a cover.

There are manufactured stones made of grits in various sizes, and a number of types of natural stone, which are all fairly fine. In the manufactured stones the grit size can be chosen, so varying degrees of coarseness are possible. But no manufactured stone can be as fine as the finest natural ones. It is possible to get manufactured stones fine on one side and coarse on the other. One of those is a good buy, otherwise you should have a moderately coarse stone for quick removal of metal and a fine one for finishing.

Most cutting edges have two existing bevels – one for grinding and a more obtuse one for sharpening. There is no need to measure exact angles when sharpening. A degree or so either way will not matter, but you should give – say – a paring chisel a finer angle than would be right for one to be used with a mallet. There are devices to attach to a tool that hold it at the correct angle in relation to the surface of the stone, usually with a roller on an arm that cramps on. However, most craftsmen rely on holding the tool freehand. What needs practice is keeping the tool at the same angle for the whole length of the stone. There is a tendency to drop your hands at the far end.

One hand grips the handle or the top of a plane iron and maintains the angle and thrust, while the fingers of the other hand provide pressure just above the edge being sharpened (fig. 8.2a). Besides wearing the steel away, the surface of the stone wears away. To keep this wear as even as possible, move a tool about on the stone as you rub it. A narrow chisel may take a figure-eight course (fig. 8.2b) and even a plane iron wider than the stone should be moved about.

With a chisel or plane iron continue rubbing on the bevelled side until you judge the edge to be sharp. Wipe off the oil with a cloth and feel with your finger on the flat side towards the edge. If you have made the surfaces meet there will be roughness at the edge. That is a 'wire edge', which is the ragged sliver of steel that was rubbed away as the surfaces met, clinging loosely to the edge. You can loosen or remove it by rubbing the other side of the tool flat on the stone with a circular action (fig. 8.2c). A slice across the edge of a piece of scrap wood will make sure it has gone.

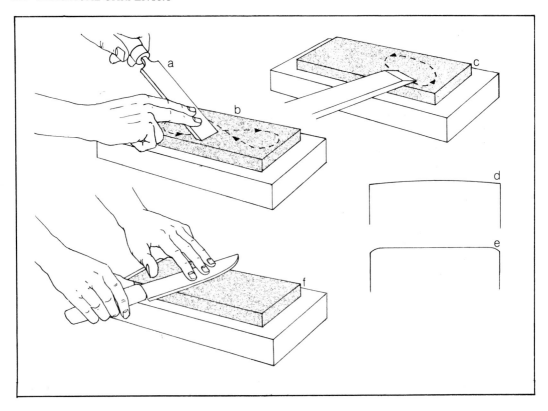

8.2 *Press and move a chisel about the stone (a,b) and finish by rubbing the other side flat (c). Plane iron edges may be rounded (d) or the corners taken off (e). Spread pressure when sharpening a knife (f).*

The edge is now as sharp as that stone will get it. If the edge is examined under a microscope it will be found to be jagged like a saw edge, with the spacing of the teeth the same as the size of grit in the stone. If you were sharpening with a coarse stone, continue sharpening on a finer stone just long enough to remove the gaps left by the coarse grit and replace them with finer ones. Rub flat again and remove the new finer wire edge, then the tool is ready for use. For delicate work you may want to go to an even finer stone. This is particularly so for carving tools, although it may also be worthwhile for a smoothing plane that is to be used on wild-grained hardwood.

Chisels are sharpened straight across and should be kept absolutely flat on one side. Exceptions are carving chisels where a slight bevel may be put on the otherwise flat side. Block planes, rebate planes and ploughs should also have their irons sharpened straight across, but with the corners rounded to prevent them causing ridges (fig. 8.2d and e). The thinner steel of a modern plane iron has the one bevel for the whole thickness instead of a grinding and a sharpening bevel.

Knives are best dealt with by rubbing equally on each

side. You can find the angle by first laying the blade flat on the stone and then lifting it until its edge just touches the surface. A hand on the handle maintains the angle, while the spread fingers of the other hand apply pressure (fig. 8.2f). Move the blade about on the stone to sharpen all parts equally. Do not turn over until you have rubbed many times on one side and can see the bevel there, then aim to get the same amount of bevel on the second side.

When the sharpening bevel of a chisel or plane iron with two bevels is getting wide, the other bevel should be re-ground, so that you can start again on the oil-stone with a narrow sharpening bevel.

A gouge sharpened on the outside can be dealt with on a flat stone by moving the edge about and rolling the blade (fig. 8.3a), although there are some hollow stones available. Continue sharpening until you can feel the wire edge inside. That has to be removed with an oil slip, which is a small oil stone with curved edges (fig. 8.3b). Use the slip like a file to rub inside, moving it about to all parts of the edge. Twist the edge on the surface of a piece of scrap wood, to make sure the wire edge has gone.

If the gouge is sharpened inside (called 'in-cannelled') sharpen with the slip, moved about the bevel equally (fig. 8.3c), then remove the wire edge by rolling the gouge while resting it flat on the main oil stone, before twisting it on a piece of scrap wood.

Turning tools are sharpened in a similar way, except the chisels are bevelled equally on both sides. Some turners

8.3 Roll a gouge as it is sharpened (a), then remove any wire edge inside with a slip stone (b). If the bevel is inside, sharpen with a slip stone (c).

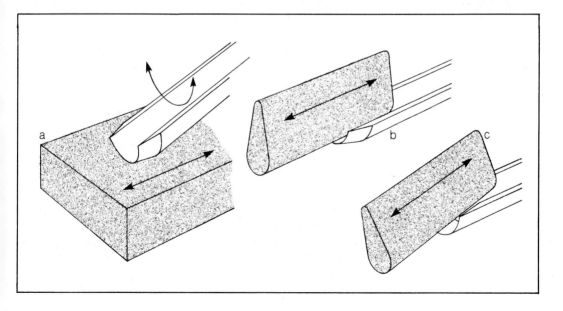

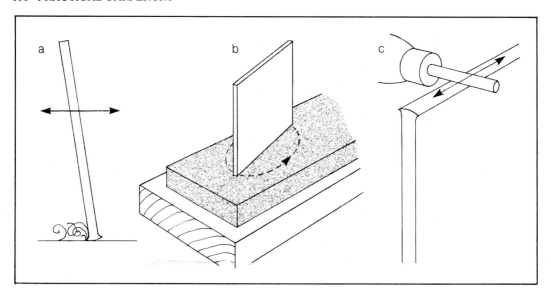

8.4 *A cabinet scraper uses a burred edge for cutting (a). To sharpen, its edge may be squared on a stone (b), then burrs turned with a burnisher (c).*

prefer to blend the sharpening bevels into the grinding bevels. Others maintain separate bevels for sharpening and grinding.

Spokeshaves are sharpened like plane irons, but you may have to turn the stone on edge in order to sharpen the type with projecting tangs.

There is a type of scraper with a replaceable hook blade, which may be sharpened with a fine file or a stone used as a file, but not many sharpenings are possible before the hook has to be replaced. A cabinet scraper is sharpened in a different way, as what makes it cut is a turned-over burr on the edge (fig. 8.4a). The scraper is tilted and pushed or pulled over the surface to take off very fine shavings.

The edge can be filed true, if necessary, and then it is rubbed on an oil stone to make the edge square and true. The flat sides can also be rubbed, followed by more rubs along the edge (fig. 8.4b). A hard steel burnisher is rubbed on the edge, first tilted slightly to one side and then to the other to turn over the cutting burr (fig. 8.4c). A gouge or chisel could be used as a burnisher. Use will turn the burr back, but the edge can be restored several times with the burnisher, before it is necessary to return to the oil-stone.

SAW SHARPENING

On a new saw the teeth are cut and sharpened by machine, so they are all the same. It is difficult to achieve the same precision by hand. Although it is possible to restore the teeth of many saws yourself, it is advisable at longer intervals to have the saw dealt with professionally, so that you start again with perfectly even teeth. Handsaws are made of a tool steel that can be filed. Some circular saws are of the same steel, but many now have tips of harder material. They go much longer before needing sharpening, but when that is due they must be dealt with by an expert with special equipment. Bandsaw blades are not resharpened, but are replaced when they are worn. It is handsaws that are normally sharpened by the owner.

Three things have to be considered. There is the set of the teeth: they are bent alternate ways to cut a kerf wider than the thickness of the blade, so that the saw does not bend in a deep cut. There is the shape of the teeth, which distinguishes a saw meant for cutting along the grain from one intended primarily for work across the grain. There is the angle given to the cutting edges of the teeth. Teeth must all finish level.

In side view, the teeth of general-purpose saws have their forward cutting edges sloping so as to sever the wood fibres (fig. 8.5a). A rip saw has the leading edge upright, or nearly so, the teeth acting more like plane irons – curling up the fibres before breaking (fig. 8.5b). In both cases the included angle is 60° (fig. 8.5c), so it is possible to file across both edges with a normal triangular file (often called a 'three-square' file). Saw files are made with fine teeth and may be reversible in their handles to give a double life. Do not use an ordinary coarser triangular file.

The first need will be touching up a saw that has got blunt for the first time. The tips of the teeth will be seen to have rounded and you have to take off enough metal to restore them to points. The saw has to be clamped with not much more than the teeth exposed and pointing upwards. There are special saw vices, but you can use two stiff pieces of wood in the normal vice (fig. 8.5d). The grip must be tight to prevent vibration, which is noisy and affects the accuracy of filing.

It is usual to sharpen fronts of the teeth set towards you, then to turn the saw round so that the alternate teeth can be sharpened in the same manner. You must guard against taking off too much from the teeth one way, which might happen if you sharpened without turning the saw round. Check the level of the tips of the teeth. If there is much unevenness use a large flat fine file to rub along a few times, but do not take off any more than absolutely necessary. If the teeth are fairly even you can omit this stage.

Look at the teeth pointing towards you. The forward cutting edges in a cross-cut saw will be seen to slope. Put the

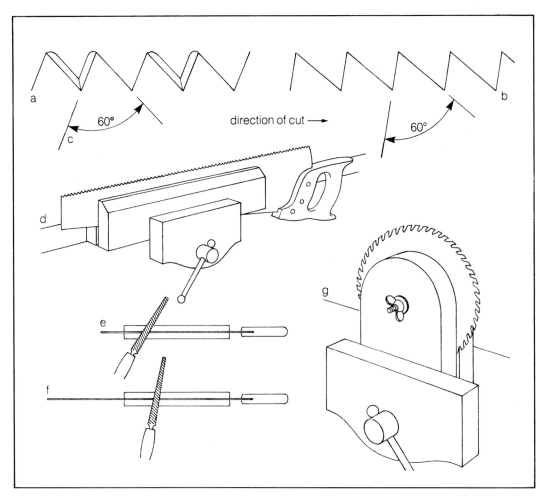

8.5 *Cross-cut saws sever fibres with a knife action (a). A rip saw cuts more like a plane (b). The included angle matches the section of a file used in sharpening (c,d,e,f). Circular saw teeth may be of a different form (g).*

file in a gap and move it until it matches that angle (fig. 8.5e). The other side of the gap will automatically be matched. Go on, using the file at the same angle in alternate gaps all along the saw edge. Have one hand on each end of the file and use steady level strokes each time. File guides that maintain the angle are obtainable. How many strokes depends on the size of the teeth and amount of wear to be corrected, but do not file any more than necessary. Go all the way along, usually starting at the tip end. Be careful not to drop the file into any wrong gaps or you will spoil the saw by bevelling some teeth the wrong way. Turn the saw round and file the alternate teeth the same, but now the file will be angled the other way. After a few teeth examine what you have done and see that the height of all the teeth filed is reasonably even.

After filing, the teeth may be very spiky. Try the saw

across a piece of wood. You may be satisfied with it as it is, but if it tends to dig in at some stages of the cut, there may be one or two high teeth. You can use a fine flat file very lightly along the teeth to remove high spots, but keep this to a minimum.

To sharpen a rip saw, file straight across the teeth pointed towards you (fig. 8.5f). Turn the saw round and do the same with the alternate teeth. You may need to lightly rub the tops and sides of the rip teeth with a flat file if it seems spiky during first cuts.

Circular saw teeth are in many forms. Some are like hand-saw teeth and may be sharpened in the same way. You can make up a vice with a curved end and a bolt for the saw blade (fig. 8.5g).

You may file teeth perhaps two or three times, but this will reduce the amount of set each time, so the kerf cut will become so slight that there is no clearance on the blade. You then have to set the teeth again. This needs control in bending or you can break a tooth off. Do not try to bend at the base of the tooth; it is only the top half that has to be bent, and that not very much (fig. 8.6a). Setting should be done before sharpening, otherwise the action of setting may blunt the teeth.

There are now several types of plier-action saw sets (sometimes spelled 'setts'). They bend the teeth one at a time as you squeeze the handles. The amount of bend and the distance from the tip is controlled by stops (fig. 8.7). The most basic type is like open pliers with stops. There are older type sets with notched edges in a plate, but their only

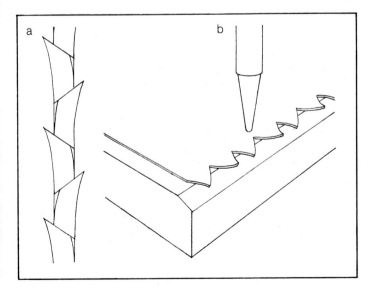

8.6 *Saw teeth are set alternate ways (a). Large teeth may be bent with a punch (b).*

8.7 A saw set uses a plier action to set saw teeth and has adjustable stops to suit the size of teeth.

use today is for the very large teeth of cross-cut saws used for logs. Bending is then done by eye.

The small teeth of tenon and dovetail saws should only be set with a plier-type tool. Teeth of hand saws at 4 or 6 per 25 mm (1 in) might be set by careful use of a punch and hammer over the edge of an iron block (fig. 8.6b), but it would be unwise for a beginner to try this method on small teeth. Too much set makes hard work of sawing. You have to judge it so that it is just enough.

POWER PLANER MAINTENANCE

A planer or jointer has a cylindrical block carrying two, three or four cutters or knives, each as long as the width of the table, the number depending on the capacity of the machine. The cutters are rotated at a very high speed. In ideal circumstances each cutting edge projects the same amount, is straight and exactly in line with the take-off table; then you get a smooth cut of even depth. A common arrangement turns the block so as to give 12 000 cuts per minute. If one blade is higher that one does most of the work at a fraction of the efficient speed, and the quality of finish suffers. Check that all blades are the same height and that this is the same over the width of the machine.

Knives are mounted in the cutter block in different ways, but in all machines there is provision for raising and lowering them, usually after slackening screws. The height of the rear table should be adjusted to the height of a blade when it is vertical and this can be checked with a straight strip of wood (fig. 8.8a). Try this at each end of the blade. Lock the knife blade at that positon and do the same with the others. With the motor disconnected, turn the block with your hand at one end, while holding the straight piece of wood in place. You will see if one edge is higher than the others as it tries to move the wood along. Ideally, at any position the cutting edges should just skim the wood. Checking may be easier if you accept a slight movement. By marking the wood opposite the edge of the rear table and putting another mark about 3 mm (⅛ in) beyond it (fig. 8.8b), you can try the wood in several positions while you turn the cutter block by hand and see if movement is nearly the same everywhere.

One way of lifting each knife level with the rear table is to use a powerful U-shaped magnet, to draw and hold up the blade while you tighten its screws (fig. 8.8c). With a broad spread it should be able to hold up both ends of the blade level at the same time.

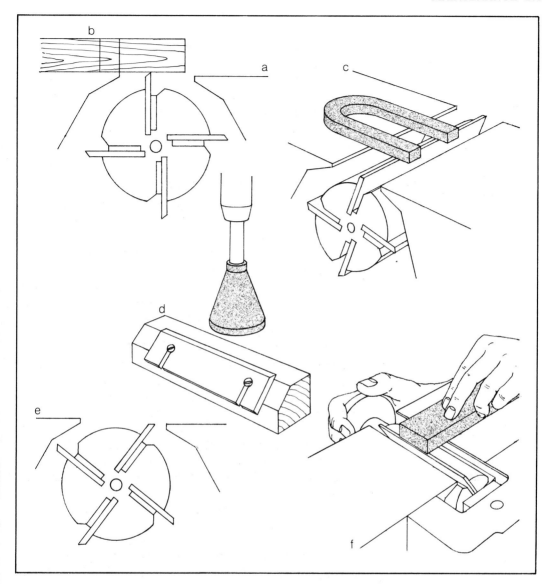

It is important that the cutting edges should be absolutely straight. The ordinary woodworking shop does not usually have facilities for grinding such edges straight and it would be unwise to attempt freehand grinding. What is needed is a means of holding the knife at the correct angle and moving it under a flat grinding surface. It might be possible to arrange something with a grinder in a drill press (fig. 8.8d), but if the knives reach a stage when they should be reground, it is better to return them to the makers or to another grinder with suitable equipment. However, it is possible to sharpen many times without removing the knives from the machine,

8.8 *Power plane blade movement and setting may be tested with a strip of wood (a,b). A magnet will hold a blade level (c). Edges must be ground straight (d), then set level with the feed table (e).*

provided that you do not have to remove deep knicks due to hitting nails or pieces of grit.

To sharpen in the machine, have the motor and belt disconnected, then lower the feed table so that its surface comes in line with the bevel on a knife (fig. 8.8e). Have a flat fairly coarse oil-stone and wrap much of its length in paper. With one hand on the pulley keep the cutter edge in position and rub the oil-stone on it, with the paper sliding on the table (fig. 8.8f). Use plenty of oil and pressure. Wipe off the oil from time to time and check that you are not taking more off one place than another. Deal with all edges in the same way, then clean off any surplus oil and test the action of the machine.

If the planer can be used for cutting rabbets at one side and you are replacing or moving knives, make sure the knives project slightly an equal amount from the cutter block at the rabbeting end.

ROUTER AND MOULDING CUTTERS

There is not much you can do to a blunted rotary cutter. Most are made of special alloy steel or are tipped, and neither will sharpen easily by hand methods. If you attempt to sharpen, only the leading face of the cutter when it is rotating should be touched. Any wearing away of the outside surface would affect the profile the tool can produce. A slim round oil slip might have some effect. A file would probably not be hard enough.

If you want to sharpen the end of a square mortise chisel, there is a special tool (usually available from the stockist who supplied the mortise chisel) something like a countersink bit with a pilot, and matched to the size of the square. When that is turned with a brace it will remove metal at the edge. To get a fine edge you can follow with a stone that has a curved cross section.

DRILL SHARPENING

To a certain extent the various woodworking boring bits have to be regarded as disposable. A limited amount of sharpening is possible, but a stage may be reached where no more can be taken off if the bit is to work. The steel of most bits is tempered soft enough for a file to cut it, but sharpening is often better done with a small oil slip, used like a file.

In many bits there is an outer spur that cuts the circle (fig. 8.9a). It must not be sharpened on the outside, or the size of the circle it cuts will be reduced and the rest of the bit may not follow into a deep hole. Sharpen inside to get a knife effect in the direction of rotation. You may have to remove a wire edge outside, but do not rub off any solid metal there. Try not to reduce the length of the spur. If there are two spurs deal with them evenly.

Inside is a lip, or a pair of lips. They are there to remove waste outlined by the spur. Their action is more wedge-like, so a very sharp edge is not so important. There must be a slight angle on the underside (fig. 8.9b) to scoop into the wood. What is important is keeping the edge of the lip higher than the cutting edge of the spur (fig. 8.9c). It is the spur that needs most sharpening, and when that gets back to the depth of the lip, the bit may have to be discarded. You can file the underside of the lip, but you should not reduce its depth very much.

Twist bits, whether for hand or power drilling, are made and sharpened in the same way. Power-drilling spade bits have a different form. It is the broad cutting edges that need attention (fig. 8.9d), but it is their outer corners that wear. If they are rounded, file the whole width of each edge until they are restored to sharpness and will cut a clean circle. Do not sharpen outside. Countersink bits go a long time without needing sharpening, but if they do you need a file with a knife edge (to get inside a rose bit) or a small round file for a snail countersink. In both cases, file the leading edges and not the outsides.

Metalworking bits, such as are used for screw holes in wood, are difficult to sharpen freehand. There are jigs for

8.9 *The spur (a) of a twist bit cuts the circle of a hole, while the lip (b) removes waste, so the spur must project further (c). A power drill spade bit is sharpened with a file (d). Cutting angles of a metalworking bit are important (e).*

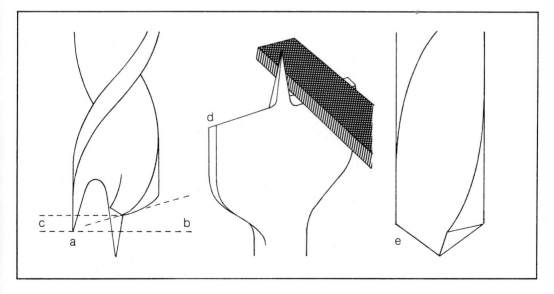

use on bench grinding wheels, but these are unsuitable for diameters of anything less than about 3 mm (⅛ in) – the assumption being that anything smaller than that will be discarded rather than resharpened. However, for wood-working we do not need the precision of cutting edge angles that are necessary for metal, and it is possible to restore a reasonable edge by hand grinding.

Your best guide is a larger drill fresh from the makers. If you look at the end of a drill at least 6 mm (¼ in) diameter, you can see the angle between the two sides and the way the underside is backed off from the cutting edge (fig. 8.9e). Without this the drill would merely slide round and not pull itself into the wood or metal. What you have to do on any size drill, down to the tiniest, is to reproduce this end. Have a high speed dry grinding wheel and touch the drill on it very lightly. A common mistake with small drills is to press hard and take off too much. If you are sharpening a broken drill, first grind the end square across, then slope each side and finally back off the edges as shown.

SERVICING OIL-STONES

Oil on a stone attracts dirt. A stone should be wiped clean after use, but if you are using a stone frequently sound practice tends to get neglected. Its case should have a cover to keep out dirt. Even if you have kept a stone clean it will gradually clog with particles of steel mixed with oil. A dirty stone does not sharpen properly.

You can soak the dirt out of a stone with paraffin. Leave it in a can of paraffin for a day or so, if possible. A scrubbing brush will remove loose dirt and you may have to change the paraffin before you complete the job. Newspaper will soak up surplus oil. What remains in the stone will help in later sharpening.

A stone regularly used for chisels and plane irons will get worn out of true. Hollow in the length is not so serious as hollow in the width, which makes it difficult to sharpen tools straight across. Spreading the points of contact when sharpening can delay hollowing, but the corners will always remain high.

To grind a stone level you need a piece of plate glass and some abrasive powder in oil, such as is sold as valve grinding compound at car supply stores. Spread ·the grinding compound on the glass and rub the stone on it with plenty of pressure, working with a mainly circular action. This is a slow process. You can rub two stones together to get a similar result, but the harder one will wear away the other.

Information

NAILS

Nails are produced in a large range of sizes and types. Most are made of iron, which may be coated with zinc or other metal to protect against rust, or made of brass, bronze or other alloy with a good resistance to corrosion. Brass is preferable to iron for furniture. Diameters are described by a gauge number, different from that for screws, but usually only one diameter is available for each length. Large heads provide the strongest grip, but small heads can be driven flush or sunk for a better appearance.

Note: Measurements in millimetres are given in **bold type**; measurements in inches are given in normal type.

TYPE	USUAL AVAILABLE LENGTHS		USE AND CHARACTERISTICS
Round wire nail	**20–150**	¾–6	General-purpose. Fairly large head.
Oval wire nail	**12–150**	½–6	Head buries, and shape reduces risk of splitting.
Cut floor nail	**12–150**	½–6	Flat, with hooked head that buries.
Clout nail	**12– 50**	½–2	Large head, for gripping roofing felt.
Panel pin	**12– 50**	½–2	Fine, with small head to punch into wood.
Hardboard pin	**9– 50**	⅜–2	Very fine, for fixing hardboard.
Tack	**6– 30**	¼–1¼	Large head, for fixing fabrics.
Sprig or glazier's point	**12 *or* 20**	½ *or* ¾	Headless, to bury under putty when fixing glass.
Annular or barbed ring nail	**20– 75**	¾–3	For boat building; teeth resist withdrawal.
Roofing or screw nail	**65**	2½	Large head and twisted body, for fixing corrugated sheets.

SCREWS

Choose wood screws, as distinct from metal-thread screws, which have threads for nuts. Wood screws are made in many lengths, from 6 mm (¼ in) up to 150 mm (6 in) and more, and diameters, indicated by a gauge number different from that used for nails, from about 2 mm (³⁄₃₂ in) to 7 mm (⁹⁄₃₂ in) and larger. The combinations of gauges and lengths shown below should suit most purposes and are normally available.

Most screws are of mild steel, but brass, stainless steel or other metals, plated or coloured, are available. Screws are boxed in 100s, but available in smaller quantities. Raised heads may only come in a few sizes.

Suggested sizes for holes suit hardwoods, and the pilot holes could be smaller in softwood and made with a bradawl for small screws.

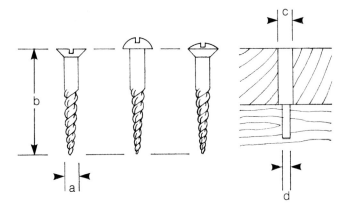

Note: Measurements in millimetres are given in **bold type**; measurements in inches are given in normal type.

GAUGE NUMBER(a)	COMMON LENGTHS (b)			CLEARANCE HOLE (c)		PILOT HOLE (d)	
2	**6**		¼	**2.5**	³⁄₃₂	**1.5**	¹⁄₁₆
3	**9.5**		⅜	**3**	⁷⁄₆₄	**1.5**	¹⁄₁₆
4	**9.5 – 19**	⅜ –	¾	**3.2**	⅛	**2**	⁵⁄₆₄
5	**12.5 – 19**	½ –	¾	**3.2**	⅛	**2**	⁵⁄₆₄
6	**12.5 – 38**	½ –	1½	**4**	⁵⁄₃₂	**2**	⁵⁄₆₄
8	**19 – 76**	¾ –	3	**5**	³⁄₁₆	**2.5**	³⁄₃₂
10	**25 – 76**	1 –	3	**5.5**	⁷⁄₃₂	**3.2**	⅛
12	**51 – 76**	2 –	3	**6**	¼	**3.2**	⅛
14	**64 – 76**	2½ –	3	**7**	⁹⁄₃₂	**5**	³⁄₁₆

ABRASIVES

Many grits are used for abrasives and may come loose, on paper or on cloth in sheet, disc, strip or endless bands. Most sheets are 280 mm (11 in) by 230 mm (9 in). Glass and garnet coating sheets for wood may not be fixed with waterproof glue. Most other abrasive materials are. Abrasive sheets described as 'wet and dry' have waterproof glues. Emery is only used on metal. Several grit classifications are used. The best refers to the fineness of the grit (used for manufactured grits and given in the first column), but other classifications are used and are listed for comparison. Steel wool for wood finishing is available in three grades, approximately comparable to abrasive grits as shown.

GRIT	GLASS OR GARNET PAPER	TRADITIONAL GRADE	EMERY CLOTH	STEEL WOOL	USE
400	–	10/0 ('ten nought')	–	–	Very fine finish
320	–	9/0	–	–	
280	–	8/0	–	–	Flatting polish
240	–	7/0	–	–	
220	–	6/0	–	–	
180	00 (flour)	5/0	0	–	Finest normally used on bare wood
150	0	4/0	FF	00	
120	1	3/0	F	–	Medium sanding
100	1½	2/0	1	1	
80	F2 (fine 2)	0	1½	–	Usual first sanding
60	M2 (middle 2)	½	2	3	
50	S2 (strong 2)	1	3	–	Rough sanding
40	2½	1½	4	–	
36	3	2	–	–	Coarse stock removal

GLUES

Many different adhesives are available, but any described as suitable for paper or card as well as wood should be avoided as not strong enough for constructional joints.

TYPE	APPLICATION	COMMENTS
Animal or fish	Heat, then rub and cramp.	Traditional type. Non-waterproof.
Casein	Mix powder with water. The joint should be cramped.	Derived from milk. Moderate damp resistance.
Cellulose	Apply and hand hold briefly.	Little strength but quick-acting and waterproof. For fixing small parts only.
Contact cement	Allow to become tacky then postion parts exactly.	For fixing plastic laminates to wood. Immediate adhesion.
Epoxy	Two-part (resin and hardener supplied separate). Apply and cramp for two days.	Strongest waterproof glue. Sticks most most materials to themselves as well as to wood. Quicker-acting type available, but not as strong.
PVA	One-part. Cramp briefly.	Non-waterproof. Dries clear. Suitable for furniture and indoor use.
Resorcinol formaldehyde	Two-part. Cramp closely.	Strong and waterproof. Red glue line. For boat building.
Urea	Two-part. Cramp closely.	Strong with good water resistance. For furniture and small boats.

FILLERS

Prepared fillers are supplied as paste to be applied with a knife, or as liquid to be brushed on, with another semi-liquid medium grade between these two extremes.

PASTE FILLER	MEDIUM FILLER	LIQUID FILLER	NO FILLER
Ash	Mahogany	Bass	Cypress
Chestnut	Rosewood	Beech	Ebony
Elm	Sapele	Birch	Gaboon
Hickory	Walnut	Cedar	Hemlock
Oak		Fir	Holly
Padouk		Maple	Pine
Teak		Sycamore	Spruce

STAINS

Stains alter the colour of wood without hiding details of grain. They are used before applying a protective finish.

TYPE	COLOURS	AS SUPPLIED	CHARACTERISTICS
Oil	Mostly to deepen natural wood tone	Liquid, ready for use	Even spread and deeper penetration than other stains.
Water	Wood shades and a few other colours	Crystals to dissolve in water	Colours not as intense as oil. Can be mixed. Little penetration. Better spread with several coats.
Spirit	Wood shades and some bright colours	Powder to dissolve in methylated spirit	Quick drying. Good penetration. Unsuitable for large areas. For small parts or touching-up.
Permanganate of potash	Colourless, but turns many woods brown	Crystals to dissolve in water	Chemical actions, so check effect on similar scrap wood to see resulting colour.

FINISHES

A finish is applied to improve appearance and to protect the wood from abrasion and the penetration of dirt and liquids. A clear finish shows grain and stain. An opaque finish hides wood detail and may be any colour.

TYPE		COMMENTS
Clear finishes	Varnish	Made from natural or synthetic lacs. Slight golden tinge. Applied by brush. Several coats needed.
	Varnish stain	Varnish with stain included, so that colour is in the finish and does not enter the grain.
	Shellac	Flakes dissolved in methylated spirit. May be brushed, but more often used as French polish.
	French polish	System of pad polishing using shellac. Ordinary polish has slight golden tinge, but bleached polish is almost clear.
	Lacquer	Synthetic sprayed finish. Clear with any degree of gloss.
	Oil polish	Pad polish with linseed oil. Slow to dry.
	Teak oil	Oil and varnish pad polish, much quicker to dry than oil only.
	Wax polish	Mixture of waxes for pad polishing. Slow to apply if used as sole finish, but may follow varnish or other finish.
Opaque finishes	Oil paint	Traditional type mostly superseded by synthetic. All colours available. Several coats needed. Gloss or matt or intermediate surface.
	Emulsion paint	Water-based paint. Not a wood finish, but may be used to seal hardboard before application of ordinary paint.

Glossary

Adam A period of furniture building and decoration. Ascribed to Robert and James Adam.

Adze A tool like an axe with the blade set at right angles to the haft, used to level surfaces.

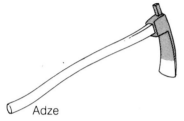
Adze

Alburnum The botanical name of sapwood.

Annual rings The concentric rings that form the grain of a tree. One ring is added each year.

Annulet A turned raised bead around a cylindrical part.

Antiquing A finish that makes modern furniture look old.

Apron A wide shaped rail in cabinetwork. Projecting ornament on a door lock rail.

Arbor A temporary tapered turned piece to hold a hollow article being turned. Also a fitment for an electric drill.

Arch back An armchair where the arms continue at the back to make an arch (as in a Windsor chair).

Architrave Outer molding around a door.

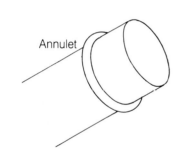
Annulet

Arris The line or sharp edge between two flat or plane surfaces.

Astragal A raised moulding or bead on a flat surface.

Auger A long drill, with its own handle, for deep drilling.

Autumn growth Part of an annual ring in a tree. It is formed by the descending sap.

Awl A pointed tool for making holes.

Axis An imaginary line about which a body can be assumed to revolve. The centre-line of a solid object.

Backboard The piece of wood closing the back of a cabinet.

Back-flap hinge A hinge designed to swing back further than a normal hinge. It is often used under a drop leaf on a table.

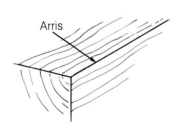
Arris

Back iron Cap on plane iron to stiffen it and break shavings.

Badger Large rabbet plane.

Ball-foot A turned round or elliptical ball on the bottom of a leg.

Balluster (baluster) Pillar to support a rail.

Banding A strip of inlay laid around and usually parallel with edges of panels, such as drawer fronts, table-tops and cabinet parts.

Auger

Bar Intermediate member dividing a window into smaller parts.

Bar cramp Alternative name for a sash cramp.

Barefaced tenon A tenon shouldered on one side only.

Base The foundation of anything or the main bottom portion in an architectural or other assembly.

Basil Grinding angle of a cutting tool.

Batten Any narrow strip of wood. A strip fitted across boards to join them, cover a gap or prevent warping.

Baulk (balk) Timber roughly squared before cutting into boards.

Beam Strong horizontal timber, load-bearing and supported by a wall or other means.

Beam compass Two points or a point and pencil adjustable along a wooden rod.

Beaumontage Wood stopping like sealing wax to melt into holes.

Bench stop A wood or metal stop on a bench top. Wood is pressed against it when planing its surface.

Bevel An angle or chamfer planed on an edge. Also the name of an adjustable tool for testing angles.

Bezel Ring around glass over the face of a clock or other instrument.

Bill hook Chopping knife used by woodcutters.

Blind Not right through. A stopped hole for a dowel or a mortise for a short tenon.

Blind nailing or screwing Using the fastener in a rabbet or elsewhere that will be covered by another part so that the head is not visible in the finished work.

Bolster A pad to withstand a thrust.

Bonnet Decorative shaping and moulding or carving at the top of any piece of cabinetwork, but particularly on a clock.

Book matched Veneers cut next to each other and laid together so that one is a mirror image of the other.

Bow back A chair back with a curved bow and spindles enclosed in it, but not necessarily an arched back.

Bowing Warping in the length only.

Bracket An angular support used particularly to support a shelf or flap.

Brad Nail cut from sheet metal, parallel in thickness and tapered in width.

Bridle joint The reverse of a mortise and tenon joint, with two ends extending at either side of a central web.

Bull-nose plane A plane with its cutting edge very close to the front of the body. Usually the edge is the full width of the body, for getting close into the end of a stopped rabbet.

Bureau A writing desk, with a closing front and storage places inside.

Burr (burl) An outgrowth on a tree. It can be cut across to

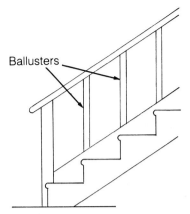

Ballusters

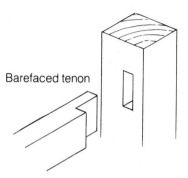

Barefaced tenon

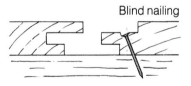

Blind nailing

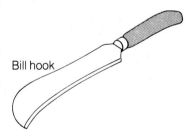

Bill hook

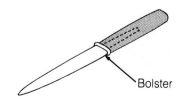

Bolster

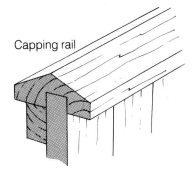

Capping rail

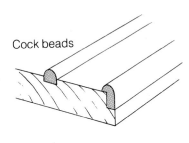

Cock beads

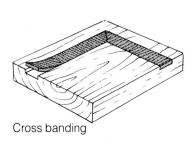

Cross banding

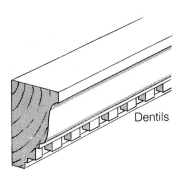

Dentils

show a very twisted grain that is valued for its decoration when cut into veneers.

Cable moulding Moulding with a rounded part carved diagonally to look like stranded rope or cable.

Cabriole leg Leg given a flourish so that it curves out from a corner in a stylized form of an animal's leg. Usually it finishes in a ball foot.

Capping The top moulding on a pedestal or post.

Capping rail Rail over top of fence or gate.

Carcase The main assembly parts that make up the skeleton of a piece of furniture, such as the framework of a table, cabinet or chest of drawers.

Casement Hinged sash window.

Cast Twisting of a surface that should be flat.

Caul Part of press for holding glued veneers.

Chaise longue Long low chair for reclining.

Chamfer An angle or bevel planed on an edge.

Cleat A small piece joining other parts together or an alternative name for a wood clamp.

Cock bead A bead standing above the surface of the wood.

Coniferous A cone-bearing sort of tree, the main source of softwoods.

Conversion The process of cutting logs into boards.

Comb An undulating edge that is found particularly on a chair back.

Core Base wood on which veneer is laid.

Cornice A moulding above eye level that projects around the top of a cabinet.

Cramp (clamp) Tool for holding parts together, particularly when gluing. Batten fixed across other boards.

Cross banding Decorative veneering that uses narrow strips cut across the grain.

Crook (crotch) Wood cut from the point where a branch leaves the tree. Cut to take advantage of the curved grain in order to get maximum strength in a shaped part or for decoration.

Cup shake Defect in lumber. A crack around the lines of annual rings.

Dado A groove in wood.

Dead pin A wedge.

Dentil Rectangular ornaments on cornice mouldings.

Distressing Intentionally damaging furniture to make it look old.

Doatiness Speckled marking in wood indicating the start of decay.

Donkey A quick-action vice used for holding work during the cutting of marquetry designs.

Dowel A cylindrical piece of wood that is particularly used as a peg in holes for making joints.

Dovetail The fan-shaped piece that projects between pins in the other part in a dovetail joint.

Dressing Planing and finishing wood.

Drift Large punch, tapered to pull holes into line.

Draw bore or draw pin A tapered peg or dowel through staggered holes in a mortise and tenon joint, to draw the parts together.

Drop leaf A flap that swings down at the edge of a table and can be supported when raised to enlarge the table-top.

Ellipse The inclined transverse section of a cylinder or cone.

Escutcheon A keyhole, or the plate covering and surrounding it.

Face marks Marks put on the first planed side and edge to indicate that further measuring and marking should be made from them.

Fall front A flap that lets down to be supported in a horizontal position. An example is the writing surface of a bureau.

Fastenings (fasteners) Anything, such as nails and screws, used for joining.

Fiddle back Grain pattern shown when wood is quarter-sawn, particularly in mahogany as used in violin backs, but also seen in sycamore, maple and some other woods.

Figure Decorative grain pattern and particularly that shown when the medullary rays are prominent in quarter-sawn wood. Especially seen in oak.

Fillet A narrow strip of wood used to fill or support a part.

Finial A turned end to a post.

Fish plates Strips of wood or metal each side of an end-to-end joint.

Flour paper Very fine glasspaper.

Flush bead moulding A bead worked into a surface, instead of standing above it, as in an astragal.

Fluting Rounded grooves that are the reverse of beads.

Folding wedges Two similar wedges used overlapping each other to provide parallel pressure.

Foxiness Reddish colour in wood indicating the onset of rot.

Foxtail wedging Using wedges driven into the end of a tenon so that they spread the wood and make it grip when it is driven into a blind mortise.

Framed construction In which the carcase is formed of strips of wood, with the spaces filled by panels.

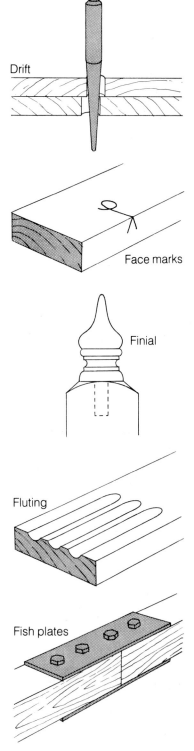

Drift

Face marks

Finial

Fluting

Fish plates

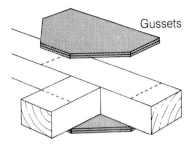

Gussets

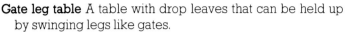

Fretwork Pierced work done with a very fine fretsaw.

Furniture Besides its usual meaning, this also applies to ironmongery for doors, windows etc.

Gate leg table A table with drop leaves that can be held up by swinging legs like gates.

Gauge A marking tool or a means of testing. A definition of size. The thickness of sheet metal or the diameters of wires or screws.

Glaziers' points Small steel triangles used like headless nails to hold glass in a frame.

Groundwork The base surface to which veneer is applied.

Groove Any slot in wood such as a dado. Less commonly a rabbet.

Growth rings See annual rings.

Gunstock stile Sort of upright at the side of a panelled door, wider beside the lower panel than beside the upper one.

Gusset Piece over frame joints to strengthen and stiffen.

Haunch

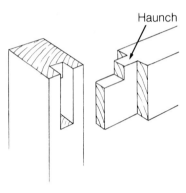

Haft The handle of a tool.

Halved joint Two pieces of wood notched to fit into each other where they meet or cross.

Hand screw A wooden cramp.

Heartwood The mature wood nearer the centre of the tree.

Handed Made in pairs.

Hanging stile The stile on which the hinges of a door are attached.

Haunch A short part of a tenon in a corner joint.

Horse Trestle. Temporary strut.

Impact adhesive Alternative name for contact adhesive.

Incising Carving below the surface.

Inlaying Setting one piece of wood in another, either in solid pieces of wood or as a veneer.

In the white Furniture completely made and ready for staining and polishing.

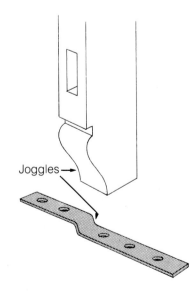

Joggles

Jamb Vertical side of a window- or door-frame.

Jig Guide for shaping.

Joggle Protection on the end, particularly beyond a mortise. A double bend.

Joist Wood to support a floor or ceiling.

Jury Anything temporary, e.g. jury strut.

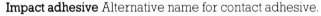

Kerf The slot made by a saw.

Keying Fitting pieces of veneer into kerfs. Used particularly to strengthen a mitre joint.

Knee Shaped bracket or brace.

Knot A flaw in wood caused where a branch left the tree.

Knuckle The pivot part of a hinge.

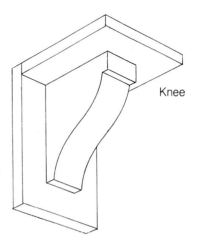

Knee

Lac Resinous substance secreted in trees by insects.

Lacquer A transparent varnish. Traditionally a brushed finish on gilded work, but now more often a sprayed finish.

Ladder back A chair back with several cross members between uprights.

Laminating Constructing in layers with several pieces of wood. Used particularly in curved work.

Lath Strip of wood of smaller section than a batten.

Lattice work Pierced strapwork.

Laying out Setting out the details of design and construction.

Lineal Specified by length only. Sometimes used when pricing quantities of wood.

Lumber American term for converted wood.

Marking out Marking ends and positions on wood before cutting shaping and drilling.

Marquetry A system of inlaying that uses many woods to produce a pattern or picture using solid wood or veneers.

Matched boarding Joining boards edge to edge with matching tongues and grooves.

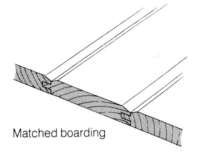

Matched boarding

Medullary rays Radiating lines from the center of a log, which can be seen in some woods radially cut but are invisible in others.

Mill work Manufacture of joinery mainly by machine.

Mitre A joint where the angle of meeting is bisected as in the corner of a picture frame.

Moulded plywood Double curvature laminates built up in layers with strips of veneer.

Moulding Decorative edge or border which may be a simple rounding or an intricate section of curves and quirks. Many are of named classical form, used in architecture and cabinetwork.

Mullet A grooved block used for testing the thickness of the edge of a panel or drawer bottom that will have to fit in a groove.

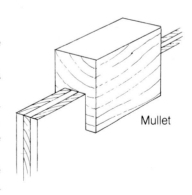

Mullet

Muntin An internal rail in a framed assembly as between the panels in a window frame.

Mullion Vertical division of a window.

Necking Turned bead on the upper part of a pillar, pedestal or finial.

Newel Post carrying the hand rail to a flight of stairs.

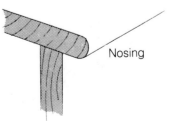

Nosing

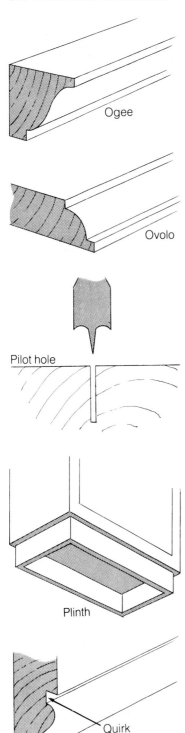

Ogee

Ovolo

Pilot hole

Plinth

Quirk

Nosing Semi-circular moulding.

Ogee moulding A moulding with a convex curve above a concave one. It is named for its likeness to a combination of the letters O and G.

Onion foot A squat version of a ball foot.

Ovolo Classic quarter circle or ellipse moulding.

Parquetry Wood-block flooring laid in geometric designs. Not to be confused with marquetry.

Patina Surfaced texture that is due particularly to old age.

Pedestal A supporting post.

Pediment A top shaped and moulded or carved. Larger than a bonnet.

Pegging Dowels or wooden pegs through joints.

Pendant, pendil, pennant A hanging turned or carved decoration. The reverse of a finial.

Piercing Decoration made by cutting through the wood, in the splat of a chair back for example. Similar to fretwork, but more robust.

Pilaster A decorative half column fitted on a flat surface.

Pilot-hole A small hole drilled as a guide before using a larger drill.

Pintle A dowel or peg on which parts pivot – the name taken from the pivotal point of a boat's rudder.

Planted Applied instead of cut in the solid. Moulding attached to a surface is planted. If it is cut in the solid wood it is stuck.

Plastic glues General name for resin-bonded adhesives.

Plinth The base part around the bottom of a piece of furniture.

Plumb Vertical.

Plywood Board made with veneers glued together with the grain of alternate layers at right angles.

Pokerwork Designs formed with red hot point. Pyrography.

Pollarding Continued lopping of the top of a tree. This produces decorative burrs in the wood.

Proud Standing above a surface, not flush with it.

Punchwork Background to carving made with punches having patterned ends.

Purlins Horizontal beams in a roof carried on the principal rafters.

Pyrography Pokerwork.

Quarter-sawn Boards cut radially from a log to minimize warping and shrinking or to show the medullary rays as 'figure' in oak and some other woods.

Quatre-foil A tracery detail based on four interlocking circles.

Quirk A narrow or V-shaped groove beside a bead, or the whole bead when worked to form part of a cover or disguise for a joint. A raised part between patterns in turned work.

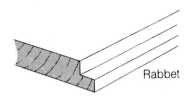

Rabbet

Rabbet (rebate) Angular cut-out in section, as in the back of a picture frame.

Racking Out of square.

Rail A horizontal member in framing.

Rake Incline to horizontal.

Rank set Having the cap iron of a plane well back from the cutting edge.

Rat rail Small round file.

Reeds Series of beads sunk on a surface.

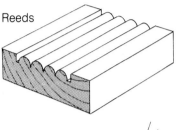

Reeds

Relief Cut back, usually to gain emphasis in appearance.

Riser Vertical front of a step.

Rive (riven) Split boards from a log instead of sawing them.

Rod back A type of Windsor chair that has many spindles, with the arms joined to spindles forming the back.

Rolled arm The arm of a chair shaped for comfort and the front finished in a scroll.

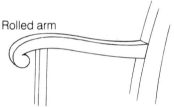

Rolled arm

Rule joint Moulded joint used between a table-top and its drop flap used with a back-flap hinge. Named for its similarity in section to the joint of a two-fold rule.

Run In an unbroken length. Timber can be quoted as 'so many feet run'.

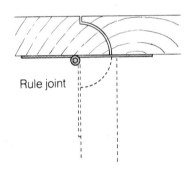

Rule joint

Saddle back Part curved both ways.

Saddling Scooping a chair seat to a comfortable shape.

Sandpaper Common, and incorrect collective name for abrasive papers.

Sapwood The wood nearer the outside of a log. Not as strong or durable as the heartwood in most trees.

Scant Slightly undersize, sometimes applied to sawn wood.

Scantlings Wood of small sections and various lengths.

Scratch moulding Small moulding cut with a scratch stock, which has a cutter sharpened like a scraper.

Scribing Cutting a joint with one part of moulding fitted into the other, instead of mitring.

Scroll Carved shape like end view of loosely rolled paper.

Seasoning Drying wood to an acceptable moisture content.

Second growth Natural growth, often from stumps, after first trees are cleared.

Segments Curved pieces of wood used to build up table rails and similar things of curved form.

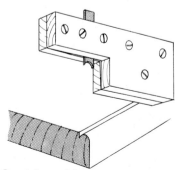

Scratch moulding

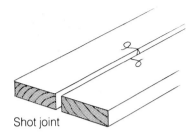

Shot joint

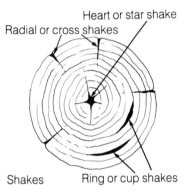

Heart or star shake
Radial or cross shakes

Shakes   Ring or cup shakes

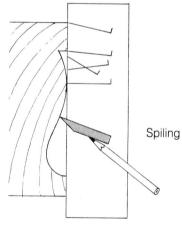

Spiling

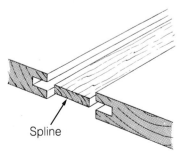

Spline

Set To punch a nail below the surface, or the tool with which this is done. The bending of saw teeth in alternate directions to produce a kerf wider than the thickness of the saw metal.

Setting out Laying out details of the whole furniture or a particular part of it.

Shooting board Device for holding wood when trimming its edge with a plane.

Shot joint Planed edges glued together.

Shoulder piece An extra bracket at the top of a leg extending under the rail or framing.

Shake A defect or crack that occurs in the growing tree, but might not be found until after conversion.

Skew Out of square or twisted.

Slabbing Squaring a log.

Slip Oil-stone with shaped sections, for sharpening inside hollow tools such as gouges.

Soffit The underside of a window or door opening.

Spandrel A shaped rail between the upright parts of a piece of furniture.

Spiling Copying a shape by using a pointed stick over a board at many positions, with the stick pencilled around and the positions repeated to transfer the shape.

Spindle Rounded slender part, usually vertical, as in a chair back.

Splat Central upright member in a chair back. Usually decorated by shaping, piercing or carving.

Splay To spread out.

Spline A narrow strip of wood fitting into grooves and strengthening two meeting faces that are glued.

Split turning A piece with semicircular section made by turning two pieces of wood glued together and separating them so that the half turning can be glued to a flat surface.

Spud A dowel at the bottom of a doorpost. A tool for removing bark.

Square turning Wood of square section, but with lengthwise shaping similar to a turned outline.

Star shake A defect in a tree shown as star lines radiating from the centre of a log.

Sticking Making moulding.

Stile The vertical part at edge of furniture framing to which rails are attached.

Stopped Not carried through, as in a stopped chamfer or rabbet.

Strap hinge Hinge with long narrow arms.

Strap work Carving that looks like interwoven crossing straps.

Stretcher A lengthwise rail between the lower parts of a chair or table.

Stuck moulding Moulding made in the solid wood, not planted.

Stud Vertical member in a partition or wall.

Surbase moulding A moulding placed between the cornice and plinth, on – for example – the table part of a bureau bookcase.

Swag Carved ornamental detail in the form of flowers or material suspended.

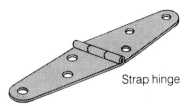
Strap hinge

Tang Pointed end of tool to fit in handle.

Tester The roof over a four-poster bed.

Thread escutcheon A metal liner for a keyhole.

Throating Groove under a projecting sill or similar member to prevent water running back.

Tote A handle (particularly on a plane).

Tread The horizontal part of a stair.

Trunnel (treenail) Peg or dowel driven through a joint.

Twist turning Spiral turning. Characteristic of Jacobean furniture.

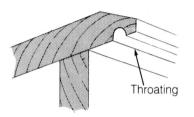
Throating

Undercutting In carving, cutting under the design to give it emphasis due to the better shadow.

Upset Cross fracture in wood. May be natural or occur in felling.

Veneer A thin piece of wood that is usually of a decorative type and intended to be glued to a backing. If very thin and cut from a rotating log, it is cut with a knife. If it is not so thin it is cut with a saw.

Veneer pin Very fine nail with a small head.

Volute A spiral scroll in carving.

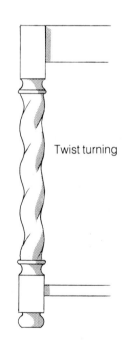
Twist turning

Wainscot This term means the panelling around a room, but it is also applied to quarter-sawn wood, such as oak, that shows figuring.

Waney edge The edge of a board that still has bark on it or is still in the pattern of the outside of the log.

Warping Distortion of a board by twisting or curving because of unequal shrinkage as moisture dries out.

Winding A board or assembled frame is said to be in winding when it is not flat and a twist can be seen when sighting from one end.

Working drawing The drawing showing elevation (side or end view), plan (view from above), sections and details from which measurements can be taken.

Index